Cyberconnecting

Abraham's impressive book on diversity as process surveys new forms of working and learning (co-creating, gamification) in current and future organisation development (Big Data and the Internet of Everything). Abraham teaches us to leverage diversity and interactions across boundaries to build meaningful connections for success in a cyberconnected business world. She holistically highlights business and digital anthropology in organisational change and development.

Philipp Amann, Transnational Threats Department,
Organization for Security and Co-operation in Europe

Cyberconnecting and its 'three lenses' closes a crucial intellectual gap about collaboration. It's a thought-provoking work on leveraging human resources and shaping your business in a virtual world. Abraham gives you the conceptual foundation and tools needed to be successful with your digital initiatives and business transformation. A must read for all those serious on becoming a Social Business.

Thomas A. Bryner, World-wide Social Business SWAT Team, IBM

Cyberconnecting is more than a good read and a resourceful handbook packed with lively examples and exciting stories illustrating the case in point. This is an up-to-date guide to one of the most important themes in professional life for today and tomorrow – a must for junior and senior professionals in a wide range of careers.

Andre Gingrich, University of Vienna, Austria

Cyberconnecting

The Three Lenses of Diversity

PRIYA E. ABRAHAM

Routledge
Taylor & Francis Group

LONDON AND NEW YORK

First published 2015 by Gower Publishing

2 Park Square, Milton Park, Abingdon, Oxfordshire OX14 4RN
52 Vanderbilt Avenue, New York, NY 10017

Routledge is an imprint of the Taylor & Francis Group, an informa business

First issued in paperback 2020

British Library Cataloguing in Publication Data
A catalogue record for this book is available from the British Library

ISBN 13: 978-1-4094-3446-7 (hbk)
ISBN 13: 978-0-367-59954-6 (pbk)

Library of Congress Cataloging-in-Publication Data

Abraham, Priya E.
  Cyberconnecting : the three lenses of diversity / by Priya E. Abraham.
    pages cm
  Includes bibliographical references and index.
    ISBN 978-1-4094-3446-7 (hardback) -- ISBN 978-1-4094-3447-4 (ebook) -- ISBN 978-1-4724-0362-9 (epub) 1. Diversity in the workplace. 2. Personnel management. 3. Employees--Effect of technological innovations on. 4. Information technology--Management. 5. Technological innovations--Management. 6. Communication in management. I. Title.

  HF5549.5.M5.A27 2015
  331.13'3--dc23
                                                              2014031287

Contents

List of Figures

List of Tables

List of Boxes

List of Abbreviations

B2B   Business to business

B2C   Business to customers

BWOR   Bank wiring observation room

BYOD   Bring your own device

CMS   Content management system

cyberIDT   cyberIdentity Development Tool

GDT   Globally distributed teams

HR   Human resources

ICT   Information and communication technology

IT   Information technology

LCMS   Learning content management system

LMS   Learning management system

MENA   Middle East and North-Africa

MOOC   Massive open online course

NGO   Non-government organisation

NOMO   No mobile device

OPEC   Organization of the Petroleum Exporting Countries

PD   Performance driver

ROI   Return on investment

SCRUM   Iterative and incremental agile software development framework
            for managing software projects

TTT   Train the trainer

UX   User experience

PART I
The Context

Chapter 1

The Cyberconnected World of Work

At the heart of this book lie one definition and two premises. For our purposes, 'cyberconnecting' will be defined as building interconnectivity in the digital world. The first premise is that the way we connect is changing; the second is that today's most innovative companies are inviting various stakeholders to be co-creators. For technology to work, it must be human-centric, and this can only be achieved through the process of co-creation.

One significant change driver among many in the world of work is the unprecedented pace of development in information technology (IT). Technology is handing back aspects of banking, travelling, health and wellbeing, and will soon inform literally every aspect of our lives. As a consequence it shapes the ways we connect with others, the ways we perceive ourselves and others, and the environment in which our interactions take place. This will have major implications for underlying business models and the ways we connect with peers, clients, competitors and stakeholders. Face-to-face and cyberinteractions are at the heart of effective relationships. In this technology-induced world of work, we need to think how best to leverage interactions for the benefit of organisation development.

The ability of organisations to cyberconnect is becoming increasingly important for superior performance. This book presents diversity as the vehicle to build interconnectivity, which means to build effective face-to-face and virtual relationships across boundaries, characteristic of today's cyberconnected world of work. In response to this need, the book presents a much-needed strategic framework required for building interconnectivity: 'The Three Lenses of Diversity', designed to organise thinking in the navigation of technological, cultural and social boundaries.

It is a solution-oriented approach to building interconnectivity in the digital age. The ramifications of diversity inherent to today's cyberconnected world of work can be examined, not isolated from business, but embedded in actual cross-boundary work situations, where an appreciation of multiple identity constructions, perception of self and others, and the environment can make a difference in outcome and performance. Cross-boundary work situations are captured in two life cases which describe projects in the telecommunications and mobile learning industries.

Building Interconnectivity

Interconnectivity is the intentional building of reciprocal relationships with awareness of the intricacies of any human interaction with other people or technology across various boundaries. It grows out of the willingness to explore, discover and span the multifaceted, coexisting layers of social, technological and cultural boundaries.

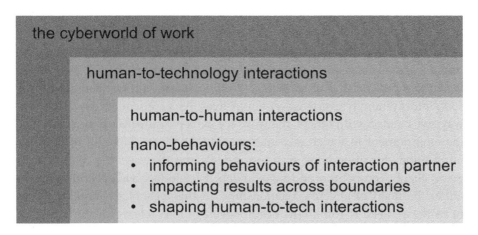

Figure 1.1   The cyberworld of work

The heart of the cyberconnected world[1] of work marks the human-to-human interactions which through human-to-technology interactions make the cyberworld fail or succeed (see Figure 1.1). The superior quality of these interactions enables people to break through the silos typical to the world of work. These entail technological, functional, cultural and hierarchical boundaries, all of which contain further vertical and horizontal boundaries.

---

1   The term 'Cyber-' rests on Norbert Wiener's work on the ramifications of the theory of messages, in which he then presented the futuristic view that one day there would be a computer system that ran on feedback. Essentially, it would be a self-governing system. Wiener 1950:15.

Nano-behaviours are the subtle, almost imperceptible behaviours over which we tend to step due to heavy workloads or which we have not developed the skills to look out for, but which greatly impact the way we interact with one another on projects that inform technology development or its adoption, irrespective of our background or expertise.

Human-to-tech interaction captures people interacting with technology in the role of end consumer or shaper. Using a laptop, exploring a smart-phone or adopting a wearable is pre-informed by the underlying human-to-human interaction in the making of the item.

Leveraging human-to-human and human-to-tech interactions is marked by spanning social, technological and cultural boundaries dominant in the cyberworld of work, which describes the non-physical place in global interaction, which is in turn made from human-to-human interaction.

The core of cyberconnecting in this book is mobile technology, its enablers and its human interface; it will be presented through a life case based on a project of the company SonaConn. Making enterprises and organisations mobile is no longer a matter for debate. Today's mobile users, customers and employees alike, expect interaction at their fingertips. Apps[2] have become a dominant delivery mechanism, generating a multi-billion industry; however, enterprise mobility goes well beyond mobile apps – it influences the way enterprises and organisations run their businesses and, in particular, how they connect and interact with their client and users.

In the quest for new opportunities in the cyberconnected world of work, enterprises and organisations are looking into new ways to attract consumer purchases and new referrals from prospective customers. They apply innovative approaches to align employee behaviour with organisational strategies, tasks and disciplinary plans, resulting in better acceptance of management plans along with increased productivity and low attrition. They develop, design and implement gamified mobile learning programmes in order to assist employees and clients in adopting positive behaviour change. At the heart of this endeavour lies gamification, that is, the selected use of game elements in

---

2   There is an ongoing debate over the definitions of the terms 'app' and 'application'. For this book, I have used 'app' to refer to a single functionality while an 'application' handles a wide variety of functionalities, regardless of the delivery mechanism, such as mobile versus desktop. In any case, the apps vs. applications concept is very important to enterprise IT security, especially with regard to protecting the valuable company asset of data.

a non-game environment. It describes the process of game thinking and game mechanics to engage users and to solve problems.

Gamification can be a component of the Internet of Things, which is embedding itself into everyday items. From toothbrushes, fridges and thermostats to cars and cities, everything around us, including health, is getting connected. The Internet of Things is part of the book inasmuch as the devices benefit from superior user experience (UX) to find ultimate user acceptance, whose materialisation requires the acknowledgement of the diversity of future users. The users' underlying identities have personal, psychological, social and commercial value. The collection and use of personal data can have benefits for individuals, organisations and government, by offering greater insights through data analysis and the development of more targeted and more effective services.

Cyberconnecting today is unthinkable without big data. Big data needs a refreshed, ethical and human-centric view of decision-making, anticipated outcomes, purpose and value to clients. In this book the focus lies on the qualitative work that provides us with insights into what people's motivation drivers really are. Thus, ethnographic significance should be integrated as a complement in collaboration with statistical significance, aiming at the complementary approach between causation and correlation.

All of the above items are embedded in the cloud, which describes the use of files and applications over the internet, and is more of a journey than a business destination, whatever the industry sector, and wherever on the globe. *Cyberconnecting* understands the cloud as a ubiquitous design principle to everything organisations deliver, a true driver to business change, bringing together a range of public and private services, to deliver agility, scalability, simplicity and speed to market.

Naturally, *Cyberconnecting* recognises the potential for criminal exploitation or misuse of data and the ways it enables people to connect. Cybercrime as such will not be covered in this book; however, it acknowledges that people require greater transparency, accountability and autonomy concerning their data. Authorities are charged not only with setting the rules in which the digital world will emerge, but also adapting their own processes towards cyberconnecting. This book takes the position that cyberconnecting is constructive, productive and fundamental to achieving positive relationships between people and commercial organisations, that is, meaningful and effective business relationships. It focuses on the mindful and ethical use of the opportunities it entails.

Who We Are – Our Identity Map

Building interconnectivity requires us to show 'who we are', usually generated by our identity. Identity is a construct. In today's cyberconnected world it refers to how we perceive ourselves and express our individuality in the world. Identity is enacted through face-to-face and online social interactions with others. We have coexisting, multifaceted and overlapping identities, whose importance shifts depending on context. The tangible identities such as gender or ethnicity are encrypted in our body, whereas the less visible characteristics of our identity, the intangible elements, are either chosen, in cases such as our political affiliations, or developed, in cases such as our further education. The latter are likely to change over the course of our life, shaped by the dialogical relationship of self-determination and control or ascription of others.

Our identity informs our role in our larger social environment, the cognition we have about others in different spaces, the way we interact with others, and thereby the way we are seen and categorised by others. The contextual nature of identity instructs the emphasis we put on selected parts of our identity: at home we might be a caring parent or a loving partner, at work we might be an innovative leader, online we might want to explore a new identity by using an avatar, for example in order to become an opinion maker.

Because online information and communication technologies have the potential to shape identity processes in meaningful ways, it is important to consider the identity implications of social media practices and other online tools in general. The knowledge about and the awareness of our identity map and those of others help build effective relationships, in the traditional face-to-face and the cyberconnected world of work.

Boundary-Spanning

Building interconnectivity in the digital age requires some important boundary-spanning competencies. These competencies enable you to establish relationships with business partners by temporarily altering the emphasis you put on selected identities of your identity portfolio. The shift in the importance of coexisting identities must happen with awareness of environmental contingencies, and the business partner's perception of self, you and other key stakeholders. For successful establishment of relationships, knowledge about global trends and socioeconomic drivers, skills such as observation and listening, and finally, the adoption of behaviours such as reflecting, redesigning, mobilising and customising are essential.

Boundary-spanners are those who have developed these competencies and actively seek to work across boundaries and find benefit in the process. In today's cyberconnected world of work, the group of boundary-spanners has grown in size and has become wider in rank. Literally everyone is concerned with boundary-spanning activities whereas formerly it was restricted to a selected and often privileged group of expats whose responsibility was to work across boundaries.

The intercultural component upon which cyberconnecting in part rests is covered throughout the book, specifically by the presentation of the SonaConn project. It features additional intercultural insights based on hands-on examples from the delivery of a large-scale change project in the Middle East and North African (MENA) region.

The Roadmap to Interconnectivity – The Three Lenses of Diversity

If in your boundary-spanning role you are required to build interconnectivity it might be useful to understand:

- the coexisting and overlapping identities people bring into interactions;

- the appraisal they have of self and the other, in connection with which perception it is important to understand and to respond to potential stereotypes; and

- the environment in which all of this happens.

The book presents a much-needed strategic framework required for building interconnectivity: 'The Three Lenses of Diversity', designed to organise thinking in the navigation of technological, cultural and social boundaries. The framework consists of:

- The Lens of Multiple Identity for the exploration of people's coexisting and overlapping identities.

- The Lens of Perception for the examination of potential stereotypes and their impact on the interaction.

- The Environmental Lens for the analysis of the geopolitical, cultural, financial and business environment.

As a central reference point, the framework is useful not only when a problem has already arisen but also as a form of inquiry and to prevent it ever happening.

The Three Lenses of Diversity rest on the research findings that show that 'Diversity is a process' generated from interactions. As such diversity is:

- dynamic;

- regenerative;

- perception-shaped; and

- environment-shaped.

Each of The Three Lenses of Diversity comes with a hands-on tool or guideline for the easy application in the world of work, explained in Part II of the book, The Practice.

The Lens of Multiple Identity is covered through the cyberIdentity Development Tool (cyberIDT), an online instrument that helps individuals to understand their own identity map and its implications for relationship-building efforts in cross-boundary work. The personal development process includes the completion of the online questionnaire; a personal feedback report containing the respondent's scores and information to help them interpret and integrate the results; and an individual virtual feedback session with a licensed coach. For the purpose of team and organisation development, the use of the cyberIDT in combination with the participation in development programmes helps to:

- increase the face-to-face and cybercollaboration in groups of people with different backgrounds (for example, cultural, social, organisational or generational); and

- shape cultural change initiatives to close the gap between current and desired cultures.

Whereas in the past it was enough to develop only a relatively small elite group
of expats for international assignments, the need now is to prepare people
throughout the organisation to span boundaries both globally and within the
same region and affiliate.

Organisation Development

Organisation development is concerned with the diagnosis of organisational
health and performance and the capability of the organisation to develop
further through change. It involves the applications of organisational
behaviour and recognition of social processes of the organisation. This
reflexion process embraces a wide range of strategies for intervention
in the social process of an organisation. These intervention strategies
aim at the development of the individual, teams and the organisation
as a whole. Specifically, the objective of organisation development is to
improve the overall performance and effectiveness of an organisation.
See Figure 1.2 for the seemingly opposing fields essential for successful
organisation development.

Figure 1.2   Organisation development through seemingly opposing fields

Traditionally in the industrial age and its understanding of great leaders, it
was top management who were charged with leading and supporting the
improvement of an organisation's visioning, empowerment, learning and
problem-solving processes. Distinctively, this book assumes that every
member of an enterprise or organisation contributes to its development. As
organisation development is not the responsibility of a single leader or a
specific department, this book presents the unique combination of approaches

from business anthropology, IT and 'Diversity as a process' for shaping the organisation's capability to improve its performance and effectiveness through its people, often without the intervention of top management.

BUSINESS ANTHROPOLOGY – THE PITH HELMET GOES MOBILE

As diversity and selected IT have already been presented, let us now turn to the third field, namely business anthropology.

Just one hundred years ago ethnographers – ethnography as a sub-discipline of anthropology is a comprehensive study of a culture at a particular place and time, captured in writing – roamed through the bushes and jungles to research exotic people and cultures. Those days of the imperialist pith helmet and leather-embroidered notebooks provided with a glass inkwell and pen are long gone.

Just over the last few years anthropologists and ethnographers have not only researched digital communities, they have actively shaped the domain to an extent that nowadays they are celebrated as the next generation of rock stars, for example, in the role of data scientists, for the critical sense-making process of big data.

Business anthropologists specialise in the study of business fields of management, operations, marketing, product design and development, consumer behaviour, organisational culture and international business. They use ethnographic methods such as participant observation, informal and structured interviews, researcher logs and digital fieldbooks to uncover people's diverse needs and expectations in today's cyberconnected world of work. Diverse identity portfolios need reflection in development solutions of face-to-face programmes and mobile applications.

There is an emerging notion of human-centred design. In this form of design, business anthropologists involve the recipients in a design process focused primarily on their needs.

Building interconnectivity requires a holistic form of understanding, analysis and problem-solving. It is a way to bring balanced, more impactful solutions to our businesses and social challenges, solutions uncovered by qualitative research methods help close the gap between human behaviour and tech to engage internal and external stakeholders.

The World of Work

THREE OUTLOOKS ON THE WORLD OF WORK

Global megatrends are widely documented on a macro-level. This section is not a prediction of the future; rather its purpose is the illustration of the ever-changing nature of the boundaries in which the world of work has already started to operate.

Even today our world of work is determined to a great extent by:

- the world population's demographic shifts, with higher life expectancy and falling birth rates;

- the increasing speed and connectivity of IT systems; and

- the orientation on the individual in all aspects of life, which in turn has implications for the world of work.

The business world of the twenty-first century is marked by rapidly expanding contact across boundaries and cultures, characterised by volatility, uncertainty, complexity and ambiguity. The three outlooks crystallise the ramifications the shifting boundaries might have on the world of work. These boundaries are increasingly brittle, sometimes strengthening one another, at other times making one another even more porous. They are shifting social, technological and cultural boundaries. Selected directions are listed below.

Shifting social boundaries:

- The economic downturn is potentially giving rise to greater social and economic polarisation between the 'haves' and 'have-nots'. The unprecedented extent of global migration will create social division and social tension.[3]

- Workplace demographics are shifting, and, as a result, shaping the future of the way we work. By 2025, over 75 per cent of the workforce will consist of millenials, often collaborating with peers in their grandparents' age bracket. Beyond daily interaction the intergenerational dynamics will force policy-makers to face the challenges of pensions and healthcare.

---

3   Reicher, Hopkins 2013.

- The 'digital natives', those who have been immersed in the cyberenvironment, are growing to adulthood: this generation of employees will have adopted a number of online identities or personae, might however feel insufficiently skilled or responsible for their cybersecurity, and at the same time, will be facing a significant reduction in the number of jobs as a result of substitution through automation.

Shifting technological boundaries:

- The long-familiar tech trend of the relentless fall in the cost of computing power (Brynjolfsson, McAfee 2014:12). Stable and mobile electrical power will likely be available to a substantially larger part of society; energy efficiency will no longer represent a hurdle to progress and will ensure boundary-free access. Secure online identity systems will allow more reliable user authentication.

- New regulatory schemes regarding intellectual property might open up commercial activity worldwide. Companies and individuals might be able to profit fairly from the intellectual property they generate.

- At the same time, security issues are increasingly pervasive: problems of ownership of the data in networked systems and the differentiation between data misuse and legitimate use will have to be solved. Further questions include what data the authorities will be able to access and use for the purposes of preventing and disrupting criminal activity and who will cover (and recover) any losses, both financial and in terms of data recovery (ICSPA 2013:3).

Shifting cultural boundaries:

- The 'big bang' of information: with the relentless fall in the cost of computing power high-speed broadband, whether fixed or mobile, will be more widely pervasive and affordable. A small solar-powered battery and a tiny computer have already done this for remote African and Indian villages. This 'big bang' of information – and education as well – is empowering millions of people, enabling them to cross boundaries not encountered before.

- Continuously growing focus on individualism: through this, people are increasingly looking for personal growth, purpose recognition, access, influence and impact. The greater autonomy will allow independents to follow their passion: the anywhere anytime is redefining the workplace.

- One size fits all: the growing individualism is expressed by our selected and imposed lifestyle, characterised by self-responsibility, autonomy and alleged independence. The increase in individualism stands in stark contrast to the mechanism and channels through which it develops, that is, products and services in connection with shopping, banking and health, made available on end user devices available anytime, anywhere, sold worldwide and made to fit all in order to streamline processes for revenue generation.

The cyberconnected world of work offers a lot of opportunities, challenges and characteristics. These have crystallised only as a consequence of recent economic developments and innovation in information and communication technology (ICT), and as a result, people flow across social, political and organisational boundaries.

In place of an extended theoretical description of the idiosyncrasies of the modern workplace, two cross-boundary life cases will accompany us through the book. These are real cases that assist you in visualising the diversity of today's workplaces and their challenges and opportunities, which impact the individual, the teams and finally the organisations.

These two real-life examples will surface and resurface throughout the book, illustrating human behaviour issues embedded in today's cyberconnected world.

More examples will be presented and briefly explained in order to bring the diversity challenges to life.

CAPTURING THE WORLD OF WORK

Some companies create and innovate technology; others use and adopt it; but in the cyberage, both must closely interconnect tech with human behaviour. Coexisting and overlapping identities of the people involved and their work relationships in cross-boundary work situations are captured in two life cases.

REAL-LIFE CASE: MANAGEMENT AND LEADERSHIP DEVELOPMENT

Carolyn will accompany us through the book. As of the writing of the book, she is a 32-year-old business consultant from Great Britain, and in this capacity a decision-maker on the first real-life case, a multimillion pound, large, complex programme in the expert area of 'change management' in the telecommunication industry in MENA, in particular, in Egypt. The UK corporation called for the worldwide implementation of performance drivers (PDs) designed to support employees in developing management and leadership skills to grow the business across the globe.

SonaConn is one of the world's leading mobile telecommunication organisations with a significant presence in Europe, the Middle East, Africa, Asia Pacific and the United States. It is a public limited company with headquarters in England and is listed on the London Stock Exchange.

Carolyn is a communications expert and a full-time employee of the British consulting firm, for whom, together with a consultant colleague, she won this project in MENA, helping the organisation to generate some major income stream.

In the context of the management and leadership development programme, PDs, primarily referred to as interpersonal skills, were viewed as a tool for promoting more effective managerial interests and herein action, that is, profitable growth. In summary, the management and organisation development programme featured challenges as follows:

- The implementation of predefined PDs, embodied in skills such as communication, dealing with a complex environment, customer orientation. The required PD skills were translated into workshop activities covering the topics entailed in the PDs.

- The learning architecture featured a mixture of large group events and PD workshops tightly knit into a compact schedule accommodating the greatest possible participant numbers (1,600 managers) in the shortest possible time (one-and-a-half-years maximum).

- Workshops needed to be designed for the needs of three managerial levels, that is, line managers, supervisors and shop managers across divisions and locations in Cairo and the whole of MENA. Large group events were intended to bridge the hierarchical gap among managerial levels. The needs analysis and the design of the large and complex project took place in only two months of development time across continents, including the period of Ramadan.

Figure 1.3 below depicts the design details:

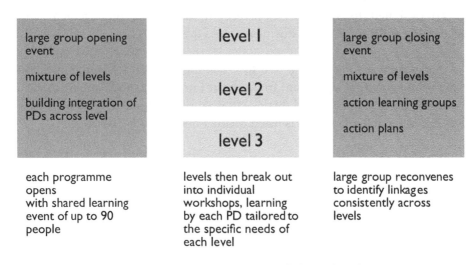

each integrated programme was 2 days in length

Figure 1.3   SonaConn – programme architecture with large group events

The programme was designed and delivered by a globally dispersed team of 20–25 members from ten different nationalities and diverse backgrounds employed by or associated with the British consulting firm. Approximately 15 of these team members worked throughout the entire duration of the project; the remaining members changed from time to time. Further project details are presented in the relevant chapters.

REAL-LIFE CASE: SUCCEEDING WITH MOBILE LEARNING

Keith, the learning and development director of A1Guard, and Nadia, the managing director of the MyMemLab start-up, will accompany us through some chapters, highlighting their challenges in going mobile.

This life case presents the development of selected mobile learning initiatives for A1Guard, a key player in the health and safety industry. For this purpose they collaborate with a start-up in the mobile learning industry, called MyMemLab, a truly virtual organisation. MyMemLab are an expert consultancy in mobility, learning and gamification. They develop, design and implement gamified mobile learning programmes, helping to deliver global mobile solutions.

The company aims to become a key player in the mobile learning industry by offering superior consulting services. Their innovative approach incorporates elements of gamification and thus revolutionises the way people learn. As a result, they shape changes of some of the paradigms in the organisation development industry.

The start-up taps into the current organisation development landscape by offering effective solutions which fulfil the needs of diverse user groups, assisting people in adopting positive behaviour change. They specifically unlock global enterprise knowledge and develop full market potential.

MyMemLab offers the full cycle of consulting services to A1Guard, essential for the successful implementation of mobile learning initiatives. These services include:

- Mobile strategy: development of a mobile learning strategy;

- Diagnosis: needs assessment of the mobile learning environment within A1Guard's market segment;

- Prototyping: building of a test model of the mobile solution;

- Application development: development in iOS, Android, Windows Mobile and Web;

- Content conversion: conversion for mobile learning apps, mobile Web and learning management systems (LMS); and

- Metrics and evaluation: return on investment (ROI) of their mobile learning initiative.

Further project details will be highlighted when relevant for the interaction between Keith and Nadia and their stakeholders.

How This Book is Organised

The book is divided into three parts (see Figure 1.4):

- Part I: Context

- Part II: Practice

- Part III: Application

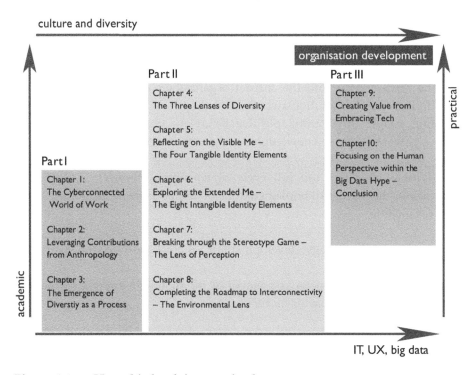

Figure 1.4   How this book is organised

Part I is designed to frame the context, also known as 'The what'.

Chapter 2 highlights the contribution anthropology has made over the decades and illustrates the approaches that helped surface matters in relation to interconnectivity. It also illustrates the key contributions from business anthropology and its merits for modern organisation development work. Finally, it provides an overview of its methods and approaches to the world of cyberconnecting.

Chapter 3 presents the history of diversity in a nutshell and so crystallises essential aspects of current understanding of Diversity as a process. It also illustrates the emergence of the intercultural field, and shows the contributions both fields make to building interconnectivity. Finally, it explains the research and the development of the connected framework, 'The Three Lenses of Diversity', and the tool developed further to the research insights, the cyberIDT, for the use of people development in cross-boundary work situations.

Part II captures the practice of the theoretical background and its use in organisation development, also known as the 'So what'.

Chapter 4 presents the dynamic framework 'The Three Lenses of Diversity' and walks you step-by-step through the overall design and each of the lenses, which are:

1.   The Lens of Multiple Identity;

2.   The Lens of Perception; and

3.   The Environmental Lens.

Once the framework has been presented, its benefits and its application for use in organisation development practice will be covered in detail.

Chapters 5, 6, 7 and 8 expand on each lens. Chapter 5 explains the difference between the tangible and the intangible identity elements and provides an in-depth illustration of each of the four tangible identity elements: Appearance, Gender, Generation and Ethnicity.

Chapter 6 demonstrates the importance of the intangible identity elements: Wellbeing, Mobility, Sociability, Communication, Geopolitics, Lifelong learning, Inclusion and Employability. Chapters 5 and 6 each provide the possibility for some self-evaluation at the end of the chapter.

Chapter 7 presents The Lens of Perception in action. The perception of the 'other' is at the heart of the quality of effective work relationships. The chapter offers ways to break through stereotypes in order to open new opportunities; uncovering potential blind spots that hamper change readiness.

Chapter 8 completes the roadmap to interconnectivity by presenting The Environmental Lens, through which the environmental contingencies that impact relationship-building efforts can be examined.

Part III, also known as the 'What next', concentrates solely on the application in organisation development. Specifically, contributions from cultural anthropology are substantiated with industry examples. Equally, technology-induced implementation developed in co-creation with anthropological practices is discussed with the aim of engaging diverse user groups internal and external to organisations.

Chapter 9 describes how the anthropological toolbox provides the basis for a thorough needs analysis, which allows diverse people's needs to be met, in turn creating superior interconnectivity.

Chapter 10 covers the value people's multiple identities have and illustrates the emerging need for a more human-centred design of applications, achieved through the application of The Three Lenses of Diversity.

I have written this book for professional managers, business educators, those engaged in personal and organisational development, those with a purely research interest and interested general readers, all of whom will benefit from its unprecedented insights into critical but little-understood processes which provide both a new view of diversity and a strong business case for the practice of organisation development.

The production of knowledge will continue and probably accelerate. The underlying research is very much a work in process.

Chapter 2
Leveraging Contributions from Anthropology

Cultural anthropology has made it into the cyberconnected world of work through its specialist sub-discipline of business anthropology. In particular, the discipline contributed to the origins of organisational behaviour and intercultural management. In general, management study approaches originate in the social science disciplines.

In light of the fact that today's cyberconnected workplaces are social constructions embedded in economic contingencies, the unique key contributions the anthropological discipline brings to the business field are manifold.

The first section of this chapter highlights the contribution anthropology has made over the decades and illustrates the routes that helped surface the 'Diversity as a process' approach essential for building interconnectivity. The second section illustrates the key contributions from the sub-discipline of business anthropology and its merits with reference to this work. Finally, the third section provides an overview of the methods and approaches stemming from anthropology and consequently business anthropology that contributed to the development of the framework 'The Three Lenses of Diversity'.

From Armchair Researcher to Globalisation and ICT Expert

Bringing the benefits of the anthropological discipline to light requires a glimpse into the early approaches and achievements of anthropology, which is the study of humanity in all its diversity. It is the study of peoples around the world, across cultures and throughout time. Today's modern anthropology is mainly concerned with the study of living peoples; however it also studies peoples whose ways of life may have long disappeared from living human societies.

THE WEST VERSUS THE REST

Traditionally, anthropology has focused either on cultures of the past (the complex nature of the discipline requires a number of sub-disciplines or fields such as archaeology or physical anthropology) or cultures in 'exotic' settings. This has largely earned the discipline the reputation of being about studying 'others' in place and time rather than 'ourselves' in the here and now. Some have even made the point in one fashion or another that sociology is about 'the West', while anthropology is about 'the rest'.

Nevertheless, since the emergence of the discipline its activities and objectives have changed over the decades and adapted in accordance with the contingencies of the environment. Each period has its unique contribution and rewards to world knowledge. Table 2.1 below presents a selection of anthropological contributions relevant for the current diversity work. The chronological list is by no means a full historical overview; on the contrary, it presents anthropology's contributions, its benefits and most importantly its relevance for current and future work on diversity as the foundation for building interconnectivity.

Table 2.1   Contributions from anthropology

Time	Representative	Contribution	Benefits	Relevance for this work
1800s	E.B. Tylor/ J.G. Frazer	Collection of first materials	Knowledge access to other cultures	First emergence of anthropology discipline
	B. Malinowski	Anthropological fieldwork	Ethnography	Multi-sited ethnography
1960s	C. Lévi-Strauss	Patterns as to how representatives of a culture solve problems	Structuralism/ Systematic processing	Structured patterns of interaction
1990s	A. Appadurai	Grassroot globalisation	'Scapes'	Understanding of environment
	U. Hannerz	Cosmpolitans	Cultural make-up	Constructivist approach of identity
2000s	A. Gingrich	Definition of terminology	Belonging versus Othering	Dialogical principle of relationship-building

In the nineteenth century the British scholars E.B. Tylor and J.G. Frazer accessed knowledge about 'the other' by working with materials collected by missionaries, colonial officials, business traders and adventurers. Diversity was then presented by a mix of previously existing sciences, notably natural history and medicine, and, in response to criticisms and self-criticisms, these practices became more refined over the decades. The Victorian representatives have tended to be dismissed as 'armchair anthropologists'. The data collected by others were viewed through their missionary or colonial lens, leading to the production of the 'other' culture on the basis of pre-informed observation.

EXPLORING THE FIELD

The British anthropologist Bronislaw Malinowski (1884–1942) helped develop the field of anthropology from a primarily evolutionary focus into sociological and psychological fields of inquiry. He is remembered for his role in developing the methods and the primacy of anthropological fieldwork, making a substantial contribution to the twentieth century becoming the century of ethnography in the anthropology discipline.

Box 2.1   Ethnography in a Nutshell

In a nutshell, an ethnography is a comprehensive study of a culture at a particular place and time, captured in writing. The outcome informs the reader through narrative immersion and storytelling techniques (often known as thick descriptions) alongside objective description and results of various interview style techniques. Ethnographic writing requires the researcher's presence on the scene for a considerable period of time, simultaneously participating in and observing the social and cultural life of the group. As opposed to the earlier method of armchair anthropologists, the ethnographer interacts with the people. The result of omitting one additional key informer such as the missionary or trader and of providing first-hand experience from observing and engaging in a dialogue is a more unbiased view of the researched culture.

Claude Lévi-Strauss (1908–2009), the disillusioned French philosopher turned anthropologist, reached rockstar-like fame through his achievements, of which his 1955 book *Tristes Tropiques* was only one among many. Although himself a technical anthropologist, he is well known as a structuralist. Lévi-Strauss proposes the idea that the human brain systematically processes organised, that is to say structured, units of information that combine and recombine to create models that sometimes explain the world we live in, sometimes suggest imaginary alternatives, and sometimes give tools with which to operate in it.

The task of the anthropologist, for Lévi-Strauss, is not to account for why a culture takes a particular form, but to understand and illustrate the principles of organisation underlying the onward process of transformation which occurs as carriers of the culture solve problems that are either practical or purely intellectual.

GOING GLOBAL

Among many trends cultural anthropology followed in the twentieth century, the dominance of globalisation in the later part of the century certainly shaped the research orientation of many anthropologists. In his work *Modernity at Large* (1996), the contemporary sociocultural anthropologist Arjun Appadurai discusses his understanding of nation states and globalisation. His 'grassroot' globalisation relies on a series of social forms, which contests and questions the top-down actions of corporate capital and the nation state system, preferring strategies, visions and horizons for globalisation on behalf of the poor, which he rephrases as 'globalisation from below'.

With this in mind, Appadurai defined a number of 'scapes' as primary sources for meta-level considerations (see Figure 2.1). These 'scapes' are:

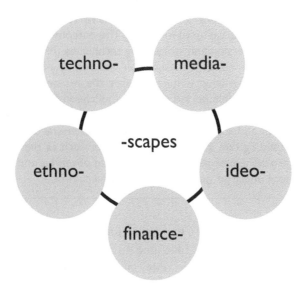

Figure 2.1   Five landscapes representing global cultural flows

- ethnoscapes as landscapes of persons who constitute the shifting world in which we live: tourists, immigrants, guest workers;

- mediascapes as image-centred, narrative-based accounts of strips of reality expressed by electronic capabilities to produce and disseminate information: newspapers, magazines, television;

- technoscapes as the global configuration of technology crossing formerly impervious boundaries;

- ideoscapes as concentration of images highly political and often directly linked to state ideologies and their power interests: freedom, welfare rights, sovereignty and democracy; and

- financescapes as disposition of global capital now mysteriously and rapidly moving: currency markets, stock exchanges, commodity speculations.

Amidst the gloabalisation hype of the 1990s, the Swedish social anthropologist Ulf Hannerz (born 1942) brought forward the notion of cultural make-up. He claims that one's own culture becomes transparent only when living, working and in general interacting in an environment other than one's own.

BRIDGING SELF AND OTHER

Finally, Andre Gingrich's work (2004) on 'Belonging' and 'Othering' makes an essential contribution to the diversity work described in this book. With reference to the relational aspect of diversity addressed in this work the notions of 'Belonging' as opposed to 'Othering' are indispensable to the regenerative character of diversity. Belonging refers to ascriptions connected with sameness of representatives participating in an interaction, whilst Othering refers to ascriptions of difference. Gingrich's definition of Belonging and Othering is as follows:

> ... *a working definition of such personal and collective identities as simultaneously including sameness and differing. These identities are multidimensional and contradictory, and they include powerrelated, dialogical ascriptions by selves and by others, which are processually configured, enacted and transformed by cognition, language, imagination, emotion, body and (additional forms of) agency.*[1]

---

1   Gingrich in Baumann, Gingrich 2004:6.

Belonging and Othering are mutually constitutive components of an interaction shaping diversity. This will be discussed in more detail in subsequent chapters.

Volumes have been filled with the history of anthropology. Over the centuries contributions from anthropology important for modern world of work are manifold. Frazer/Tyler substantially built the discipline; Malinowski brought it to life by introducing hands-on research practices. Lévi-Strauss turned around world thinking on patterns. Appadurai offers 'landscapes' for the illustration of global cultural flows. Hannerz provides a concept for cosmopolitans, who became omnipresent with the new dominance of gloabalisation and migration, and finally Gingrich offers a contribution on perception paramount for this development.

With this in mind, contributions from anthropology relevant for *Cyberconnecting* are as follows:

- multi-sited and nowadays digital ethnography;

- structured patterns of interaction;

- understanding of the environment;

- constructivist approach of identity;

- dialogical principle of relationship-building.

All of these will be reflected on in detail in the following chapters.

The next section concentrates on the significant domains of business anthropology, which in the course of research became important for building interconnectivity, leading in turn to this book.

Business Anthropology – The Shapers and their Domains

Cultural anthropology and its approaches and methods have brought a number of achievements to the business world. The research methods originating in the 'exotic field' have been widely accepted in organisations and have been adopted by a number of different academic disciplines such as sociology and psychology.

Business anthropologists specialise in the study of business fields of management, operations, marketing, product design and development, consumer behaviour, organisational culture, human resources management and international business, using anthropological methods, particularly ethnographic methods such as participant observation, informal and structured interviews and other anthropology-based research methods.

The term 'business anthropology' became more popular and widely used in the 1980s, when anthropologists were hired full time to conduct research in relation to consumer behaviour and marketing. Prior to that time, the terms 'industrial anthropology', 'anthropology of work', or 'applied anthropology in industry' were more frequently used to denote areas of research and practice focused on business-related phenomena. More recently, the term 'business anthropology' has begun to be used more generically to refer to any application of anthropology to business-orientated problems. Currently 'business anthropology' is recognised as a sub-field of the discipline in applied anthropology, substantially adding value to perspectives on organisations. Current research initiatives concentrate on:

- organisational theory and culture;

- international business, especially international marketing, intercultural management and intercultural communication;

- marketing and consumer behaviour;

- product design and development.

It was in fact Bronislaw Malinowski, mentioned above, who opened the door to what is today known as business anthropology.

THE BIRTH OF ORGANISATIONAL BEHAVIOUR

In the context of the increase of industrial technology in the early twentieth century and the related boost in unionisation, a major research project took place. In the mid 1920s at the Western Electric Company[2] near Chicago a series of experiments aimed at increasing the productivity of the workforce and reducing worker fatigue and dissatisfaction was conducted by Fritz Roethlisberger, an engineer and philosopher, and his research associate William J. Dickson.

---

2   Now Lucent Technology.

Their hypothesis was to manipulate one single variable, specifically, increasing the factory illumination; however, results showed that productivity also increased when lighting was dramatically decreased. The result of the initial illumination tests was inexplicable on the basis of the theory available at the time. Due to the failure of the linear causality of illumination on productivity, researchers turned to the complexity of relationships among variables in the social system and their impact on productivity.

The major research known as the Hawthorne studies was conducted in three independent stages – illumination tests, relay-assembly tests and bank-wiring tests. Although each was a separate experiment, the second and third developed out of the preceding series of tests.

The second stage was a massive project consisting of more than 20,000 interviews, for which the Hawthorne researchers called on the help of the psychologist Elton Mayo, who had established a friendship with the two anthropologists Bronsilaw Malinowski and A.R. Radcliffe-Brown and therefore knew that anthropologists study the natural social systems in the field. It was this approach that Mayo wanted to apply in the third phase of the project.

One of Radcliffe-Brown's students, W. Lloyd Warner, designed and partly conducted the third stage of the Hawthorne project, known as the Bank Wiring Observation Room (BWOR). This phase of the project focused on the exploration of what workers actually *did* on the job as opposed to what they *said* during interview they would do. A group of trained observers and interviewers collected the data, which was then analysed in the anthropological tradition derived from studying a small society such as a tribe.

Consequently, the business anthropology discipline owes its life to the developments on the Hawthorne project.

Beyond the application of an existing discipline in a new area, the Hawthorne studies triggered a number of other results:

- the use of the term 'Hawthorne effect' to describe how the presence of researchers produces a bias and unduly influences the outcome of an experiment;

- several important published works, foremost of which were Mayo's *The Human Problems of an Industrial Civilization* and Roethlisberger et al.'s *Management and the Worker*;

- a clear definition of the 'human relations' school;

- an emphasis on the practice of personnel counselling;

- the enormous growth of academic programmes in organisational behaviour at American colleges and universities, and eventually worldwide.

The severe economic deprivation unfolding in the 1930s and the accompanying lack of resources for organisational research resulted in the newly established branch of anthropology being fragmented into several branches, the main ones being:

1.   Marxist and neo-Marxist critiques of industry at home and abroad;

2.   the ethnography of industrial occupations and professions; and

3.   the study of industrialisation processes outside the West.

ORIGINAL INTERCULTURAL ASPECTS

Only in the 1960s did the next hype of business anthropology occur, primarily for three reasons relating to economics:

1.   the West began to form relationships with former colonial states;

2.   the United States increased economic and technical aid to Third World countries; and

3.   Japan and the Organization of Petroleum Exporting Countries (OPEC) countries achieved considerable economic success.

These economic developments raised the need to understand the mentality of 'the other side', greatly contributing to the first stage development of the 'culture shock industry'. One anthropologist, Edward Hall, unintentionally but certainly powerfully led to the packaging of culture in the current intercultural industry. In his effort to present cultural understanding in an accessible form to non-academics and practitioners, Hall focused on microbehaviour, such as space and time perceptions in different cultures, which to date is still a commonly used intercultural approach.

Hall's focus on micro-behaviours represented the start of what later became the intercultural industry. Well-known representatives are Geert Hofstede, Fons Trompenaars and Charles Hampden-Turner, who in the 1980s and 1990s each developed Hall's initial steps further in their unique ways. Dutch business anthropologists praised Hofstede's and Tromenpaars' theories for their focus on national culture. In fact, the proposed national cultural maps have helped organisations to understand the reasons behind cultural differences among countries and increased their understanding of these differences with regard to management behaviour in different cultural contexts.

However, the maps were fiercely criticised for their emphasis on difference within culture and the static character of their cultural analysis. Specifically, business anthropologists criticised the static notion of the concept of culture, making followers of the concept believe that Hofstede's dimensions were an unambiguously specifiable collective programming of people in an organisation.

CULTURE AS ROOT METAPHOR

Organisational anthropologist Linda Smircich advances the view that organisations should be understood as cultures. This moves beyond the view that a culture is something that an organisation *has*, in favour of the view that a culture is something an organisation *is* (Smircich 1983). This makes culture the foundation or root metaphor of an organisation as opposed to the commonly held assumption that it is just one part of an organisation. The latter, for example, is portrayed in the McKinsey 7S model. However, this assumes that decision-makers in charge of organisational analysis, often consultants in cooperation with senior management, understand the organisation's culture as a root metaphor as opposed to an instrument.

The instrumental approach is in accordance with the 'has' culture, the view that a culture is something that an organisation *has*, rather than something an organisation *is* (Smircich 1983). The *is–has* dichotomy is linked to the notions of 'organisational culture' and 'corporate culture'. 'Corporate culture' is typically expressed as:

- what an organisation *has*;

- what dominant members value;

- what senior managers' value and how they prefer to do things; and finally

- what additional variables can be manipulated.

In contrast, the characteristics of 'organisational culture' are depicted as follows:

- what an organisation *is*;

- how meaning that emerges from social interaction is negotiated and shared; and

- how senior managers play an integral part in the continuous process of creation, although they are not able to control it.

Business anthropology is largely concerned with research on organisational theory and culture. Building on his field research on British Rail's Advanced Passenger Train, the British business anthropologist Paul Bate (1994) proclaimed the then-innovative assumption that culture and in particular organisational culture is the synonym for an organisation's strategy. He successfully argued that strategic change is similar to cultural change and that as a consequence, the two terms 'culture' and 'strategy' could be used interchangeably. With this proposition he took a strong position against the mainstream strategy research of that time, which claimed that strategic change and cultural change are two independent aspects of organisational change.

His study on the British Rails was the first work in the expert area of 'change management' conducted by a business anthropologist, proposing a new perspective on organisations.

It was during the late 1990s that this author introduced anthropological approaches to management and organisation development. Abraham's publication *Cross Cultural Training: Lévi-Strauss for Managers* (1999) aimed to introduce the geology model based on Lévi-Strauss' structuralist approach to a wider business audience. After a short introduction of the model, the article examines its application in cross-cultural/intercultural training in order to show the complexity of culture in a structured yet open-ended way.

The advantages of this model on a micro-level are that it can help delegates to:

- understand that various culture-bearing elements are not necessarily in hierarchic order;

- understand that culture is not a closed system;

- recognise more easily the reciprocal action of elements within a culture;

- see the dynamic aspect of culture;

- start with mutualities within a culture or among cultures rather than with differences.

The benefit on a macro-level is that the language and the symbolic representation is more loosely aligned to executives' usual communication style. It thus overcomes some of the gaps between the academic and the business world.

The increasing internationalisation and globalisation of business relations and networks in the 1990s were reflected in a number of contributions from the field. The process of globalisation creates a connection among sites, resulting in multi-sited ethnography. Multi-sited ethnography moves beyond the single sites and local situations of conventional ethnographic research designed to examine the circulation of cultural meanings, objects and identities in diffuse time-space.

Appadurai's view of global processes of migration and communication leads to the deterritorialisation of identities in a world which will become culturally hybridised through the growth of diasporic public spheres and cultural global flows. The decline of the nation state replaces territoriality with translocalities. The related concept of 'scapes' has already been presented in the section 'From armchair researcher to globalisation and ICT expert'.

Marietta Baba (2001, 2006) studies distributed work and provides an ethnographic account of an American-based global firm's attempt to transfer a marketing methodology to a French retailing company via a global virtual team. Her multi-sited fieldwork offers helpful insights on terminology and key idiosyncrasies of globally distributed teams.

> A globally distributed team (or GDT) is a work group whose members represent and are based in two or more nations or regions, yet must work interdependently to achieve a common purpose related to the firm's global strategy.[3]

---

3 Baba 2001:2.

GDT key idiosyncrasies are a) technology-supported communication; b) differentiation between core team and extended or full team; c) non-collated workplace; d) multicultural and multifunctional.[4] The ethnographic account also revealed that the geographical distribution patterns of people and resources on the ground are relevant to the processes of distributed cognition and to the ways in which leaders exploit historical, cultural and linguistic resources to further their own agendas.

THE DISCIPLINE GOES MOBILE

One of the recent developments in business anthropology is research in and on the information and communication technology (ICT) industry with its emerging sub-discipline known as digital anthropology. Anthropologists have moved into the ICT industry as a research topic; at the same time they make use of ICT tools to present the outcomes.

As a result of this research area, also known as 'the social anthropology of technological development', it is now common to find anthropologists working within the corridors of hi-tech companies specifically covering three topic areas. These are:

- Anthropologists enter emerging market divisions in order to conduct content analysis on employees' behaviours such as the topics people work on, how they work on these topics and how they collaborate. This concerns small enterprises, including start-ups as well as multinationals in a more mature state of the business.

- Beyond the organisation boundaries, consumer behaviours and needs are of prime interest, aiming to gain a better understanding in order to develop more user-friendly products, to identify new areas of application, and overall to push technology forward.

- Beyond organisations, anthropological explorations of ICTs primarily focus on communities and on youth practices in urban settings. Equally, studies of ICT devices and their ramifications on behaviours are subjects of research.

In the same way that ICT issues have become the latest research trend, technology made available by the industry has become an essential vehicle for

---

4   Baba 2001:2.

conducting research. Mobile phone anthropology is an equally popular means for data collection, analysis and presentation. Research outcomes are no longer presented in thick descriptions, but feature storytelling via photo collections presented on blogs, which in turn are disseminated by social media tools. Thus, the research content is mirrored in the research method as the research method is mirrored in the content.

Table 2.2 below summarises the contributions from business anthropology.

Table 2.2   Contributions from business anthropology

Time	Domain	Shapers	Benefits	Relevance for this work
1930s	'Hawthorne' study on changing a single variable in connection with productivity	Initiator F. Roethlisberger, W.J. Dickson, later E. Mayo	Introduction of academic programmes in organisational behaviour	Complexity of relationships among variables
1960s	Economy-based relationships between the 'West' and the rest	E.T. Hall	Ground work for the intercultural field	Intercultural aspects
1980s	Understanding of culture in organisations	L. Smircich	Differentiation between organisation and corporate culture	Culture as root metaphor
1990s	Change management	P. Bate	Interchangeable use of 'culture' and 'strategy'	Culture *is* strategy
	Cultural hybridisation	A. Appadurai	'Scapes'	Decline of importance of nation state
2000s	Globally distributed work	M. Baba	GDTs	Multi-site research and collaboration
2010s	ICT	Various researchers	Deeper understanding of stakeholder behaviour	Mobile/digital ethnography

RELEVANCE FOR BUILDING INTERCONNECTIVITY IN THE DIGITAL AGE

The ground-breaking Hawthorne study not only opened the floor for the then-new discipline of organisational behaviour and connected extensive research conducted over centuries; it also paved the way to research the complexity of relationships among variables, which in building interconnectivity are the relationships among multiple identity constructions of the people involved, the perceptions of themselves and others, and the environment in which they move.

Hall and subsequent shapers opened the domain of the intercultural field, which reached an unparalleled popularity at the globalisation hype of the 1980s and 1990s.

Since Interculturalists tend to treat different cultures as fixed entities, they thus impose limitations on the dynamics of social transaction. Their concepts no longer offer any solutions to the challenges of the modern interconnected workplace. Interculturalist aspects are certainly relevant for diversity in the evolutionary sense of the subject matter and will be addressed later.

Smircich's most essential differentiation between organisational and corporate culture brought clarity as to the importance of concentrating on the 'is' culture present on the researched project. This specifically includes what people thought, felt, said, and finally did.

The 'is' culture requires the participation and engagement of each individual in the organisation and thus opens the floor for building interconnectivity. Bate's contribution of the different way to look at the organisation is indispensable for this book, that is, not to think about culture but to think culturally. Baba's research on GDTs makes a substantial contribution to the specialist topic area of diversity in teams, and hence will be of essential importance to this book. Technology, and in particular, ICT is a prerequisite for cyberconnecting both on the content level as illustrated in one of the live cases and as a research approach, as in digital ethnography.

The Toolbox

What is an Anthropologist Doing on a 737 or in a Board Meeting?

Anthropology and business have long been perceived as separate worlds; nevertheless the former's methodology, that is, qualitative research in organisations, has over the centuries become popular routine.

As illustrated in the sections above, 'From Armchair Researcher to Globalisation and ICT Expert' and 'Business Anthropology – The Shapers and their Domains', anthropologists brought a number of innovative approaches to organisations. Even in today's business world largely interconnected by ICT, the discipline's qualitative fieldwork techniques are priceless contributions to businesses and industries. Their value has been recognised by other disciplines such as marketing, product development and customer relationship management, whose professionals now apply these techniques in their work.

This section presents a description of the techniques that led to the approach of building interconnectivity, the framework 'The Three Lenses of Diversity', which will be illustrated in detail in subsequent chapters. The section does not comprise a full overview of all techniques available, but focuses only on the tools that have been used on the live cases presented in Chapter 1 and beyond. These tools are participant observation, sociogrammes, structured interviews, focus groups and field books.

PARTICIPANT OBSERVATION

Participant observation describes the process of gathering data about people's daily routines, in which the researcher takes on a role in the social situation under observation. The anthropologists immerse themselves in the researched social or organisational situation, whose success often depends on the researcher's relationship-building capacity with the key stakeholders. Originally this technique, known as ethnography, was developed to capture in writing the study of people at a particular place at a particular time.

As mentioned earlier, Bronislaw Malinowski is the 'creator' of ethnography and, in conjunction, participant observation in the traditional space of research. Undoubtedly he was present on the scene in the Trobriand Islands in Melanesia for a considerable period of time, simultaneously participating in and observing the social and cultural life of the group. Nowadays this is a widely used business technique.

Observational skills are applied as soon as the anthropologist arrives at the organisation, whether that be at the airport, in the parking lot of the company site or in the office buildings.

There is more than one function a researcher can assume in an organisation. The anthropologist can:

- become an organisational member; or

- enter the organisation as a consultant; or

- be introduced as a researcher conducting a survey.

Any function entitles the researcher to become immersed in 'participant observation' or in 'direct observation'. The latter role describes a situation where the researcher is present as an observer, but not as a participant. In reality, the arbitrary differentiation between 'participant observer' and 'direct observer' may not be so clear when taking on an assignment, since in reality, work often requires a hybrid role. This in turn is ignited by the multi-sited and interconnected research necessitated by today's business world. As a result, researchers cannot engage in every single action, so direct observation is necessary or even unavoidable.

An ideal situation allows the researcher to assume the role of overt observer. This includes full transparency regarding the researcher's presence in the field of study, typically presuming permission of all people of the studied community. In addition, it presumes a sponsor whose support is indispensable for the outcome of the research.

In contrast, there is also the approach of 'covert observation', often used in settings where overt observation would be difficult, for example, a mental hospital. Nonetheless, covert observation raises a number of ethical issues such as the researcher getting involved in inappropriate or even criminal situations or the risk that the researcher may 'go native'.

Anthropologists employing participant observation as a tool aim to understand the individual's or community's reality from the actor's perspective by simultaneously maintaining a necessary level of objectivity. Boundary-crossing has generated the notion of 'the other', which anthropology has dwelt on over centuries, expressed in the placing of 'the other' in a distant time and often place. More on 'the other' will follow in the next chapters.

Organisations offer many opportunities for analysis. An in-depth organisational analysis requires a thorough understanding of the people and processes in the organisation. Beyond participant observation there are several other types of exploration that anthropologists use, ranging from interviewing to working with focus groups. The rich data stemming from these methods in turn require modes of processing in order to identify patterns and meaningful results, for example coding.

INTERVIEWING

In addition to participant observation, one major research technique in anthropology is interviewing. It is one of the most common anthropological techniques used in the studies of organisations and people in general, and specifically of consumers. There is a wide variety of approaches, from informal interviews in the course of participant observation to highly structured interviews in formal settings, specifically arranged for this purpose.

Key informant interviewing can be conducted face-to-face, on the phone, via voice-over-IP services such as Skype, and even in writing. The latter form is usually disseminated by email, inviting respondents to reply electronically. One common format is word-processing or database files with prefabricated text fields for respondents to capture their insights. The other common form is real-time online surveys, assisting the researcher to design a questionnaire quickly and easily.

Informal interviewing in organisations typically occurs during participant observation or casual forms of investigation such as chats at the coffee machine. It is used throughout fieldwork to establish vital rapport with stakeholders and to unearth new topics that might remain undiscovered. Whilst the process of informal interviewing should appear to be a lightweight conversation to the key informants, the researcher needs to stay focused to adhere to the research agenda. At the end of the field day, it can feel like hard work to the researcher.

In highly structured interviews, by contrast, people are asked to respond to the same or an identical set of questions, which where digital dissemination of the questionnaire is concerned requires a brief introduction at the beginning of the questionnaire and a deadline by which the online questionnaire should be completed. In the case of face-to-face interviews the process requires an interview schedule and an explicit set of instructions for the interviewer.

The most commonly used form of interview techniques is the semi-structured interview. This consists of a written list of questions and topics to be covered in the interview. Despite the structure there is a quality of free flow which allows the anthropologist to follow new leads. It probably offers the best balance between free flow and full control in the course of an interview.

Prior to the start of the application of the interviewing techniques in an organisation some important issues need to be considered. These include setting up the interviews, the role of the anthropologist, the importance of language and the appropriate methods for data recording.

SOCIOGRAMMES

Sociogrammes are a form of visual representation of social relations. Typically, sociogrammes are diagrams of points and lines that illustrate the structure and patterns of group interactions. A sociogramme is an abstraction, a map representing the socio-geographic positions of group members and their relationships with every other person in the group. Commonly used symbols in anthropology are the triangle △ to flag male members of the group and the circle ○ to identify female members of the group.

When working with participants during the previously mentioned Hawthorne project, Roethlisberger, Dickson and Mayo paid special attention to the relationships among the workers. In the process, they discovered the 'informal organisation' of the organisation – the hidden social structure which seemed to have as much effect on worker productivity as anything in the 'formal company'.

Distinctively, sociogrammes can be drawn on the basis of many different criteria such as channels of influence, lines of communication and monitoring conversational turn-taking to identify power structures.

Whilst some social researchers use sociogrammes on the basis of pre-informed criterion, business anthropologists habitually use this type of chart to detect the unknown.

Nevertheless, in organisations the method is often applied on the pre-informed basis of process optimisation. The aims of its application are to help business units and whole organisations rethink the way they work, in order to fundamentally improve customer service, cut operational costs and ultimately to overtake competition in the sector of operation.

Airlines, for example, use the technique to chart the steps of cabin crew during food and beverage logistics. The analysis of these charts led to small changes in the preparation of the trolleys and the size of the glasses used, which resulted in better customer service and significant cost savings.

FOCUS GROUPS

In today's business world no marketing or research department would relinquish focus groups for consumer behaviour investigation. Prior to its long history in qualitative research dating back to the 1950s, the technique was also used much earlier in anthropological fieldwork in order to record people's real-time reactions. The 'Radio Research' work of Paul Lazarsfeld and Robert Merton crystallised its commercial benefits and the method thus became popular in organisations.

The overall purpose of focus group research is the exploration of respondents' attitudes, feelings, beliefs, experiences and reactions to a certain topic. Core approaches applied are loosely structured or semi-structured interview guidelines presenting questions or scenarios, which the group members discuss among themselves. The researcher's role is to facilitate the process.

The recommended number of participants for focus groups is six to ten people; the process usually requires one to four hours and is typically facilitated in on-site meeting rooms. The selection of the participants is often in the hands of one of the key informants and decision-makers of the organisation, coordinated upon the guidelines provided by the anthropologist researcher.

Organising and moderating focus groups in organisations can be quite a challenge; so is the data recording process. Nevertheless, one major advantage of this qualitative research method in organisations and specifically to clients, users, participants or consumers is that they can become a forum for change, as early as at the stage of initial inquiry.

THE FIELD BOOK GOING DIGITAL

Organisational exploration requires the capturing of data. The days of the imperialist pith helmet and leather-embroidered notebooks provided with a glass inkwell and pen are long gone.

Fieldwork and, specifically, participant observation is still considered the adventure part of the entire process. Writing up notes, in contrast, is viewed as the least sexy part of the venture.

The term 'field book' is used here to illustrate different types of field notes. These are:

- scratch notes: plotting random notes about actions, encounters, unexpected occurrences in the course of a field day;

- diary: personal notes about the fieldwork, designed to capture feelings serving as a tool in challenging or even stressful situations;

- log: research plan on fieldwork time scheduled versus fieldwork time invested;

- field notes: the meat of all fieldwork; mostly descriptive notes from watching and listening, sometimes also methodological notes or analytical notes.

Whilst all of these types of field notes used to be handwritten, they now have largely become digital.

Available tools and applications are numerous. Whilst this section summarises just a few of these ideas, worldwide thousands are being developed and put online. Figure 2.2 below provides an overview of the changes during the move into the digital age of anthropological fieldwork in organisations:

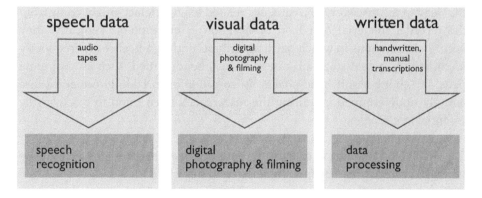

Figure 2.2   **From analogue to digital field research methods**

In today's cyberconnected business world the application of these methods and related considerations such as internet access and data protection have become daily routine. When conducting research in organisations situated in more remote places, some of these issues require careful consideration and alternative solutions. Nonetheless even coding, that is, the analysis of the collected date, has gone digital. The next section presents a brief introduction to coding, after which we will consider these options.

CODING

Coding is an important technique in qualitative research. The objective of coding is the extraction of key words and other 'meaningful chunks' from the rich data collected by anthropological research methods. As described in the sections above, these are participant observation, structured interviews, sociogrammes and focus groups that will allow new insights and approaches.

Coding gives explanations for patterns of behaviour that are relevant and important for the people involved. The exploration of significant categories and associated relationships can also lead to a complete theory.

The process of identifying patterns, codes and categories is usually long and exhausting, when done manually. It requires testing and retesting assumptions and finally the triangulation of discovered codes and categories. The work includes repeated word-by-word analysis, which traditionally has been done manually. Over the last few years the process has been automated by the help of rich-text databases and algorithms developed for this purpose.

One important step in the process of coding is the identification and labelling of categories, such as 'the use of a certain artefact' or a way of 'greeting'. Codes that lead to the discovery of a category related to an 'artefact' might come from the recorded material based on observation of encounters. Typically, they occur in interactions in which particular rituals and significance are frequently identified. As a next step, sub-categories can be identified, such as 'corporate pens' or 'giving a soft hand-shake'. In so-called open coding, categories are entirely undetermined, requiring the researcher's open mind to discover the essential material.

Finally, the labelling of categories is important as this provides a handle by which the category can be thought about and discussed.

Traditionally, coding has been a manual process, often starting with the identification of 'eye-catchers' in the mountain of materials. Over time the process went digital. In line with technological development and market availability, hierarchical database systems first became popular in social sciences. This type of database, however, captures only 1:n relationships, also known as parent–child relationships, linking together records like a family tree with one single source. For the complexity inherent in social science research 1:n databases soon proved to be incomplete, and thus with the emergence of relational databases the complexity of social relations was more easily mirrored digitally. Relational databases accommodate a collection of tables of data items, all of which are formally described and organised according to the relational model, allowing a quick comparison of information due to the arrangement of data in rows and columns. The possibility to describe many-to-many or n:m relationships among data items together with the uniformity of relational databases further allows the researcher to build completely new tables from existing tables, using structured query language. Strictly speaking, the n:m database encodes the logical relationships between data items through a normalisation process with a view to ensuring data consistency and to increasing the speed and versatility of the database.

With today's social network opportunities anthropologists leverage the tools made available from this environment. Materials collected from organisational research can now be presented online. Digital photo-books, narrative accounts, stories and so on invite audiences to run the analysis, identify eye-catchers, design polls, win prizes – in brief, they design a gamified process to motivate audiences to do the coding for you.

Mobile research has become an indispensable attribute in modern organisations for learning and development across contexts, enabling users to take advantage of the discovery opportunities offered by mobile technologies. 'Gamification' refers to the application of selected game thinking and game mechanics in a non-game context such as organisations, for the use of and benefit to employees and stakeholder engagement. Gamification in this context has become one import vehicle to support motivation and learning outcomes in diverse audiences.

One research area anthropologists have just started to investigate is the next frontier of innovation, competition and productivity, all soundly resting on human behaviour, that is, big data.

Today's most-hyped technology of big data describes the massiveness of the amount of data now created each day and collected by organisations. It also describes the speed at which this data is analysed, and finally the diversity of the type of data that is generated and collected, including text, audio, web logs and more. Common ways to describe big data are 'volume, fuzziness, correlation and reuse'.

In general, social science disciplines distinguish between two types of human behaviour data. The first, quantitative or 'thin' data, comes from digital sources: for example, he is 38 years old, drives an SUV and buys diapers. The second, to which cultural and business anthropology largely contributes, is qualitative or 'rich' data, often captured in thick descriptions and rich text. It delivers an understanding of how people actually experience the world. For example, he likes the baby's smell, his eyes brighten up when he looks at the baby, buying sanitary products for the child makes him feel special.

Big data analytics is a tool. Available big data algorithms predominantly focus on correlation, paying little attention to causality, and, as a result, provide limited feedback into what humans actually think and feel. The reality is that deeper insights into human behaviour remain elusive for most organisations. Small data insights from qualitative research are essential for making meaning out of patterns in big data by uncovering the causality of behaviours.

At the same time, the exclusive days of small data are gone. Data is simply becoming too much bigger and more complex. Anthropologists, who over the centuries have solely concentrated on small data, will not only have to start thinking differently about how they work meaningfully with the phenomenon of big data, but also about how to shape ways of working responsibly and aiming to role model ethically sound behaviour in the big data industry.

Ethical and legal dilemmas occur at all stages of anthropological research. Business anthropologists are responsible for anticipating and resolving the issues related to ethical standards. They need to act in accordance with data protection rules provided by the client organisation and with ethical norms outlined by various bodies covering anthropological research in order to protect research participants and contributions to research knowledge. Within these competing duties and conflicting interests business anthropologists should strive to maintain integrity in the conduct of anthropological research.

In summary, the unique contributions from business anthropology to the process of building interconnectivity work are as follows:

1.   'Inside-out insights through immersion': the method of fieldwork activity. The unique contribution of anthropology is the conduct of ethnographic fieldwork by means of participant observation.

2.   'The paradigm shift': the critical look at organisations as a cultural phenomenon. Organisations are viewed as tribes with specific values and norms that inform and re-inform their members.

3.   'The rich text writing': the narrative style of writing of ethnographies by anthropologists distinguishes business anthropology from other organisation research disciplines to an extent that it can include thick descriptions and storytelling.

4.   Globalisation, boundary-spanning, interconnecting: combining seemingly opposing topics and approaches in the cyberconnected world of work.

The Fresh Perspective on Organisations – How Much Culture is in it?

The anthropological discipline presents the opportunity to gain a holistic view of an organisation. The featured methods are typically 'emic', which originates from 'phonemic' and in general refers to speech sound that carries meaning. Emic thus describes observed behaviours and behavioural patterns presented in a way that is meaningful to the owner of the behaviour, or actor. Obviously, the relevance of a meaning can be recognised only by people familiar with the differentiation to the meaning of other phonemes. Literally anything from within an organisational culture can inform an emic account. As a result, organisational surveys based on anthropological methods can take unexpected turns and surface unforeseen results.

Anthropological methods encourage looking at a more open-ended research area, for example, surfacing multiple identity constructions as key success factors in cross-boundary work.

DEPTH OF FINDINGS – RICH TEXT VERSUS SHORT MESSAGE

One other unique contribution from anthropology is the depth of findings. In the business world, where the research takes place, efficiency is critical to the survival of businesses. All activities focus on generating profit, which naturally requires a different perception of what is of primary importance. In brief, priorities of organisations in the business world are typically speed and usefulness.

In contrast, in the social sciences the focus lies on the processes. Conducting research with appropriate methods produces valid results with a primary emphasis on the validity of findings rather than their usefulness. The specified research methods acknowledged in the social science field are designed to provide depth and typically allow no shortcuts. As a result findings might be complex and thus perceived as inadequate in the speedy and result-oriented business world.

DEALING WITH COMPLEXITY

In recent years, businesses have indicated an increasing need to dealing with complexity and diversity in the business world. Leading and managing across boundaries has become a gradually more complex task where simple answers no longer provide suitable solutions.

Academic procedures and solutions are needed in the business world. Due to the fact that findings might be out of the routine scope of business, there seems to be a limited understanding of which of the conclusions are valid or invalid and, even more, relevant for business.

The richness from cross-disciplinary research is being increasingly acknowledged. Findings from minority disciplines are being heard. Ways to analyse, think and reach valid conclusions are growing in importance. This capability should be used to translate findings from research in such a way that they can become meaningful for leaders in the interconnected business world and thus inherent diversity.

The Practice – The Anthropological Ingredient of The Three Lenses of Diversity

In Part II of this book, 'The Practice', outcomes from the anthropological research are reflected as summarised in Box 2.2:

**Box 2.2   The Anthropological Ingredient of
The Three Lenses of Diversity**

This is the study of people in organisations, including the self and the other. Multi-sited ethnography focused on people's interactions, continuously questioning potentially pre-informed perception. Related data analysis led to the identification of structured patterns of interaction that describe diversity in a global business situation, which enabled the creation of a framework called The Three Lenses of Diversity that provides practical alternatives with which people in similar global business situations can operate. The Three Lenses of Diversity, when applied to future cross-boundary interactions, functions as a roadmap that helps people leverage their full diversity portfolio for success in business.

The Application – The Toolbox in Action

In Part III of this book, 'The Application', approaches from the anthropological disciplines are presented in full detail.

In summary of the above and as a preview of the coming chapters, Table 2.3 provides you with an overview of the selected technique (tool), its method and purpose, and the objective for the further development of a prototype of a gamified road safety mobile application. Gamification in the business world is used to motivate and engage an audience to achieve a desired outcome by positively influencing an anticipated behaviour change beneficial to the organisation output.

Table 2.3   The anthropology toolbox

Tool	Methods	Purpose	Objectives
Researcher Log	Testing in own context – App installation on research team devices	Analysis of emotions and behaviours in own context Data collection merges into overall findings	Getting to know the application and potential own observable behaviour changes
User Log	Group of 200 employees record experience with app in own context over a few days time	Collection of a larger data set, directly stemming from the users	Key insights from larger user group in excess to existing primary research outcome (22 users)
Participant Observation	Driving session user and researcher, Location, number of users, timing and so on to be identified	Analysis of emotions and behaviours in driver's context	Exploration of potential observable behaviours of drivers
In-depth Interviews	One-to-one interviews with drivers subsequent to driving session	Following up on observed behaviours, identifying causes and drivers for displayed behaviours	Uncovering motivation to change behaviour, Winning insights on suitable gamification elements
Focus Groups	Small group exploration of experience	Exploration of driving experience and use of gamified version of app	Immediate feedback of experience

Chapter 3

The Emergence of Diversity
as a Process

The previous chapter highlights the contribution anthropology, specifically business anthropology, has made to the business world over the decades, and illustrates the approaches required to help build interconnectivity.

This chapter now adds additional key ingredients from two key management development fields that shape the 'Diversity as a process' approach: namely, the diversity field and the intercultural field. The first part of the chapter briefly presents the history of diversity in a nutshell and so crystallises essential aspects of current understanding of Diversity as a process. The second part of the chapter illustrates the emergence of the intercultural field and its connected industry, and brings to light its relevance for understanding of Diversity as a process. The third part explains how the source live case originated from anthropological fieldwork, and finally the inauguration of Diversity as a process, its connected framework, 'The Three Lenses of Diversity', and the tool building on the research insights, the cyberIdentity Development Tool (cyberIDT) are presented.

Key concepts of the first two sections of the chapter are outlined below. Concepts were selected based upon the influence they had at the point of emergence in their respective discipline and the importance they have for Diversity as a process (see Table 3.1).

The sections 'The Emergence of Diversity' and 'The Rise of the Intercultural Industry' present a concise view of the growth of each field over the last few decades. Clearly, the coverage is by no means full; however, it illustrates the complexity of these fields. Moreover, two brief illustrations crystallise the different agendas of the fields. On the one hand, the traditional understanding of the diversity field looks at national agendas with the goal of minimising discrimination and achieving equality and inclusion for minority groups. On the other hand, the intercultural field seeks to provide understanding of the 'other' primarily in the business field. By realising this, the connected intercultural industry often over-essentialises the 'other' to the benefit of profit generation and maximisation.

Table 3.1   Key concepts of the diversity and the cross-cultural/intercultural disciplines

	Diversity	Cross-cultural/Intercultural industry
1950s/1960s	Civil and women's rights, national US matter	Theoretical field of cross-cultural psychology and applied field of cross-cultural training due to continuous expansion of international business community
	Civil Rights Act Women's movement grew out of Civil Rights Movement for African Americans About rights/discrimination based on race and gender At different times added other elements, for example, sexual orientation	Culture assimilator for specific groups with particular needs
1980s/1990s	From national agenda to organisational agenda	Culture by dimensions/Dilemma theory
	From legalistic to value	Culture-general assimilator
	Social identity theory versus investigating single dimensions of diversity	Culture clash and culture shock publications
	Inclusion and capability approach	Development of interpersonal skills specific for intercultural management challenges
2000s	From focus on difference towards focus on relationship	Basic human values as bridging strategy
	Identity negotiation mainly on the basis of visible traits	Psychometric tools

The Emergence of Diversity

The new understanding of Diversity as a process mirrors the world and its fast-changing circumstances and challenges: a significant increase in natural catastrophes with immeasurable impact on people and organisations, attempts at political change in regions where change on this scale was not expected, an increase in migration of unknown volume and extent, and an unparalleled shift towards individual responsibility and accountability, to name but a few. The uncertainties inherent in these challenges reflect the necessity for the new paradigm of diversity and its application to the phenomena people are subject to in the workplace context.

THE RISE OF CIVIL RIGHTS

When the topic of diversity rose in popularity in the mid-twentieth century, it focused first on women's rights and civil rights at the national level in the US. In a nationally televised address on 6 June 1963, President John F. Kennedy urged the nation to take action towards guaranteeing equal treatment of every American regardless of race. Soon after, Kennedy proposed that Congress consider civil rights legislation to address voting rights, public accommodation, school desegregation, nondiscrimination in federally assisted programmes and more. Despite Kennedy's assassination in November 1963, only one year later Title VII of the Civil Rights Act became law in the United States, outlawing discrimination in employment in any business on the basis of race, religion, sex or national origin. For black and white, male and female, the doors to opportunity opened.

In that same year:

- Thomas Kurtz and John Kemeny created BASIC, an easy-to-learn programming language, for their students at Dartmouth College, United Kingdom.

- Bob Dylan's songs of social protest to conditions in American society became increasingly popular.

- The Beatles arrived in America.

- Nelson Mandela was sentenced to life imprisonment in South Africa.

As of this writing, 1964 is already a half-century in the past. The world then, its events and configurations feel very distant from today's interconnected world. The roots of interconnectedness were already there, however, as evidenced by the following two examples from that year:

1.   IBM announced the System/360, a family of six mutually compatible computers and 40 peripherals that could work together. The initial investment of $5 billion was quickly returned as orders for the system climbed to 1,000 per month within two years. At the time IBM released the System/360, the company was making a transition from discrete transistors to integrated circuits, and its major source of revenue changed from punched-card equipment to electronic computer systems.[1]

2.   First signs of connections within Europe were expressed by the British and French Governments as they agreed a deal for the construction of a Channel Tunnel. The twin tunnelled rail link was expected to take five years to build; it was finally opened 30 years later.

In the later twentieth century the scope of the 'strategic imperative to increase the representation of minorities and help achieve ethnicity and gender targets'[2] shifted from the national to the organisational, with organisations soon viewing equality as a cost factor.[3]

VALUING DIVERSITY

In parallel, an additional shift occurred: due to growing globalisation and its inherent interconnectedness of cooperation and interaction during the last decades of the twentieth century, the focus shifted from a legalistic approach to one of 'valuing diversity'.[4] This development took place to avoid two potential dangers:

1.   damage to the organisation's reputation externally; and

2.   internally rising costs caused by high interpersonal conflict and increased employee turnover.[5]

In its attempt to avoid potential harm, the new orientation of valuing diversity promotes two advantages for organisations:

---

1   http://www.computerhistory.org/timeline/?year=1964.
2   Burnett, Kettleborough 2007:102.
3   April, Shockley 2007:23.
4   April, Shockley 2007:357.
5   Bennet-Alexander 2000:103.

1.   diversity as competitive advantage as organisations utilise a broad
        diversity to enhance the organisation's sensing capability for new
        market opportunities;[6] and

2.   equal valuation and treatment for all in compliance with social
        justice and corporate social responsibility.[7]

In the early 2000s the concept of inclusion first appeared on the scene. Inclusion
describes the approach of 'creating environments where all people can prosper
and progress irrespective of race, colour, gender, physical ability, age, religion,
sexual orientation, or belief'.[8] At the same time, the 'capability approach'[9] found
its echo in commercial, governmental and not-for-profit organisations. In the
1980s, the capability approach was first articulated by the Indian philosopher
Amartya Sen; it is defined by its choice of focus on the moral significance of
individuals' capability of achieving the kind of lives they have reason to value.
In the 2000s, the ethical theory earned attention in the workplace equality
agenda, which can be viewed as an explicit ethics of equality.

In the late 1990s and early 2000s the recognition of the potential value of
diversity motivated two major streams of research (see Figure 3.1).

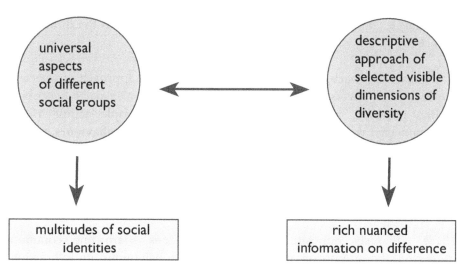

Figure 3.1   Late 1990s/early 2000s: Two major streams of research

---

6   April, Shockley 2007:56.
7   Appiah 2005; Cornelius 2002; Fukukawa et al. 2007.
8   Burnett, Kettleborough 2007:103.
9   Gagnon, Cornelius 2002:32.

Organisational researchers specialising in the tradition of social identity theory explored insights into the universal aspects of encounters with diversity. These universal aspects describe the ways people view others and interact with those who belong to a different social group, regardless how the group is defined, for example by gender, race, nationality, occupation, tenure or some combination of demographic dimensions. The aim is to surface those intergroup dynamics that are likely to emerge as the result of any type of difference, making hardly any distinctions among the multitude of social identities that may differentiate people. Reduced interest in these distinctions happens at the expense of the differences that shape experiences with certain specific kinds of diversity, such as race and gender.

The other stream of that time presents the opposite direction, investigating single dimensions of diversity. Volumes have been filled with rich and nuanced information, specifically on the unique implications of race, gender and nationality presenting distinct concerns, challenges and opportunities inherent in these specific dimensions on social interaction. This stream fully investigates aspects such as power and status differences that stem from societal and historical contingencies. This approach supports the examination of the types of relationships among categories of people representing the mentioned dimensions of diversity and how they differ, for example, the difference between Whites and Blacks on the dimension of race.

Neither approach, that is, neither the descriptive approach of selected dimensions of diversity nor the approach of universal aspects described earlier, however, offers the necessary solutions people acting in an interconnected workplace require, namely, outlooks on behaviours people with different social identities or different selected dimension of diversity might display.

NEGOTIATING IDENTITY

These obviously opposite research approaches share one common challenge: the prediction of diverse people's behaviour in interaction (see Figure 3.2). Predictions and outlooks for just two people interacting seem impossible; even more so are predictions and ramifications for the complexity of intergroup interactions among people with overlapping of distinct characteristics.

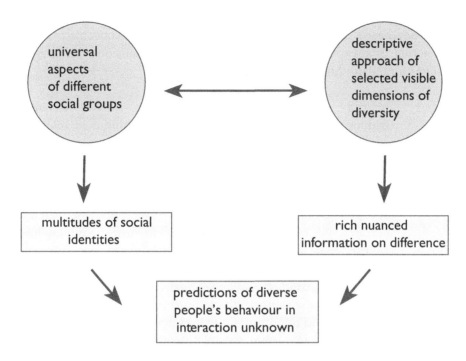

Figure 3.2   Challenge of both streams of research

Identity negotiation first became a prominent topic a few years into the new millennium. Identity negotiation describes the cognitions that people have about themselves, which they call 'self-views', and the cognitions they have about others, also called 'appraisals', the correspondence of the two, and the affective and behavioural manifestations of these cognitions.[10] The approach is based on the early work of symbolic interactionists, dating back to the early twentieth century, who proposed that people make sense from the world based on self-views and interpret other's behaviours towards them.

Individuals interpret and draw meaning from past interactions and experiences while informing future interactions based on former episodes. Misalignment of self-views and appraisals is of clear concern to targets and perceivers individually; it also has serious implications for their collective attitudes and experiences in interactions.[11] Group identity, social integration, relationship conflict and collective performance are all subject to the overall degree of correspondence between self-views and appraisals in a group of people, referred to as interpersonal congruence.

---

10 Polzer, Caruso 2008:92 in Diversity at Work.
11 Polzer et al. 2002.

Today nearly all medium to large organisations are concerned with the promotion of diversity in one of the portrayed dimensions. In designing systems for the promotion of diversity, organisations:

- typically run recurring and compulsory training to inform employees about their duties and responsibilities in relation to equal employment opportunities;

- introduce human resources (HR) processes that help to design, monitor and evaluate the implementation of diversity policies and practices, whose assessment is extended into the managers' performance reviews, through which, in turn, accountability is believed to be achieved;

- periodically conduct organisational 'temperature checks' by systemically analysing feedback from employees about perceptions of barriers and opportunities to career advancement. These audits are designed to surface potential institutional bias in relation to diversity and inclusion matters. Results help to shape and design cultural change initiatives to close the gap between the current and the desired cultures.

The success of any of these initiatives requires authentic leadership and thus commitment and role-modelling from senior leaders in order to demonstrate true substance as opposed to mere symbolism.

Since the introduction of the Civil Rights Act in 1964 cross-boundary interconnectedness has exponentially increased:

- digital information is today measured in petabytes, that is, 10^{15} bytes or 1,000 terabytes, now available to decision-makers about people's, and specifically customer's behaviours;

- social media platforms have created superstars long before they boarded a plane;

- the nature of learning has changed from individualistic perspective to interconnected approach, team learning and Massive Open Online Courses (MOOCs).

The cyberconnected workplace is the expression of these developments and events. In the majority of organisations, HR departments are in charge of diversity policies and practices. The interconnectedness of the modern workplace now requires a new form of diversity beyond policies and practices. Diversity now needs to meet the requirements of the people for whom boundary-spanning is paramount for success in business, available at their fingertips.

For this purpose diversity changes from an HR department responsibility to a personal responsibility and opportunity.

The Rise of the Intercultural Industry

This section captures the rise of the intercultural industry, highlighting its benefit: the understanding of the 'other' on the interpersonal agenda for the benefit of business success.

Before exploring a more detailed illustration of the intercultural field, it is certainly essential to clarify the word 'intercultural' as opposed to 'cross-cultural'. These two terms tend to be used interchangeably, causing a lack of clarity in both definition and application. One of the definitions of 'cross-cultural' is as follows:

> ... It is important to make a distinction between cross-cultural and intercultural (communication). Nevertheless, boundaries are fuzzy and a critical review of publications illustrates, that writers and researchers use the two terms interchangeably. Cross-cultural (communication) refers to comparing communication and behaviours of different groups when considered abstractly or when members of different groups are directly engaged with each other, i. e. two groups of different national identity.[12]

In contrast, one definition of 'intercultural' is as follows:

> ... Intercultural (communication) refers to people in social interaction with each other (not upon conceived differences between members of different groups).[13]

---

12 Scollon, Scollon 1995:13.
13 Scollon, Scollon 1995:13.

As boundaries in a cyberconnected workplace and thus interactions by people in these settings become ever fuzzier, this section will continue to use the term 'intercultural', but will apply the term 'cross-cultural' where necessary to context and in quoted research.

Subsequent to the clarification of terminology let us look to the emergence of 'business anthropology'.

As captured in Chapter 2 'Leveraging Contributions from Anthropology', the emergence of business anthropology took place as early as the 1920s.

THE RISE OF THE INTERCULTURAL INDUSTRY

The anthropologist Edward Hall unintentionally but certainly powerfully led to the packaging of culture, still popular in today's Interculturalist industry. In his effort to present cultural understanding in an accessible form to nonacademics,[14] Hall focused on microbehaviour, such as space and time perceptions in different cultures, which largely shaped the first intercultural hype in the 1960s. As described in the previous chapter, times were favourable for the emergence of the intercultural industry then, primarily for three economy-based reasons. These were:

1.   The West began to form relationships with former colonised states;

2.   The United States increased economic and technical aid to Third World countries; and

3.   Japan and the OPEC countries achieved economic success.[15]

This economic development raised the need to understand the mentality of 'the other side', greatly contributing to the first stage of development of the 'culture shock industry'.[16] Whilst a number of anthropologists, such as the earlier mentioned Edward Hall, were leading figures in business anthropology, a parallel industry became increasingly popular, namely the Interculturalists, whose aim was to package culture suitably for the needs of the business world. The offering of the Interculturalists to their target groups would be largely the assorting of different cultures in the form of entities, who in turn would engage in social transaction.

---

14 Dahlen 1997:42.
15 Dahlen 1997:11.
16 Hannerz 1996:9.

Looking back in the history of the intercultural industry it is essential to recognise three main streams which emerged over the last six decades with the industry in place. These three streams are presented in the section below, whereby the first two streams are still labelled 'cross-cultural' and whilst the third by self-definition is called 'intercultural'.

The first stream emerged in the 1960s when the intercultural industry became increasingly popular due the continuous expansion of the international business community and an increase of migration. In the United States organisations such as the Peace Corps and various missionary organisations sent greater numbers of people to overseas destinations.[17] Cushner and Brislin argue that:

> ... the theoretical field of cross-cultural psychology and the applied field
> of cross cultural or intercultural training have both continued to grow
> in response to these circumstances.[18]

One of the methods they developed, known as the culture assimilator, has become increasingly popular. The culture assimilator features a critical-incident approach. These incidents are captured in short vignettes presenting examples of culture clashes between individuals from different groups, who in their interaction intend to pursue a common goal.[19]

This publication on the culture assimilator presents a number of incidents from the Middle East without any further specification such as geographic location. The one exception takes place in Saudi Arabia, again with no further specification, and is presented below. The short description is followed by selection of alternative suggestions prompting the reader to select the best possible explanation.

Box 3.1   Opening a Medical Office*

Dr Tom McDivern, a physician from New York City, was offered a two-year assignment to practice medicine in a growing urban centre in Saudi Arabia. Many of the residents in the area he was assigned to were recent immigrants from the much smaller outlying rural areas. Because Western medicine was relatively unknown to many of these people, one of Dr McDivern's main responsibilities was to introduce himself and his services to those in the community. A meeting

---

17 Cushner, Brislin 1996:1.
18 Cushner, Brislin 1996:1.
19 Cushner, Brislin 1996:13.

at a local school was organised for that specific purpose. Many people turned out, and Tom's presentation went well. Some local residents also presented their experiences with Western medicine so that others could understand the value of using his services. Some of Tom's office staff were also present to make appointments for those interested in seeing him when his doors opened a week later. The meeting was an obvious success; his opening day was booked solid.

When that day finally arrived, Tom was anxious to greet his first patients. Thirty minutes had passed, however, and neither of his first two patients had arrived. Tom began to worry about the future of his practice as he wondered where his patients were.

What was the major cause of Tom's worries?

1. Although in Tom's mind and by his standards his presentation was a success, people actually only made appointments so as not to hurt his feelings. They really had no intentions of using his services, as modern medicine was so foreign to their past experiences.

2. Given the time lag between sign-up and the actual day of their appointments, people had time to rethink their decisions. They had just changed their minds.

3. Views concerning units of time differ between Arabs and Americans. Whereas Tom believed his patients were very late, the Arab patients could still arrive and consider themselves to be on time.

4. Tom's patients were seeing their own traditional healers from their own culture; after that, they could go on to see the new doctor.

*Cushner, Brislin 1996:160.

Further to each incident the reader is then provided with rationales for alternative explanations, which also indicate the best answer.

Until the mid-1980s the culture assimilator was developed for specific groups with particular needs. The incidents of the culture-specific assimilator were designed to prepare individuals from one cultural group for interaction with people from another specific group.[20]

Around this time Brislin developed the culture-general assimilator largely based on a rich and diverse body of research identifying similarities in people's

---

20 Cushner, Brislin 1996:13.

experiences despite the wide range of roles they had and the many different countries in which they lived.[21]

In the 1980s and 1990s a great number of 'culture clash' publications[22] with the aim of explaining how to achieve better results when doing business with 'the other' appeared on the market. Justifying the need for these publications necessitated that authors point out the problem, as depicted in the example below:

> ... Cultural diversity is not something that is going to go away tomorrow, enabling us to plan our strategies on the assumption of mutual understanding.

This early development of this industry raised the need to understand the mentality of 'the other side' by regularly pointing to the difficulties connected to it, thus greatly contributing to the first stage of acceleration of the 'culture shock industry'.[23]

The use of 'Othering' serves as the key assumption for more or less developed research in the field and is reflected in almost all publications, one of them being Richard Lewis' *When Cultures Collide*. In the introduction the concept of 'Othering' is embedded within the boundaries of various nation states, which are then labelled as national characteristics. Disconcertingly, the author claims that working with the concept of 'national characteristics' is treading a minefield of inaccurate assessment and surprising exception.[24]

Idiosyncratic to these publications are the following two facts:

1.   It would appear to be an advantage to conceive of culture as something with its own properties, rather tangible, bounded, atemporal and internally homogeneous;[25] and

2.   Cultures need to be categorised in order to become manageable, that is, 'the several hundred national and regional cultures of the world can roughly be categorised into three groups'.[26]

---

21   Cushner, Brislin 1996:25.
22   Dahlen 1997:13.
23   Hannerz 1996:9.
24   Lewis 1999:3.
25   Dahlen 1997:178.
26   Lewis 1996:36.

Further to this clarification of the understanding of culture, a list of cultural characteristics organised by nationalities is usually offered. As some of the source data was collected in Egypt, below is a taster[27] typically labelled as Middle East:

- The West sees Arab society as one which is in decline, propped up temporarily by oil revenues. The Arabs, by contrast, are very conscious that their civilisation once led the world and believe they are capable of doing so again (in a moral sense).

- Arabs move around less than Westerners, therefore they are more conservative.

- Arabs stand or sit much closer to their interlocutors than do Westerners. It is normal to breathe on them and touch them frequently.

- Pork is taboo to Arabs, unlike in the West.

The repertoire of this type of publications is further enhanced by literature presenting one country or region such *Understanding the Arabs*[28] or *Don't They Know It's Friday?*,[29] frequently offering more detailed descriptions, nevertheless still presenting a range of stereotypes.

The concept of culture as something with its own properties and as a tangible and internally homogeneous entity is promoted not only in specialist publications, but equally in student textbooks such as the one below on organisational behaviour:

> … *Behaviour is any form of human action. For example, based on their culture, Middle Easterners stand closer together (a behaviour) than do North Americans, whereas Japanese stand farther apart than do either North Americans or Middle Easterners. Latin Americans touch each other more frequently during business negotiations than do North Americans, and both touch more frequently than do Japanese. People's behaviour is defined by their culture.*[30]

---

27 Lewis 1996:334 ff.
28 Nydell 1996.
29 Williams 1998.
30 Adler 2002:18.

PRIME TIME POPULARITY

The second stream, which was introduced by Geert Hofstede, organises culture by dimensions. His definition of culture is 'the collective programming of the mind which distinguishes the members of one category of people from another'.[31]

Hofstede's work has become common knowledge not only among people related to the intercultural field, but to a wider community such as individuals who have participated in management development programmes. At this point it is significant to note that most people's knowledge about Hofstede's concept was collected by third party sources presenting the initial four dimensions.[32]

Hofstede's now widely known concept stems from data gathered from a survey on work-related values conducted between 1967 and 1973, in which 88,000 employees from across IBM took part. The data derived were processed by factor analysis and results were presented in a four-field diagram.[33] A number of publications were extricated from the base findings. In brief, the four dimensions are:[34]

- power distance, which describes dependency relations in society;

- uncertainty avoidance, which refers to the anxiety people have towards the future, and which humans have tried to cope with through technology, law and religion;

- individualism, which describes the relationship between the individual and the collective, pointing to examples such as that in some societies people live in nuclear families whilst others live in tribal units based on kinship; and

- masculinity, which refers to assertiveness, as opposed to femininity, which refers to nurturing.

Along these dimensions Hofstede ranks 40 national cultures from high to low.

Hofstede's work has been widely criticised, specifically for the absence of any substantial methodology and its Western bias. From an anthropological

---

31 Hofstede 1980 in Lewis 1996:25.
32 Dahlen 1997:63.
33 Dahlen 1997:109.
34 Hofstede 1980:11.

point of view the most outrageous factor is the narrow conceptualisation of culture, using culture as a synonym for nation. One hair-raising example of the application of this narrow use of culture is the all-White sample to represent South Africa, due to the Apartheid system at the time of the data collection.

Another popular concept based on dimensions is Charles Hampden-Turner and Fons Trompenaars' study published in 'Building cross-cultural competence. How to create wealth from conflicting values'. They identified seven dimensions from the results of questionnaires, which presented the respondents with a straight choice between universal rules versus particular exceptions, individual advantages versus community responsibilities, specific versus diffuse criteria of judgement, and more.[35]

The Trompenaars and Hampden-Turner study[36] identified seven dimensions on which the values of diverse cultures vary. These concepts are highly abstract terms, deliberately so as the authors claim that we seek to include a large number of 'family resemblances' beneath each bifurcation. These 'families' are:

- Human Relationships, comprising Universalism versus Particularism, which seeks to discover whether one's prime allegiance is to rules and rulebound classifications, or to exceptional, unique circumstances;

- Individualism versus Communitarianism, which measures the extent to which managers see the individual employee and shareholder, his or her development, enrichment, fulfilment as paramount or to what extent the corporation, customers and the wider group should be the beneficiaries of all personal efforts;

- Specific versus Diffuse, which measures the tendency to analyse, reduce and break down the field of experience, or to synthesise, augment and construct experience;

- Neutral versus Affective, which concerns the legitimacy of showing or controlling emotions while at work;

- Achieved status versus Ascribed status, which is about why status is conferred on people. Is this because of what they have

---

35 Hampden-Turner, Trompenaars 2000:353.
36 Also see Hampden-Turner, Trompenaars 2000.

achieved or because of what they 'are', that is, human beings, male, of good background;

- Time, comprising Sequential time versus Synchronous time, which has to do with whether one sees time as passing in a sequence, or coming around again and again; and

- Nature, again covering only one dimension, Innerdirected versus Outerdirected, which concerns the 'locus of control'. Is it inside each of us, or outside in our environments to which we must adapt?

Even though based on the dimension concept, this study presents a ground-breaking perspective as it is applicable to any kind of situation beyond the national concept, be it private, organisational or public.

This approach is enhanced by the development of the dilemma theory, which clearly distances the approach from an either-or dichotomy towards reconciliation of conflict situations. As opposed to the Hofstede study, whose data source is one organisation, the data of the Hampden-Turner and Trompenaars study was collected across different organisations in different industries located in different nation states.[37] Hampden-Turner and Trompenaars, oblivious to the pending impact of their study, found themselves selling the book far beyond the intercultural industry.

THE PERSONALISATION OF CULTURE

The third stream emerged with the rise of the new economy in the early 2000s, which increasingly required people to collaborate beyond the boundaries dominant in the 1990s, namely organisational boundaries and national borders.

The intercultural industry responded by offering practical tools based on concepts predominantly focusing on interpersonal skills. The revival and more sophisticated expression of some of the self-assessment tools applied from the 1960s throughout the 1990s with the aim of exploring one's perception found their expression in the form of psychometric instruments. These tools require candidates to complete online questionnaires and provide them with personal feedback, mostly delivered in one-to-one sessions but also designed for group settings, circumstances permitting.

---

37 Hampden-Turner, Trompenaars 2000:357.

One recent trend in the third stream is the focus on basic human values. Shalom Schwartz, a social psychologist, presents a theory on this topic[38] which discusses the nature of values and spells out the features that are common to all values and what distinguishes one value from another. The theory identifies ten basic personal values that are recognised across cultures and explains their origins. At the heart of the theory is the idea that values form a circular structure reflecting the motivations that each value expresses and that are appraised to be culturally universal. As is characteristic for recent developments in this area, the Theory of Basic Values can be measured by two major methods, the Schwartz Value Survey and the Portrait Values Questionnaire.

Diversity Management and the Intercultural Field – Complimentary yet Divergent

In summary of the illustration of the emergence of diversity and the rise of the intercultural industry presented above, Table 3.2 shows the respective agendas.

Table 3.2   Agendas of diversity management and the intercultural field in comparison

	Diversity	**Cross-cultural/Intercultural**
Market	Minority group interests Governments and organisations	Business people Respective counterparts: 'The other'
Objective	Minimisation of discrimination of minority groups as integral part of a nation's political agenda	Maximisation of organisation's profits from international business as key strategic objective
Method	Overall agenda focus on quotas	Intercultural training and development
Vision	Contribution to social justice based on tangible aspects of difference	Tolerance of world difference based on culture concepts as entities with describable boundaries

There have been two key management development fields for supporting awareness of diversity in recent years:

---

38 Schwartz 2012.

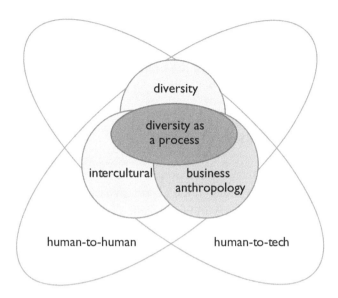

Figure 3.3   Three key components of Diversity as a process

1.   The Intercultural field, where the key objective has been to understand the 'other' in terms of diverse national cultural values and practices in the workplace, and the challenges that this brings to global collaboration.

2.   The Diversity field, where the key objective has been to reduce discriminatory practices against minority groups in the workplace, and thus support governmental agendas for greater social justice and integration.

In addition to these two key management development fields, which are in some ways divergent yet complimentary, a third ingredient forms the basis of the Diversity as a process approach, that is, the contributions from cultural anthropology, and specifically, business anthropology (see Figure 3.3).

The Genesis of Diversity as a Process

The third part of this chapter explains how business anthropology gave birth to the real-life cases.

This part further provides a short description of other relevant projects reflected in the research and presents the real-life case essential for continuous testing and illustration of Diversity as a process concepts.

This part also provides the key thinking of Diversity as a process and a glimpse into the connected framework called Diversity as a process matters. It closes with a preview of the tool developed on the basis of the key findings of the research, the cyberIdentity Development Tool, also known as the cyberIDT.

THE ORIGINS OF DIVERSITY AS A PROCESS

The source data for the Diversity as a process findings primarily originate from a large and complex programme in the expert area of 'change management' in the telecommunication industry in Egypt, called SonaConn. The programme's objective was the worldwide implementation of performance drivers (PDs) designed to support employees in developing skills to grow the business across the globe.

This inductive macro-ethnographic research dwells on rich data stemming from extensive fieldwork conducted by this author in the hybrid role of anthropologist and senior consultant. First order findings, that is, data presented from anthropological research approaches, lead into second order findings,[39] that is, the re-interpretation from micro-level outcome. The second order level allows for drawing on a wider range of projects. The study includes, it goes without saying, the core of the local and the global, and therefore represents an appropriate example of analysing a macro-level process for a wide range of international projects in the business world.

Other projects whose data merged into the research were equally large and complex projects overcoming a great number of horizontal and vertical boundaries. Specifically, they all took place in the management and organisation development area covering a number of strategic challenges in the airline and energy industries with headquarters in Europe whilst project stakeholders were spread across the globe. One core project that finds reflection in this book is the growth strategy of a start-up in the technology-driven learning industry called MyMemLab, briefly described in Chapter 1. The latter life case is the basis for continued testing of the further illustration of the Diversity as a process approach.

On the SonaConn project, first order findings come from a wide range of sources such as interaction by writing, that is, mostly asynchronous communication, such as email; interaction by speaking; interaction by watching; and interaction by doing.

---

39 Kriwet 1997:36.

Data, specifically from this complex project for first order findings, include the following:

- participant observation from 316 days' presence of the researcher in Cairo;

- 27 semi-structured interviews from the needs analysis period;

- ten informal interviews with senior management;

- four feedback sessions with focus groups, each comprised of up to eight participants;

- approximately 800 feedback forms from PD workshops completed by participants immediately following each workshop and six weeks after workshop dates;

- approximately 55 workshop activities building around PDs serving as basis for knowledge transfer;

- approximately 547 emails from the project team as basis for conversational analysis;

- numerous stories from team members, participants and individuals related but external to the project;

- approximately 35 follow-up interviews with the project team for data verification.

The chart in Figure 3.4 below provides an overview of the research flow and specifically the ways the first order findings progressed to second order findings. The collected data were carefully reviewed with the help of tools from cultural anthropology, which included identifying patterns, coding meaningful repetitions, labelling significant iterations and repeating the process several times.

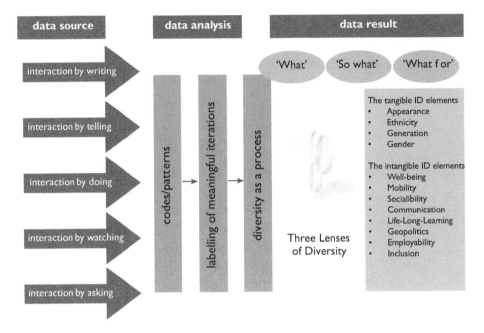

Figure 3.4   Summary of the research process

The actual research question examined the contributions from diversity. The contributions that were the second order findings were identified by filtering the available data through the subsequently developed framework. Now the research outcome can be organised into a hierarchy of three components: the overarching domain, a framework and finally a hands-on tool. Figure 3.5 below provides an overview and presents the key influencers necessary for the exhibition of the pyramid. Key influencers are:

• the three key ingredients as presented earlier; and

• the long-term experience in leadership and organisation development by the author.

The foundation is the Diversity as a process approach and its connected corollaries, the second layer is the framework 'Three Lenses of Diversity', which was one result of the data analysis and subsequently developed for this research and the third is the identity elements whose activation shapes the success or failure of connecting and effectively working across boundaries, which were subsequent to the actual research further developed and are now reflected in the psychometric development tool, the cyberIDT.

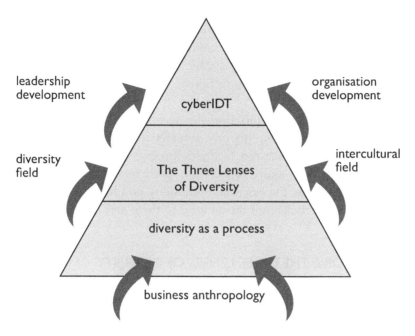

Figure 3.5   **The diversity as a process pyramid**

THE COROLLARIES OF DIVERSITY AS A PROCESS

Diversity as a process offers new perspectives and solutions to the personal and structural challenges people are facing in the cyberconnected world. Diversity as a process lies in the recognition of new insights gained from the research, which are summarised in the following four corollaries:

Corollary One: Diversity is dynamic.
Diversity is not just there. It is a process, which is created in dyadic or intergroup interactions.

Corollary Two: Diversity is regenerative.
The nature of diversity is changing in alignment with the multiple identity constructions people bring into these interactions.

Corollary Three: Diversity is perception-shaped.
The quality of diversity is shaped by the views and appraisals people bring into interactions and informs the readiness for adopting new behaviours.

Corollary Four: Diversity is environment-shaped.

Diversity is exposed to external configurations. Insights generated from these configurations are indispensable for the strategic orientation of the anticipated outcomes from interactions.

The complexity inherent in this domain necessitates a framework to help organise thinking in relation to any interaction in cross-boundary work situations. Equally, a structured feedback process on the ways people use their identity portfolio equips interaction participants with the necessary background knowledge, the essential vocabulary and finally the capability to find solutions to the challenges meaningful to them and the context in which they happen.

THE FRAMEWORK: THE THREE LENSES OF DIVERSITY

The Three Lenses of Diversity is a dynamic framework which is designed to organise thinking in relation to any interaction in cross-boundary work situations (see Table 3.3).

It consists of three 'lenses' through which interaction partners, be they managers, staff, clients or other stakeholders, can 'filter' any interaction that happens in the course of working across boundaries. Interactions refer to dialogues in meetings, casual conversations, email or social media communication and to any connection made in the modern interconnected business world.

Table 3.3   Preview of The Three Lenses of Diversity

The Three Lenses are:

- The Lens of Multiple Identity
- The Lens of Perception
- The Environmental Lens

The Three Lenses can be imagined as lenses which filter beams of light. Like physical lenses, the lenses of diversity diverge encounters and interactions between individuals and groups into a kaleidoscope of diversity. This kaleidoscope is often difficult to grasp, and oversimplified explanations may result.

- The Lens of Multiple Identity helps us to understand the full identity portfolio that people bring into an interaction, that is, their own identity portfolio and those of others.

- The Lens of Perception refers to the ways we see others as well as the ways we are seen by others in these interactions. This process applies to individuals and groups equally.

- The Environmental Lens helps us to examine the environments in which the interaction takes place. These may be the organisation, the geopolitics of its location, the media and communication, and the technological and financial configuration within which the interaction is embedded.

The framework, its benefits and its application in the analogue and digital world will be covered in detail in Chapter 4.

THE TOOL: THE CYBERIDENTITY DEVELOPMENT TOOL (CYBERIDT)

Based on the findings of the contributions from Diversity research, the psychometric tool, called cyberIDT, is designed for use in the context of the 'Diversity and Inclusion' agendas of commercial, governmental and not-for-profit organisations. The online questionnaire and feedback process is designed as a personal development tool to help people build effective business relationships across functional, hierarchical and cultural boundaries in an organisational context. It does this by surfacing the intangible as well as tangible elements of people's identity map, and exploring the impact this might have on how people relate to others.

The personal development process includes:

- completion of the questionnaire online;

- a personal feedback report containing respondent's scores and information to help them interpret and integrate the results;

- individual telephone/virtual feedback session with a licensed coach;

- potential participation in a workshop to work with others and finalise a development plan.

The underlying 12 identity elements, the tool's benefits and its application will be covered in detail in Chapters 5 and 6.

Diversity as a process

This chapter explains how Diversity as a process emerged from the following key ingredients: the existing diversity field, the intercultural field, and finally, business anthropology. Diversity as a process brought alive the framework, The Three Lenses of Diversity and the psychometric tool, the cyberIDT.

The sections above summarise the understanding of diversity from the days of its rise, all the way through to its understanding in today's cyberconnected world of work.

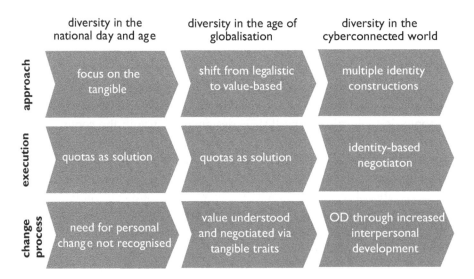

Figure 3.6   Diversity – from national to cyberconnected

Diversity as a process reflects the personal and structural challenges and opportunities people and organisations are facing in today's cyberconnected world, and thus brings a number of benefits to people and organisations (see Figure 3.6). The future will show the way insights from Diversity as a process will resolve fundamental intellectual debates that currently have the potential to advance and present solutions or polarise and further heat the debate and to what extent practitioners, participants and organisations will adopt the new approach and its instruments. Specifically, its framework, The Three Lenses of Diversity, and its psychometric instrument, offer a number of opportunities.

Benefits on the individual level are:

- a hands-on tool enabling people to shape effective business relationships across boundaries;

- insights on personal identity construction, framed within coexisting and overlapping identities that everyone activates in interactions;

- improved ability to build constructive business relationships across boundaries of differing identities.

Benefits on the team level are:

- improved team cohesion and communication with colleagues and stakeholders;

- increased collaboration in groups of people with different backgrounds (for example, cultural, social, organisational and generational);

- improved ability for the team to find creative solutions to problems using the differing experiences and identities of team members.

Benefits on the organisational level are:

- identification of institutional biases in relation to diversity and inclusion issues beyond tangible traits formerly focused upon;

- help in shaping cultural change initiatives to close the gap between current and desired cultures;

- provision of a more person-centred approach to Diversity and Inclusion agendas within organisations.

In today's cyberconnected work of world, diversity needs to offer a modern and dynamic solution, acknowledging people's multiple identities to equip them for their efforts in building interconnectivity by spanning social, technological and cultural boundaries for success in business. Whilst in the past it was sufficient for organisations to develop only a relatively small elite group of international sales force or expats for international assignments, the need now is to prepare people throughout the organisation to span boundaries both globally and within the same region and affiliate. For this reason, diversity changes from an HR department responsibility to a personal responsibility and opportunity for everyone in the organisation.

PART II
The Practice

Chapter 4

The Three Lenses of Diversity

The increase in social plurality, meaning that people's coexisting and overlapping identities are becoming even more varied and less bound to traditional social categories, is reflected in organisations' diverse workforces. The unprecedented speed of technology development informs the ways enterprises and organisations connect with their employees, clients and stakeholders, helping them to build meaningful connections with increasingly individualistic people whose independent and unique needs require acknowledgement to develop lasting relationships away from costly one-time transactions.

The previous chapter introduced the understanding of Diversity as a process and the four corollaries for building interconnectivity in the digital age, in particular:

- the dynamic understanding of diversity, which features the relational aspect of diversity;

- the developmental component of diversity;

- the strength of the less tangible aspects of identity; and

- the contingency of diversity to the environment.

This novel understanding of diversity helps people in organisations take a different perspective to shape new thinking, which eventually leads to new approaches and solutions, services and products, including ways to connect with people inside and outside the organisation.

New services and products consist of:

- approaches and solutions, negotiated, developed and delivered through human-to-human interaction among individuals and groups; and

- approaches and solutions through human-to-tech interaction, including digital strategies, for example, mobile interaction among individuals and groups.

Building Interconnectivity

Building interconnectivity is an endeavour with no clear start and no clear end. In order to make it practical, the previous chapter provided you with a glimpse into the comprehensive framework called 'The Three Lenses of Diversity', designed for the sense-making process of the complexity inherent in any interaction in cross-boundary work situations, helping to make smart decisions. This entails the identification of diverse stakeholder needs, whereby stakeholders encompass:

- participants, delegates and shapers of face-to-face development programmes;

- users and designers of tools, applications and technological development in the cybersystem;

- both of which entail internal and external clients (business to business or B2B) and end consumers (business to consumer or B2C).

Chapter 4 now picks up on the dynamic framework and walks you step-by-step through the overall design and each of the lenses, which are:

1. The Lens of Multiple Identity;

2. The Lens of Perception; and

3. The Environmental Lens.

Once the framework has been presented, its benefits and its application for use in organisation development practice will be covered in detail. The process of divergence will be explained, and the implications for people's interaction and organisational processes will be highlighted.

Examples from the two life cases presented in Chapter 1 illustrate the hands-on application of the framework, whereas the SonaConn case largely covers the human-to-human interaction with technology as interconnectivity enabler, and the MyMemLab case presents human-to-human interaction with technology in the role of interconnectivity solution.

Box 4.1   The Emergence of the Framework 'The Three Lenses of Diversity'

The Three Lenses of Diversity are a product of the application of methods from business anthropology in the modern interconnected workplace, mostly in the shape of complex business projects across Europe and the Middle East and North Africa (MENA). The author's hybrid role of leader and researcher provided the necessary exposure and background for the construction of the framework.

The collection of rich data was generated by a combination of methods from business anthropology including semi-structured interviews, participant observation, focus groups, structured face-to-face and virtual communication, written communication and informal conversations. The data analysis concentrated on the interaction among stakeholders and groupings and its impact on relationships, processes and innovation. It included identifying patterns, coding meaningful repetitions and labelling significant iterations. The result of the data analysis produced The Three Lenses of Diversity, designed to help organise thinking in relation to any human-to-human and human-to-tech interaction in cross-boundary work situations.

The smart application of approaches from social science in a business environment helps to externalise knowledge that otherwise lies unfolded.

RECOGNISING BOUNDARIES

This book understands diversity as the best vehicle to build interconnectivity, which means to build effective face-to-face and virtual relationships across social, technological and cultural boundaries. These boundaries are further diversified into horizontal and vertical boundaries, each presenting a complexity of stakeholder interests, with each individual, in turn, bringing coexisting, overlapping and often contradictory identities.

As just presented in Chapter 3, The Three Lenses of Diversity is a dynamic framework which makes the understanding of Diversity as a process operable.

The framework consists of three 'lenses' through which you can 'filter' any interaction that happens in the course of working across these boundaries.

Interactions refer to dialogues in meetings, casual conversations, email or social media communication or apps, so covering any analogue or digital connection made in the modern interconnected business world.

In brief, The Three Lenses of Diversity helps organise strategic thinking in relation to any human-to-human or tech interaction in cross-boundary work situations. So, let us look at the key characteristics of interactions in cross-boundary work (see Figure 4.1).

Interactions happen across boundaries:

- interpersonal connections;

- intra-organisational processes;

- products and services on a global scale.

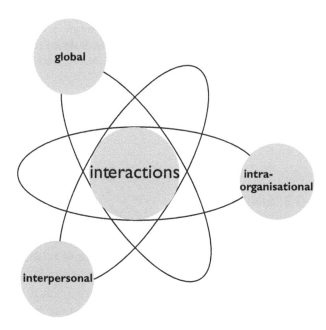

Figure 4.1   Levels of interaction

Interpersonal interaction is the cornerstone of all levels of interaction and is thus paramount for the alignment of organisational objectives. On a day-to-day basis, interpersonal and group communication processes are the key contributors to an organisation's strategy implementation.

Interactions are result-orientated

Most interactions in organisations happen on the basis of anticipated outcome. These interactions may include casual conversations at the coffee machine in the corridor, in the canteen, and as most commonly acknowledged, in official face-to-face or virtual meetings with official and hidden agendas.

Interactions lead to a decision

In order to achieve results people need to make decisions. These happen on a daily basis, informally and formally. For that purpose, let us revisit the informal canteen culture, as in chats at the coffee machine or on the way to the parking lot. Situations where decisions are made also include formal conversations as in performance reviews, strategy meetings or board meetings. Irrespective of the situation, interactions lead to decisions, which turn out to be more or less informed, and of which you are at one or the other end a shaper, participant or recipient.

The interaction–decision relationship

Volumes have been filled about decision-making processes. Decision-making concerns us all. It is omnipresent in our private and profession lives. Some decisions are minor and bear no serious consequences; others are big and affect our personal lives and those of others.

This section highlights the fact that any decision-making process is preceded by some degree of interaction that is heavily interpretation-loaded, often informed by prejudgements and former experience. The consequence of this is decisions of differing quality, as Figures 4.2, 4.3 and 4.4 below show.

The quality of decision-making processes lies in the differentiation between observation and interpretation. The Three Lenses provide the necessary aid for this substantial difference, preventing the decision-maker from making quick and often toxic assumptions and, finally, jumping to conclusions.

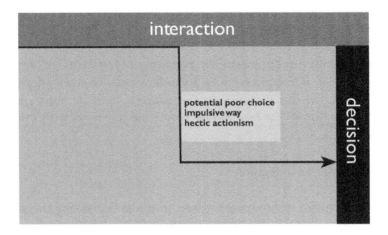

Figure 4.2   Poor result: preconceived decision

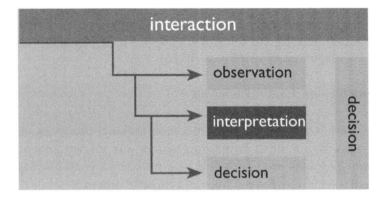

Figure 4.3   Less biased result: more informed decision

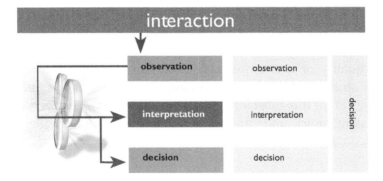

Figure 4.4   Excellent result: decision filtered through The Three Lenses of Diversity

ACKNOWLEDGING PEOPLE'S IDENTITY FOOTPRINT

Filtering your decisions through The Three Lenses of Diversity allows you to focus more effectively on your stakeholders' diversity.

Box 4.2   Key Benefits of the Framework

Shifting the mindset from transactions to relationships: today's interconnected business world is so much more than just transactions with our clients and consumers. They are individuals with individual and thus diverse interests and needs. The Three Lenses of Diversity enable us to understand, connect with and deliver to them in more relevant and personalised ways, face-to-face or digital.

Key benefits of the framework are:

- offering a strong relational aspect, in both face-to-face and virtual communication through pronounced process orientation;

- focusing on people's identity map, which impacts any interaction; and

- helping make informed decisions on the basis of observation, not interpretation.

One of the key assets of the framework is its reflection of the relational aspect of diversity. As organisations, their products and services are processes rather than structures and this dynamic is likewise mirrored in any interaction taking place in the organisational setting. In turn, the dynamic component of interactions is reflected back into the organisational processes. The strength of the framework lies in the acknowledgement of these complimentary dynamics.

The underlying research identified the key components of the framework: the multiple identity composition of all stakeholders involved in cross-boundary work with an explicit focus on the intangible nature of diversity, the perception inherent in stakeholders' socialisation processes and external influences, and the contingencies inherent in stakeholder environments.

The comprehensive framework for building interconnectivity nurtures the recognition of the intangible and implicit nature of diversity, through which people generate outcomes critical for the success of cross-boundary work.

Thus the process of divergence provides an in-depth view of interactions which otherwise might be interpreted in a simplistic way, generating heuristic assumptions. These in turn often result in short-sighted or misguided business decisions with catastrophic consequences. Conversely, the lenses of diversity diverge encounters and interactions between individuals and groups into a kaleidoscope of diversity.

The Three Lenses can be imagined as lenses which filter beams of light. The resulting kaleidoscope is often difficult to grasp, and oversimplified explanations may result. The framework of The Three Lenses serves as an orientation system for meaningful interpretations drawn from observations (see Figure 4.5).

The Three Lenses are

1.   The Lens of Multiple Identity;

2.   The Lens of Perception; and

3.   The Environmental Lens.

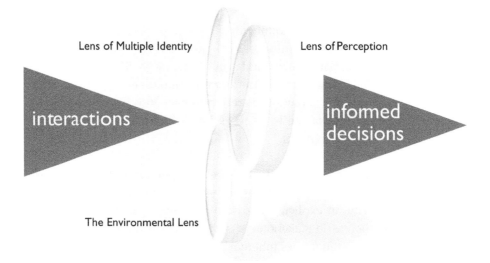

Figure 4.5   The framework – The Three Lenses of Diversity

The anticipated outcome of the application of The Three Lenses of Diversity is informed decisions solidly based on meaningful interpretations which will enable you to build effective interconnectivity, thus breaking through silos, and as a consequence, achieving better business results.

The process aims at the observations collected from interactions filtered through each lens to come to meaningful interpretations without jumping to conclusions. Table 4.1 outlines the key meanings and key benefits of The Three Lenses of Diversity.

Table 4.1   **Key meaning and key benefit of The Three Lenses of Diversity**

Key meaning		Key benefit
The Lens of Multiple Identity helps us to understand the full identity portfolio that people bring into an interaction, that is, their own identity portfolio and those of others.	→	The Lens of Multiple Identity will provide insights from your personal identity profile and will help you to make sense of the meaningful application of the multiple identity construction approach. • Identifying culturally diverse participants' needs and expectations. • Understanding and responding to diverse user needs.
The Lens of Perception refers to the ways we see others as well as the ways we are seen by others in these interactions. This process applies to individuals and groups equally.	→	The Lens of Perception will help bring your own preinformed judgements to the surface and thus help you to become more flexible in a changing, interconnected business world. • Increasing your own flexibility in a rapidly changing interconnected business world. • Developing customer and stakeholder intimacy by overcoming stereotypes.
The Environmental Lens helps us to examine the environments in which the interaction takes place. These may be the organisation, the geopolitics of its location, the media and communication, or the technological and financial configuration within which the interaction is embedded.	→	The Environmental Lens will uncover symptoms of what happens at a broader level in the organisation, its markets, and environments across boundaries. • Acting upon the contingencies delivered by the environment. • Balancing localisation against standardisation.

The Lens of Multiple Identity

Having introduced The Three Lenses, we now move on to a more thorough introduction of each lens, starting with The Lens of Multiple Identity.

Multiple identity constructions have moved beyond being merely a buzzword. They are a reality of everyday interaction which has become everyday business practice. To get you into the mood for this section, here is an opening example from SonaConn:

Box 4.3   Carolyn, the Communications Expert

Carolyn says, 'I am a member of a team delivering a complex project: the implementation of the performance driver programme. I am a communications expert in charge of the design and delivery of two different workshops, "Communicating for Impact" and "Performing through our People"; I am also in charge of the quality management of the subject matter. I am a white, 32-year-old British female, am aware of my British accent and Anglo-Saxon appearance and wonder if it might be appropriate to downplay this aspect of my identity, even though the stakeholders involved know about it. From my previous work experience in the Middle East I gather that there is some sensitivity here to the history of relations between my country and the Middle East and Northern Africa.'

The questions below provide some food for thought:

- What identity elements other than the obvious ones of age, gender and ethnicity could she emphasise in order to make a winning impression?

- What identity elements are the key stakeholders likely to bring into the working relationship?

- In what ways can the team and the organisation support Carolyn in her efforts towards effective relationship-building with the key decision-makers on the client's end and with the workshop participants?

GETTING TO GRIPS WITH THE LENS OF MULTIPLE IDENTITY

The Lens of Multiple Identity helps us to understand the full identity portfolio anyone brings into any interaction, which consists of that individual's own portfolio and those of others.

This lens allows the analysis of the composition of people's identity in the context of the interaction. It is designed to address the visible parts of our identity such as age and gender as well as the intangible parts of our identity such as geopolitics and wellbeing. In addition, it is process-orientated, since the activation of single or multiple elements of the kaleidoscope of one's identity is ever-changing, and is interesting and fruitful ground for analysis of one's own identity portfolio and those of others.

Altogether there are 12 identity elements, which are the key success factors for building meaningful relationships across boundaries and thus success in business. They emerged from the underlying research, which as such was subject to academic scrutiny. The 12 are divided into tangible and intangible elements.

Tangible elements

Let's take a geology model: the tangible identity elements correspond to the elements situated at the top or visible part of the geology model, such as trees, lakes and mountains. You can easily see and notice these elements in first encounters; they inform first impressions in the two-way process. They are 'Appearance', 'Ethnicity', 'Generation' and 'Gender'.

Intangible elements

The intangible or less tangible identity elements can be imagined as situated below the ground, so invisible at first sight (see Figure 4.6). Thus these elements are more complex to explore and to identify in oneself and others.

They include 'Wellbeing', 'Mobility', 'Sociability', 'Communication', 'Geopolitics', 'Lifelong learning', 'Employability' and 'Inclusion'.

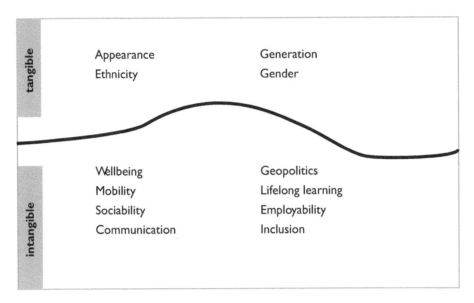

Figure 4.6   The tangible and intangible elements of identity

KEEPING IT SIMPLE

Twelve components might sound complex, however this number is essential to mirror the diversity we all bring into interactions. Specifically it is important to acknowledge the intangible elements in order not to over-essentialise tangible elements. All 12 identity elements will be covered fully in Chapters 5 and 6. For now the following points are important:

- understanding what the 12 identity elements are;

- knowing your strong points and how to maximise the identity elements you typically activate frequently;

- learning how to leverage these fully as you work to improve yourself;

- identifying which of the identity elements you are unaware of and which you wish to develop further;

- focusing on three or four out of 12 to make progress on.

So let's make this manageable by looking at the earlier challenge that Carolyn is facing.

Whether implicitly or explicitly, automatically or deliberately, Carolyn exchanges information about her identity through the obvious visible elements such as her appearance and the fact that she is a white woman in her early 30s speaking with a British accent. This information enables all stakeholder involved to attend to, evaluate, incorporate or dismiss.

However, Carolyn's identity repertoire offers a great variety for conscious selection of identity affiliations more suitable in the environmental context of Cairo. To compensate she might emphasise her role as communications expert or the fact that she has invested quite a lot of energy in her ongoing education – that she is up to speed with recent developments in communication, including social media communication. In a different context it might be the other way around. In conclusion, the context of the interaction partially defines which parts of her identity she might want to favour for building sound relationships on this cross-boundary project.

THE IMPORTANCE OF INTANGIBLE IDENTITY ELEMENTS

As stressed in Chapter 3, the diversity controversy has so far mainly stressed the tangible traits of diversity. In practice, this is reflected in the perception that Carolyn is confronted with, that she is blond, white, British and in her early 30s. Her challenge is to break through these first-sight ascriptions.

The example below from the same cross-boundary project, the SonaConn real-case, illustrates the elements that are often ignored, omitted or simply not considered important.

On the SonaConn cross-boundary project it was specifically some of the project stakeholders' historical identities that helped build common ground, although their place of origin and interaction did not initially indicate any commonness. While engaged during meeting breaks in more informal conversations on the historical context of some of the nation states represented in the venture, individuals in some of the different subgroups discovered a common interest in the great political leader Bruno Kreisky and his period[1] in Sweden. Before serving as chancellor of Austria between 1970 and 1983, the Social Democrat spent the six years from 1939 to 1945 in Sweden, where he held several representative appointments.[2] Kreisky's experience in Sweden certainly helped

---

1   Austria's Federal Chancellor between 1970 and 1983 was the only Jewish politician to ever rule a German-speaking nation. Kreisky proved in many respects to be a pioneer in forming European attitudes.
2   Roth, Turrini 1981:108.

shape systems in Austria during his political leadership period (for example, the introduction of ideas from the Swedish welfare state model, particularly in the 1970s) and so provided common ground between project stakeholders representing those two countries. In this discovery tangible attributes such as age and gender of the individuals involved had no relevance. The hook was the similarity in the two countries' political systems and leadership understanding in general. The reference point in these conversations was 'What did the leader (the political figure) then do in a difficult situation?', as difficult situations certainly emerge on complex cross-boundary projects.

Specifically, The Lens of Multiple Identity is a useful source for anyone on a team to build connections with venture stakeholders. The benefits are that the greater the diversity among the stakeholders is, the more ground it provides for a versatile range of contacts and coverage of topics that typically emerge when working cross-boundary by displaying and role-modelling leadership in bringing up less popular topics such as historical common ground.

It is often the less tangible attributes that help create a connection between representatives in the workplace. Individuals working on international business ventures often engage in informal conversations with their counterparts. These 'coffee machine conversations' or 'canteen conversations' in off-guard moments allow participants to lower potential barriers. These conversations might surface one's place of origin, which is often different from either the workplace or the project place. The identity profiles of the people engaged in the conversation thus become more developed and might offer ground for making connections in order to build sound business relationships.

So, benefits for Carolyn and all of us are:

- insights into personal identity constructions, framed within predefined elements that everyone activates in interactions;

- a hands-on tool enabling people to shape effective business relationships across boundaries;

- improved ability to build constructive business relationships across boundaries of differing identities; and

- opportunities for self-reflection as to what aspects of your identity portfolio you would like to activate in managing the boundaries around you.

The application of The Lens of Multiple Identity in the digital space, specifically in the development of mobile development applications will be covered in depth in Part III: The Application.

The Lens of Perception

Having introduced The Lens of Multiple Identity, we now carry on to a detailed introduction of The Lens of Perception; these two lenses are inextricably linked. The Lens of Perception refers to the way we see others and likewise the way we are seen by others; we perceive new approaches, and the extent and speed at which we adopt them. This process applies to individuals and groups equally.

Let us crystallise the perception challenge with the two scenarios shown in Table 4.2:

Table 4.2 The Lens of Perception – two scenarios

Scenario 1	Scenario 2
The 42-year-old from Germany leads a complex project on performance driver (PD) implementation in Cairo as described in Chapter 1. On a regular basis she returns to her current home base in London to spend the weekend, reconnect with her local network, spend some of her spare time in the London neighbourhood where she still keeps a home, does her shopping, engages in friendly neighbourhood chats, plays the odd game of golf at the local club at the weekend and connects with old friends from the international community. At the occasional social event she would upon inquiry report on her work and the fact that she currently leads a project in Cairo.	The 42-year-old from Germany leads a complex project on PD implementation in Cairo as described in Chapter 1. On a regular basis he returns to his current home base in London to spend the weekend, reconnect with his local network, spend some of his spare time in the London neighbourhood where he still keeps a home, does his shopping, engages in friendly neighbourhood chats, plays the odd game of golf at the local club at the weekend and connects with old friends from the international community. At the occasional social event he would upon inquiry report on his work and the fact that he currently leads a project in Cairo.
Based on this short glimpse of the dual life she leads and her attempts to maintain social networks at her current home base in London, what do you believe that people in her social environment would ask her about her current assignment? List three questions you believe people would ask her in one-to-one conversations:	Based on this short glimpse of the dual life he leads and his attempts to maintain social networks at his current home base in London, what do you believe that people in his social environment would ask him about his current assignment? List three questions you believe people would ask him in one-to-one conversations:
1.	1.
2.	2.
3.	3.

REALITY STRIKES

You might have captured some ideas on the ways you believe people engage with the female or male leader of the complex cross-boundary project. Let us take a closer look at the opening life case on perception. Obviously, the example leads to one of the over-essentialised tangible identity elements, that is, gender and its connected assumptions. The reason the selection took place presents the responses the leaders received, each displaying their individual identity portfolio whilst facing the same professional challenge. They were as follows:

- The female leader predominantly needed to respond to questions as to how she handled the difficulties she experienced in the role of a female leader in an Arabic environment. The lead question was: 'Isn't it difficult as a woman to lead a complex project like this specifically in the Arab World?'

- The male leader needed to respond to professional issues such as the project management of this complex multi-stakeholder programme with a particular emphasis on meeting deadlines in Egypt.

Evidently, the conversation partners walked right into the stereotype trap. Stereotypes are generalisations reached by individuals and are a result of the general cognitive process of categorising. The main function of stereotyping is to simplify and systematise the abundance and complexity of the information received by image-centred, narrative-based strips of reality disseminated by media.

In general, differing or negative impressions tend to be more accessible to memory retrieval than are average instances. They are over-represented in memory and judgement and are thus more likely to be included in stereotypes. In the opening life case, gender images and narratives are immediately exposed in the interaction with the female leader, but not in the interaction with the male leader. It puts the female leader into a defensive position whilst the male leader can merely focus on the business details.

This two-way process can lead to increased stereotyping unless the interaction partners change direction so as not to reach a dead-end. For this purpose, we will now look into the process of Belonging and Othering.

'BELONGING' AND 'OTHERING'

'Belonging' and 'Othering' are the two key ingredients of the relationship-building process in a modern interconnected business world. Both 'Belonging' and 'Othering' can be either highly constructive or destructive for success in business. Understanding the process and responding appropriately to its contingencies are essential for productive business relationships.

'Belonging' refers to the identity-building process based on sameness, similarity and shared traits among two or more interacting individuals. The initial process is often built on the visible elements of identity such as age, appearance or areas of commonness that are explored in the first encounter. For example, one's national identity or outward appearance can be good starting points for 'Belonging'. On further acquaintance, less visible aspects of identity such as the need for inclusion may come into play. These different elements of identity in a business relationship form a changing and dynamic field as the relationship matures. In daily language and organisational rhetoric the term 'we' is in many cases a signal for the expression of 'Belonging'. When taken to the extreme, 'Belonging' is inclined to criticise and condemn nearly any reference to difference or 'the other', often by denouncing it.

In contrast, 'Othering' refers to difference, variation and otherness. This logic often overrates and places excessive emphasis on 'difference'. In fact, whole industries have exploited 'the other' for commercial and political purposes. In daily language the expression 'they' is in many cases a sign for 'Othering'.

In reality, however, 'Belonging' and 'Othering' are mutually constitutive parts of identity, often forming a seamless relationship. The process can bring harmony; however it can also quite quickly create potential conflicts.

Interactions and their quality primarily depend on the individuals involved and the extent to which they activate selected elements of their identity. In this way they create either 'Belonging' or 'Othering' (see Figure 4.7). As a result, the identity elements rotate between the two extremes, generating two options:

- building Belonging through difference aiming to establish some common ground; and

- generating Othering through sameness with the overall objective of breaking through groupthink.

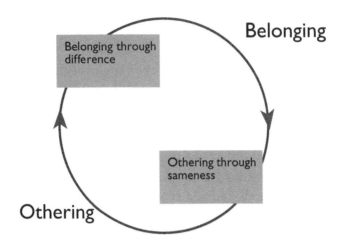

Figure 4.7   The process – Belonging and Othering

The seamless dialogical relationship between 'Belonging' and 'Othering' can happen within one single interaction between only two individuals. Individuals in interaction dwell heavily on selected elements of their identity, whether these are age, education, history and politics, or citizenship; each can create 'Belonging' for one of individuals whilst another element can create 'Othering'.

As discussed earlier, diversity is relational. The attention is redirected from the ends to the texture in between. As a conclusion the relational understanding of diversity demonstrates that diversity is not just there, but it is elicited in interactions (see Figure 4.8).

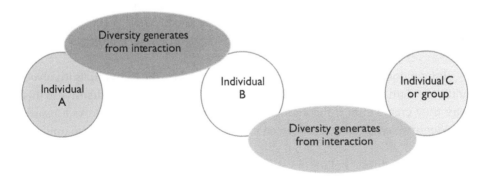

Figure 4.8   The diversity vehicle powered by interaction

As a consequence the texture of diversity changes with the individuals participating in the interaction. The identity portfolios of two or more individuals interacting shape the quality of the diversity between them.

With respect to this new understanding, interactions include any form of individuals and groups engaging with one another. Therefore, diversity is a multifaceted dynamic process and its outcome depends on a number of contingencies, which include:

- who the key players of the interaction are;

- what 'face' they show, where 'face' means the voluntary and involuntary display of selected identity elements; and

- what the context of the interaction is and where it takes place.

This view incorporates the dynamic aspect of diversity by looking at the interaction between and among individuals and groups, acknowledging its ever-changing nature due to context. It is a regenerative process created in interaction.

The space in between provides you with the opportunity to challenge stereotypes. Far more, it serves for renewal, introspection and reflection, challenging your own assumptions and preconceived information. Belonging and Othering provide insights into how to leverage the space in between.

In the opening life case, the responses to the female leader are mostly characterised by 'Othering'. She has the options of confirming the 'Othering' presented to her or reworking the situation to consciously create 'Belonging'. The informal conversations in her spare time at her home base might serve as good practice for potential similar situations in the workplace.

Group identity, social integration, relationship conflict and collective performance are all subject to the overall degree of correspondence between the selected identity elements of the interaction partners. However, people's interactions and their activated identity elements rarely correspond; it is thus the process of alignment of the selected identity elements that creates 'Belonging'. The correspondence between self-views and appraisals in a group of people without losing one's authenticity is a further key to moving beyond transactions to building meaningful relationships.

SHARPENING PERCEPTION – THE KEY TO UNLOCKING MISUNDERSTANDINGS

On the SonaConn project, the expression 'The communications department is always late' referred to some negative experience of the strategy team with deadlines. In reality, deadlines were adhered to; however the two groups had different ways of reaching them punctually. In fact the expression simply reflects a different approach towards a set of processes by the group using the expression. This value-loaded categorisation can lead to self-fulfilling prophecies which describe a false definition of a situation, evoking a new behaviour and making the originally false conception become true.[3] So, the strategy department blaming the communications department might show behaviours, for example, inappropriate email reminders and other denigrating behaviour that could cause the people in the communications department to behave according to expectation. This example is particularly important because many projects, as a result of stereotyping and self-fulfilling prophecies, end with severe delays costing millions more than forecasted.

The perception commonly accepted by one group can easily lead to over-essentialising 'the other', which can point to any group that does things differently on a business venture. The Lens of Perception helps to test the process of stereotyping and the potential development of self-fulfilling prophecies. Particular attention needs to be paid to the rhetoric used among individuals and groups on a project that can lead to a change in behaviours and so reinforce the stereotypes.

Specifically, leaders in their role model function should pay attention to verbal expressions by the team that hint at the potential production of 'the other', typically expressed by 'they are …' Once verbal patterns are clear, the leader should address them in order to avoid a costly self-fulfilling prophecy.

BENEFITS OF THE APPLICATION OF THE LENS OF PERCEPTION

- Building trusted collaboration in groups of people with different backgrounds (for example, cultural, social, technological, organisational, generational differences).

- Improving the team's ability to find creative solutions to problems by using the team members' differing experiences and identities.

---

3   Merton 1948:195.

- Breaking through formerly impervious stereotypes to identify true stakeholder and consumer wants and needs incorporating meaningful difference.

The impact of The Lens of Perception in the digital space will be explored in detail in Chapter 7.

The Environmental Lens

Let us now move on to the third lens of the framework, the Environmental Lens, which is again inextricably linked to the two other lenses, The Lens of Multiple Identity and The Lens of Perception.

The Environmental Lens helps us to examine the environments in which the interaction takes place. These may be the organisation, the geopolitics of its location, the media landscape, or the technological and financial configuration within which the interaction is embedded.

Organisation development practices need to consider and reflect upon the impact the landscapes of media, technology, ideology and financial configuration have on any initiative in order to ensure its contribution to performance.

Key insights from The Environmental Lens are indispensable for the development, design and implementation of organisation development initiatives. The real-life case 'Succeeding with Mobile Learning' illustrates diversity in the environmental landscapes from the perspective of MyMemLab, who wish to pursue their growth strategy through the successful implementation of a mobile learning initiative at A1Guard.

LEVERAGING OPPORTUNITIES PRESENTED BY THE IMMEDIATE ENVIRONMENT

In the role of start-up and expert consultant in mobile learning, MyMemLab develop, design and implement gamified mobile learning programmes, helping to deliver global mobile solutions. MyMemLab's key people pay close attention to key industry drivers from the financial industry investing in mobile learning technology. Equally, they keep abreast of innovation and competition in the sector in order to recognise and shape trends in the fast-moving industry.

Nadia, the managing director of MyMemLab, and her team won a contract for the design, development and implementation of a mobile learning programme for A1Guard, a key player in the health and safety industry. Among their broad portfolio of services to the predominantly B2B client base they provide training, learning and development solutions in the health and safety area. They now aim to transform some of their learning programmes from the traditional paradigm of classroom learning to the contemporary approach of mobile learning. Concretely, A1Guard is interested in offering a selection of classroom training on mobile devices, enabling learners to complete the learning and development courses on their smart phones and tablets.

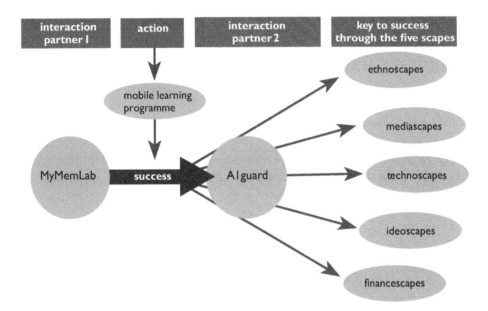

Figure 4.9 Key success through the five scapes

The Environmental Lens shows a physical representation of the environment, describing the sum of the habitats which organisations and their people have successfully managed to become part of; be they urban centres, deserts or even places in the ice. The habitat shapes people just as the people shape the habitat.

The Environmental Lens also has a less tangible, non-physical representation featuring systems such as political systems and ideologies, regional culture and organisational culture (for example, headquarters and subsidiaries), the media and communication setup with its digital configuration and finally the financial configuration.

The Environmental Lens is organised in 'scapes' which ensure the operability of the analysis required to capture the complexity of the environmental landscapes. The five scapes, listed in Figure 4.9 above and introduced in Chapter 2, are:

- Ethnoscapes: The landscapes of people, constituting the shifting worlds of organisation development: migrants, guest workers and expats in the role of internal and external stakeholders.

- Mediascapes: The image-centred strips of reality produced and disseminated by analogue and digital formats.

- Technoscapes: The global configuration of technology, crossing formerly impervious boundaries.

- Ideoscapes: The concentration of images of politics, ideologies and power interests: freedom, welfare rights, sovereignty and democracy.

- Financescapes: The disposition of global capital and financial flow available to stakeholders.

In the world of work people come into interactions with heavy cultural and social baggage obtained from interactions in a variety of environmental contexts.

Moving into new cross-boundary settings, this environmentally loaded baggage informs any face-to-face or digital interaction. We can assume that the baggage is unloaded in interactions, mostly unconsciously, or eventually upon reflection repacked. Within each of the five scapes, multiple realities exist as ideas or images which change their context depending on the interaction partner. With the meaning of ideas or images changing depending on the interaction partner ingesting them, the existence of an 'imagined world' in which one reality is no more real than somebody else's needs to acknowledged. In the strategic context of an organisation development project the five scapes deliver the much-needed vocabulary and guideline for analysis.

For MyMemLab growth strategy it is essential to perform through A1Guard successfully in order to attract a wider range of potential investors from which the entrepreneurs can select the best fit.

Key success factors for MyMemLab are:

- presenting up-to-speed expertise in mobile learning technology for client benefit;

- implementing a successful change process enabling the end users to adopt mobile learning processes; and

- designing a product that meets diverse client and end user expectations and, as a result, becomes a great success for future references.

Performance through a client brings a number of challenges for which the Environmental Lens offers the necessary support to examine the environments in which the diverse interactions of the venture takes place.

- Ethnoscapes describe the landscapes of people concerned with the mobile learning programme. They concern their identity profiles, such as age, gender, learning experiences and preferred communication styles. Of specific importance for the success of this programme is the analysis of end user learning needs and expectations, all culturally loaded across boundaries.

- Mediascapes are strips of reality expressed by electronic capabilities to produce and disseminate information. These comprise traditional channels such as newspapers and magazines and more recent technologies such as digital communication with a specific view to web 2.0 communication tools. For all stakeholders to have the skills to meaningfully apply these tools is critical to the success of the growth strategy for MyMemLab.

- Technoscapes describe the configuration of technology crossing the boundaries between humans and computers at large. A closer investigation into the IT architecture at A1Guard and the mobile fit is equally important, as is the analysis of people's 'mobile fluency'. This includes the person in charge of the development and the implementation of the mobile learning programme (a non-IT person) as well as the end user capabilities. The investigation's outcome informs the influencing skills necessary for success through the client and is thus is important for the interaction.

- Ideoscapes describe the concentration of political images often directly linked to the organisational mindset. They concern the shift from traditional learning approaches to the modern way of learning. Whilst compulsory health and safety training often produces demotivated participants, the new learning landscape offers great opportunity for successful change in training and development, given that MyMemLab includes both the clients' and the end users' potential resistance in the change process.

- Financescapes describe the disposition of rapidly moving global capital, of which MyMemLab aims to win a small share, enabled through the success and the subsequent improved attractiveness to potential investors.

The analysis using the scapes enables the MyMemLab decision-makers to make informed decisions on proactive business perspectives concerning how to generate business value through a client by earning their trust.

BENEFITS FROM THE APPLICATION OF THE ENVIRONMENTAL LENS

- Sharpening understanding of contingencies from the environment, which might be the habitat, the culture, or the cyberspace the various stakeholder organisation are embedded in.

- Uncovering symptoms of what happens at a broader level in the organisation, its markets and its environment when working across functional, cultural, technological and economic boundaries.

- Structuring readily available information for better strategic decision-making.

We have walked you step-by-step through the overall design of the framework, each of the lenses:

1.   The Lens of Multiple Identity;

2.   The Lens of Perception; and

3.   The Environmental Lens,

and related hands-on real-life examples for each lens. The following section now presents the underlying concepts of the framework in more detail.

The Academic Background

The key academic concepts which contributed to the development of The Three Lenses of Diversity are as follows:

THE LENS OF MULTIPLE IDENTITY

This lens amalgamates two key concepts, firstly Hannerz' cultural make-up[4] and secondly Sen's plural identity, sensitive to context.[5] This lens builds on the assumption that people do not own a culture but are rather owned by it. In many cases, one's own culture becomes transparent only when living, working and more generally interacting in an environment other than one's own. Viewing this cultural make-up as a continuum implies that there are two opposite ends. At one end people may develop the skill of re-creating their cultural make-up, whilst at the other end of the continuum they may hold on to their original make-up.

At this point, Sen's plural identity merges into this lens, claiming that identity depends on social context. Specifically, this means that individuals draw on selected affiliations of their cultural make-up, in particular when the context requires them to do so.

Sen illustrates as follows:

> ... for one thing, the importance of a particular identity will depend on the social context. For example, when going to a dinner, one's identity as a vegetarian may be rather more crucial than one's identity as a linguist, whereas the latter may be particularly important if one considers going to a lecture on linguistic studies. This variability does nothing to rehabilitate the assumption of singular affiliation, but it illustrates the need to see the role of choice in a context-specific way.[6]

---

4   Hannerz 1996:58.
5   Sen 2006:25.
6   Sen 2006:25

This lens allows the analysis and application of multiple identities in different contexts, whether they qualify as tangible elements such as ethnicity and gender or as intangible elements such as sociability, lifelong learning or wellbeing. Moreover, the analysis and application is process-oriented since the activation of single or multiple identity elements out of the overall portfolio of one's identity is ever-changing and hence developmental.

THE LENS OF PERCEPTION

The underlying core concept of The Lens of Perception is 'the other'. This is critically important to the diversity discussion, as 'the other' is needed to start the process of generating diversity, which eventually generates selected ascriptions of sameness or Belonging. Key concepts of 'the other' are stereotypes, and, as a result, self-fulfilling prophecies.

As previously stated, stereotypes are by definition generalisations reached by individuals. They are a result of the general cognitive process of categorising. The main function is to simplify and systematise the abundance and complexity of the information received from the environment.[7] Stereotypes can become social when they are shared by large numbers of people within a group or entity.[8] Tajfel further refers to the finding[9] that extreme events are more accessible to memory retrieval than are average instances. In this sense, negative behaviours of subcultures are likely to be over-represented in memory and judgement. Here it is worthwhile noting the difference between social categorisations which are neutral and those which are value-loaded,[10] Typically, if a group is endowed with strong value differential it might lead to self-fulfilling prophecy. Merton's description of self-fulfilling prophecy is as follows:

> ... *The self-fulfilling prophecy is, in the beginning, a false definition of the situation evoking a new behaviour which makes the originally false conception become true. The specious validity of the self-fulfilling prophecy perpetuates a reign of error.*[11]

---

7   Tajfel 1981 in Turner, Giles 1981:142.
8   Tajfel 1981 in Turner, Giles 1981:147.
9   Rothbart 1978: 237 in Turner, Giles 1981:153.
10   Tajfel 1981 in Turner, Giles 1981:156.
11   Merton 1948:195.

Stereotypes, and as a result self-fulfilling prophecies, can lead to 'Belonging' and 'Othering', where the first refers to ascriptions connected with sameness whilst the second refers to ascriptions with difference.

THE ENVIRONMENTAL LENS

The Environmental Lens covers the macro-aspect of diversity, by expanding on Hannerz's 'ecology', that is, at large, the sum of habitats and the ways in which people have successfully managed to become part of them. Specifically for the non-physical representation of the habitats, Appadurai's 'scapes' deliver the operability for these meta-level considerations. These scapes are different landscapes representing different cultural flows.[12] The five scapes are:

- Ethnoscapes as landscapes of people in constant motion such as migrants, refugees, guest workers or even tourists who 'affect the politics of (and between) nations to a hitherto unprecedented degree'.[13]

- Mediascapes as image-centred, narrative-based accounts of strips of reality expressed by electronic capabilities to produce and disseminate information: newspapers, magazines and television; film. These forms of media provide the 'narrative' to which different communities live their lives and form 'imagined worlds' as reality and fiction become indistinct from one another.

- Technoscapes as the global configuration of technology crossing formerly impervious boundaries. Whereas technologies were once orchestrated through political agendas and large-scale economies, they now bring about new types of cultural interactions and exchanges through the power of technology, which can happen at unprecedented speeds.

- Ideoscapes as concentration of images highly political and often directly linked to state ideologies and their power interests: freedom, welfare rights, sovereignty and democracy. Ideoscapes centre on the ideologies of a leading body and those that oppose it and are highly dependent on the context of the people in the interaction.

---

12 Appadurai 2006.
13 Appadurai 1996:33.

- Financescapes as disposition of global capital now mysteriously and rapidly moving: currency markets, stock exchanges, commodity speculations. Technology as such is very closely tied to the economy, which is constantly in flux and, despite our best efforts to manipulate, is wildly unpredictable.

The academic background of The Three Lenses largely stems from researchers and thinkers from the anthropological field such as Appadurai, Gingrich, Hannerz and Sen. These authors and the relevant key concepts have been presented in more detail in Chapter 2 'Leveraging Contributions from Anthropology' and in Chapter 3 'The Emergence of Diversity as a Process'.

To summarise our exploration of The Three Lenses of Diversity and its application in different cross-boundary settings, let us review the key assets of the framework.

One Size Does Not Fit All

Around the world we see organisations adapting to and operating in a rapidly changing and increasingly interconnected environment. To succeed, they need to transform their relationships with clients and consumers, internal and external, to further differentiate themselves in the marketplace, and to expand their global presence.

Whilst the discussion of localisation versus standardisation has continued for decades in the traditional consumer product and service world, it is only now starting to be paid tribute to in organisations shaping or adopting digital strategies. With stakeholders and consumers reachable at unprecedented speed and volume, building lasting relationships, not just offering transactions, is becoming more important than ever.

The dynamic framework of The Three Lenses of Diversity delivers crucial perspectives for the transformation journey:

- Inherent in interconnectivity, the framework of The Three Lenses is dynamic. It looks into change over time. Above all, the framework looks into the past, the present and the future, meeting the exceptional stretch between face-to-face communication and the digital world we all bridge routinely on a daily basis.

- All three lenses can be explored with a given representation of people, who may be employees, clients, consumers and stakeholders. For meeting diverse people's needs, each lens should be investigated at individual, team and organisational levels.

Interactions are the heart of any transaction or relationship. The Three Lenses can help to shape the quality of these interactions and to achieve informed decisions on how to move from transactions to effective and sustainable relationships. They deliver the following benefits:

- leveraging culturally diverse client and consumer needs and expectations through thorough analysis of multiple identity constructions of targeted user audience;

- developing customer and stakeholder intimacy by overcoming potential stereotypes;

- acting upon the contingencies delivered by the environment;

- developing customised programmes, services and products by careful evaluation of the balance between localisation and standardisation.

For practical application, each lens features a tool or model helping the user to filter the interactions through the lens, yielding concrete results upon which decision-makers can take action (see Figure 4.10).

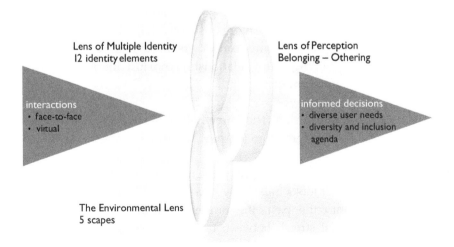

Figure 4.10   The Three Lenses and their tools

The Lens of Multiple Identity uses the 12 Identity Elements, organised in two groups:

- tangible and

- intangible identity elements.

The Lens of Perception uses the model of Belonging and Othering, offering the options of

- building Belonging through difference aiming to establish some common ground; and

- generating Othering through sameness with the overall objective of breaking through groupthink.

The Environmental Lens uses the approach of the five scapes. These are:

- ethnoscapes

- mediascapes

- technoscapes

- ideoscapes and

- financescapes.

With the boundaries of the three lenses being permeable, the framework considering the micro- and macro-level of cultural diversity mirrors the hybrid world. Our interconnected world lacks sufficient suitable frameworks and models, and the Three Lenses is one tool which helps business people to navigate through its hybridity.

- It mirrors the hybrid world that demands hybrid skills. It encourages rethinking existing models and frameworks. It furthers encourages rethinking existing organisational cultures and envisioning and building new or adapting existing products and services.

- It enables us to understand the technological, demographical and cultural diversity of stakeholders and markets.

- It establishes deeper participant, user, client and consumer insights, allowing companies to create more compelling user experiences.

- It strengthens the ability to make consumers feel special, to increase engagement and to develop intimacy as never before.

Chapter 5

Reflecting on the Visible Me – The Four Tangible Identity Elements

Succeeding in today's ever-increasingly cyberconnected business world requires not just responding, but actively shaping the opportunity it offers, that is, building interconnectivity.

Building interconnectivity in the cyberage entails:

- spanning technological, social and cultural boundaries;

- considering the behaviours people bring into these cross-boundary interactions, shaped by their heritage, experiences, perceptions, in brief, by their identity portfolio;

- examining the ramifications the digital deluge has on people and the new ways these impact their interactions;

- The Three Lenses of Diversity is a framework that navigates you through the largely uncharted pathways of successful mastery of building interconnectivity. It is designed to organise strategic thinking in the navigation of technological, cultural and social boundaries.

The key meaning and key benefit of The Lens of Multiple Identity (see Figure 5.1) are summarised in Table 5.1.

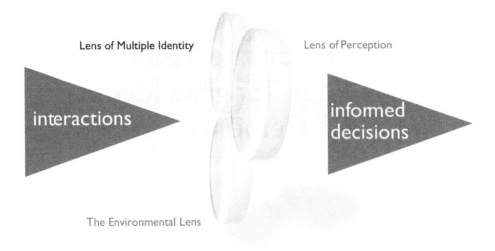

Lens of Multiple Identity

Lens of Perception

interactions

informed decisions

The Environmental Lens

Figure 5.1   The Lens of Multiple Identity

Table 5.1   Key meaning and key benefit of The Lens of Multiple Identity

Key meaning		Key benefit
The Lens of Multiple Identity helps us to understand the full identity portfolio that people bring into an interaction, that is, their own identity portfolio and those of others.	→	The Lens of Multiple Identity will provide insights from your personal identity profile and will help you to make sense of the meaningful application of the multiple identity construction approach: • identifying culturally diverse participants' needs and expectations; • understanding and responding to diverse user needs.

The Lens of Multiple Identity helps you as an individual to manage diversity by focusing on the issue of your identity. It helps you to make informed decisions as to the extent to which you activate key aspects of your 'identity portfolio' when involved in critical work-based relationships – in other words, the key aspects of who you are that enable you to build commonality and mark differences with others. It identifies a kaleidoscope of elements that comprise your identity. The 12 identity elements of The Lens of Multiple Identity are the ingredients for the surface work needed to build effective business relationships in:

- human-to-human interactions; and

- technology-to-human interactions.

Chapters 5 and 6 describe the 12 elements of the identity portfolio that form our personal diversity and that we bring into any interaction. It is essential to know the portfolio's ingredients, to understand them and to manage them. In an informed state, we also understand the impact of our identity portfolio on others. These chapters provide you with a high-level description of the meaning of each element, enabling you to 'guestimate' your personal identity portfolio.

Benefits of reflecting on and exploring your identity portfolio:

- becoming familiar with the terminology;

- understanding the meaning of each element;

- identifying your strong points and the potential impact this has on your interaction partner;

- exploring potential blind spots in your identity map and possible development steps.

Carolyn explicitly shares selected elements of her identity in her recent introduction:

Box 5.1   Carolyn's Display of Identity Elements

I am a communications expert in charge of the design and delivery of two different workshops, 'Communicating for Impact' and 'Performing through Our People'; I am also in charge of the quality management of the subject matter. I am a white, 32-year-old British female and am aware of my British accent and Anglo-Saxon appearance.

Some disproportional attention has been paid to the visible part of identity. This long-standing overemphasis is clearly shown in the way Carolyn is seen in her work environment, where she visibly stands out. As demonstrated in The Lens of Multiple Identity in Chapter 4, she is confronted with characteristics such as: she is blond, white, British and in her mid-30s. Her challenge is apparently to break through these first-sight ascriptions.

The tangible elements deserve their own chapter, called 'Reflecting'. An increasing degree of familiarity with and understanding of the meaning of the four elements will help put their importance into perspective and dig deeper than first impressions.

First impressions are formed in milliseconds. A recent study by Willis and Todorov shows that the exposure time of just 100 ms to a face suffices for people to make a trait inference. Earlier research claims that just 33 ms were above chance for the accuracy of decisions on first impressions.[1] Independent of the exact number of milliseconds needed, the judgements are already anchored on the initial inference; trait inferences from facial appearance can be characterised as fast, intuitive and effortless. Results suggest that additional time may simply boost confidence in judgements.[2]

'Reflecting' goes beyond milliseconds; it gives you a second chance to make informed decisions based on more than your first unreflected impressions.

The Four Tangible Identity Elements

This chapter specifically focuses on the tangible elements of the identity portfolio, which shape the first impression we gain from people primarily in face-to-face interactions and virtual communication. As stated, the 12 identity elements are organised in four tangible and eight intangible elements. The four tangible elements are: 'Appearance', 'Ethnicity', 'Generation' and 'Gender' (see Figure 5.2).

---

1   Grill-Spector, Kanwisher (2005) in Willis, Todorov 2006:597.
2   People often draw trait inferences from the facial appearance of other people. We investigated the minimal conditions under which people make such inferences. In five experiments, each focusing on a specific trait judgment, we manipulated the exposure time of unfamiliar faces. Judgments made after a 100-ms exposure correlated highly with judgments made in the absence of time constraints, suggesting that this exposure time was sufficient for participants to form an impression. In fact, for all judgments – attractiveness, likeability, trustworthiness, competence and aggressiveness – increased exposure time did not significantly increase the correlations. When exposure time increased from 100 to 500 ms, participants' judgments became more negative, response times for judgments decreased and confidence in judgments increased. When exposure time increased from 500 to 1,000 ms, trait judgements and response times did not change significantly (with one exception), but confidence increased for some of the judgments; this result suggests that additional time may simply boost confidence in judgments.

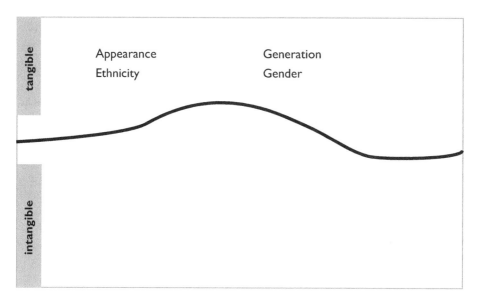

Figure 5.2   The tangible identity elements

The term 'identity' has been frequently used in this book so far. What is the understanding of identity in today's cyberconnected world?

Identity is a person's conception and expression of their individuality or group affiliations. Fundamentally, identity concerns the cognitions people have about themselves and cognitions they have about others, known as appraisal,[3] face-to-face and in cyberspace respectively, and the dialogue of the self and other cognitions in the different spaces.

Identity constructions are a constructivist approach. Identity construction and multiple identity composition are constructed in the human being when information comes into contact with existing knowledge that has been developed by experiences. It lays emphasis on the ways selected elements are created and shaped in order to adapt to the world. Constructs are the different types of filters we choose to place over our realities to change those realities from chaos to order. Consequently, identity construction is a lifetime process.

Tangible refers to visibility, to first impressions and their impact on interactions. Intangible elements are somewhat neglected aspects; they deserve their own chapter.

---

3   Adapted from Polzer, Caruso, 2010:93.

You can easily see and notice the four tangible elements in first encounters; they inform first impressions in the two-way process. 'Reflecting' on the 'Visible Me' aims to bring the overly essentialised tangible into perspective. The descriptions of the four elements provide you with the opportunity to reflect on the elements that typically receive a lot of attention. Subsequent to your thorough reflection on the entire identity portfolio, you might want to put the importance of the tangible elements into perspective.

Once Digital Icing on the Cake – Now a Key Ingredient

The digital nature of the 12 identity elements is subject to change according to the availability of vast bodies of digital data, the feeding of that information and the unprecedented speed at which this happens.

We as representatives of information society communities are not only consumers of data processed in a certain format; we are so much more. On the basis of our identity portfolio, we are unintentional producers or active generators contributing to data. For example, our data on what we learn and the way we learn, our mobility and the ways we socialise are continuously being captured, processed, traded and more or less ethically reused. As a result, our identity portfolio is influenced, shaped and transformed. Any of the roles people adopt in the digital age shapes a new sense of identity, complemented with values, may it be pride, anxiety or ignorance. In any case, this new sense of identity requires new ways of thinking for the individual and governing bodies worldwide.

With an unprecedented volume of data underway, the next generation of sense of identity is already under construction. Let us reconnect with Carolyn, who, as of this writing, is 32 years of age.

- If Carolyn was now 20 years of age, she would be a social media native.

- If Carolyn was just about to turn eight, she would be a digital native.[4] In her teenage days, truly functional augmented reality would be a given to her, available with premium services tailored to personal needs and wants. She would see data in 3D right in front of her eyes, responding to her gestures flawlessly, and retina display would be mainstream soon.[5]

---

4   Also known as Generation C, that is, born after 1990.
5   Adapted from ICSPA 2013:10.

The digital icing on the cake of some people's identity portfolio, specifically the early adopters of new technology, has become a key ingredient to each of the 12 elements. As diversity is dynamic, regenerative, perception-shaped and environment-shaped, so is the digital core of each element. The speed at which the digital changes one's identity portfolio informs the elements overall.

The Activation of the Identity Elements

Each of the 12 elements can be more or less activated in an interaction, producing the regenerative nature of diversity (see Figure 5.3). The quality of the relationship largely depends on the interplay or negotiated balance of the portfolio of identity elements.

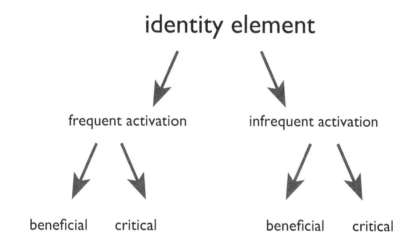

Figure 5.3   Activation level of identity element

A frequent activation of one element can have either a beneficial or a critical impact on the interaction partner, depending on the person's activation level of the identity elements. The same applies to infrequent activation.

Equally, it will enable observation of other people's behaviours, allowing you to understand the activation level of selected elements in other people. A detailed guideline on the understanding and use of activation levels for building interconnectivity follows in Chapter 7: Breaking through the Stereotype Game – The Lens of Perception.

Further, the element descriptions of the four tangible identity elements provide the insights necessary to evaluate your own activation level. For the purpose of first familiarisation with the tangible part of your identity portfolio, at the end of this chapter you will find a chart to plot your assumed activation levels. Try to designate two 'frequent' and two 'infrequent' activations for the four tangible elements. If required from your perspective, try to mark only one of the elements in the middle. The same activity is available to you for the intangible elements at the end of Chapter 6.

Now, let us move to the descriptions of the four tangible elements, breaking each into three component parts: explanations of the term involved, the digital component and your personal perception.

APPEARANCE

Box 5.2   Nerds Rule

'Nerds rule' is the slogan spotted on a t-shirt worn by a guy attending a start-up event sponsored by Microsoft Austria, providing software, support, visibility and community to promising start-ups and visionary start-ups.

Appearance as a multimillion industry

Appearance is a highly visible form of establishing membership in groups or in sub-populations of interest to express belonging to a certain profession, to mediate social status or socioeconomic class, to communicate one's religion or to underpin one's ethnicity. In a world where you can change almost anything on your body, appearance is one of the first identifiers for other people's appraisal. The appearance industry is a multimillion business consisting of fashion, accessories and sportswear.

Also, the appearance enhancement industry is one of today's fastest growing business sectors; professions like cosmetologists, aestheticians, natural hair stylists and nail specialists form a significant group of revenue-generating professionals, not to mention the plastic surgery industry. More people than ever are turning to scalpel or needle in the quest for a perfect appearance, while nonsurgical treatments to smooth wrinkles and lines or to remove hair even outnumber surgical procedures (ISAPS 2011:11).

Smart appearance matters not only in the hospitality industry, but anywhere any form of appearance is closely associated with a variety of judgements such as attractiveness, likeability, trustworthiness, competence or aggressiveness.

Fashion and fashion accessories may provide the perfect finishing touch. In addition, features and items related to Appearance convey meaning, which create Belonging or Othering in interaction with other people.

In the world of work appearance might have to be in accordance with the functional, hierarchical, and social and cultural expectations. The required appearance might be a business suit, a uniform, a safety overall or casual clothing. Regional differences might be reflected in the overall styling. Irrespective if one works in the financial industry in The City of London, the IT industry in Silicon Valley or the tourism industry in the Austrian countryside, a fit with the respective organisation culture and industry might show.

Digital Appearance

The importance we assign to appearance differs for each of us. The same applies for the digital interaction people immerse in; some pay careful attention to their self-presentation, whilst others are less concerned about it, whether they 'show their face' or use an avatar. Appearance in the cyberworld might, at first glance, appear more of an intangible element, as it seems to be hidden in the ones and zeros. However, appearance has earned phenomenal importance in cyberspace, for example in avatars, logos or self-presentation on social media networks.

This presence will be carefully designed to shape your digital reputation; it will be everything for you as an individual, for your workplace, the enterprise you might own, governments, businesses and citizens alike. Your digital presence might be diversified into a number of identities, such as your business identity shown on respective regional or international business networks or your social identity, showing a completely different face on a different set of social networks.

The widespread use of multiple identities with varying levels of verification, pseudonymity and anonymity is likely to give rise to new identity management services and tools. Damage in connection with cyberappearance will be instantaneous and increasingly difficult to repair. An emerging market for outsourced corporate online reputation management (ICSPA 2013:5) with varying degrees of success is a current signal for this. Digital appearance and related services will experience unparalleled attention and growth in the light of the absence of clarity between legitimate use and misuse of personas and the consistency of digital identities.

Your personal perspective on Appearance

Your appearance imparts an image of yourself which affects how other people think and feel about you and how they interact with you. You may, therefore, choose to project a particular persona. Features of your appearance might include business suits, uniforms, overalls, avatars, and logos or symbols. In both face-to-face and virtual interaction you may also choose to include elements that express your national heritage or your religious beliefs and other integral elements of your belief system.

Equally, you may find that other aspects of your identity are more important in order to interconnect and to gain trust and respect with your partners in the world of work. Because of the tangible nature of this identity element, it will be easy for you to identify people who place more importance on their personal appearance and the digital presentation.

Hands-on guidelines for self-evaluation

The section for the self-evaluation is at the end of the chapter. The following points might assist you in your reflection:

- What does this identity element mean to me? How do I bring it to life in digital space and in face-to-face interactions?

- What behaviours do I activate? In what ways do I shape this element in interaction with others?

- What is my contribution to the industry? In what way am I an active member? Or, am I just an end consumer?

- How much do I spend on Appearance per year?

GENDER

Gender as a self-fulfilling industry

Sex makes us, speaking in binary terms, male or female. Gender makes us, again in the limiting binary, masculine or feminine. Gender refers to those social, cultural and psychological traits linked to males and females through particular social contexts (Wharton 2012:8).

Socialisation into a gender identity starts early. A broad range of industries has generated gender division for the purpose of profit maximisation, well embedded in the biological characteristics distinguishing male and female. For example, contrast the predominantly pink covers of books such as The Beautiful Girls' Colouring Book – garlanded with butterflies, cakes and flowers – with the navy-blue The Brilliant Boys' Colouring Book – armoured with axes, helmets and a space-zapper. The campaigners suggest that publishers are sending out very limiting messages to children about what kinds of things are appropriate for girls or for boys.

Look at the gender marketing of toys and sexual objectification of women, both of which box people into very narrow, old-fashioned gender models. The implication is a culture which values physicality above all other attributes. Interest groups, mainly parents, have already persuaded retailers such as Toys R Us, Boots and Tesco to market toys in a more inclusive fashion.[6]

Gender is an achieved status because it must be learned. Its code is reflected through one's lifetime, from micro things such the colour code of sports wear, from cap to shoes, all the way through to macro issues such as the acquisition of property and the generation of wealth.

Only recently has a growing awareness of gender assignment arisen, away from the binary option of female or male. In Europe, Germany took the leadership role in offering a third gender option.

Alongside the categories of 'M' and 'F' there is a new category: 'X'. Now, the German government and legal experts are keen to stress that this third blank box isn't an official third gender, or the 'other' box – so it doesn't actually mean that there are now three recognised genders in Germany. The third option is considered as a temporary solution for very specific intersex cases. The children are expected to make a decision to be male or female at a non-specified point in the future, which represents a big achievement for intersex people.[7]

---

6   http://www.theguardian.com/world/2013/dec/23/stores-agree-end-gendered-toys-displays-campaign.

7   http://www.theguardian.com/commentisfree/2013/nov/10/germany-third-gender-birth-certificate.

Gender in the digital space

Once celebrated as an ambassador of equality, cyberspace and its connected tools soon turned out to foster gender-based stereotypes.

Quite the reverse of expectations, gender has emerged as one of the defining demographics of interest on the internet. Demographically targeted advertising has attracted the interest of online marketers in many different sectors. Online marketers and advertisers can now more precisely understand who their clients are and are able to better estimate the characteristics of website visitors through patterns revealed by big data. Marketing and advertising strategists indicate that gender is a key attribute and predictor of intent to purchase; however, research shows that gender-oriented key phrases do not generate more sales but can cost more for advertisers relative to gender-neutral queries (Jansen et al. 2013:301).[8]

Gender is also a recurrent determinant in digital learning. In the digital learning industry, data show that most Massive Open Online Course (MOOC) students are well-educated, employed, young and male. They are younger mirror images of most of the instructors, many of whom are celebrated as 'stars', made so by the large numbers of students, irrespective of completion rates. Some recent articles entitled 'Masculine Open Online Courses'[9] illustrate that MOOCs may be taking academia back to the days when senior scholars were mostly men. The absence of role models for students with a differing identity portfolio is, as in any other situation, detrimental for the development of a more diverse approach in this area.

Far from democratising education, critics argue that MOOCs will only reinforce those with power and weaken those without it. Early evidence from MOOCs suggests significant drop-out rates.[10]

Early in 2014, Facebook broke through the limiting binary gender game by introducing a new range of options in the gender landscape.[11] Now, the users of the social media site have well over 50 gender options at their fingertips,

---

8   The dataset of the research was quite substantial, with nearly seven million records over a lengthy data collection period (that is, 33 months spanning four calendar years). The dataset also included a varied set of search and consumer behaviour and interactions (for example, impressions, clicks, orders placed, items ordered and money spent).

9   The term has been used widely; the original source seems to be unknown.

10 The reasons for the poor completion rates will be revisited in Chapter 10.

11 http://www.theguardian.com/technology/shortcuts/2014/feb/16/facebook-should-remove-all-gender-options.

including trans categories. Some of the new categories were head-scratching to some, such as, 'cisgender,' 'androgyne' or 'genderqueer', requiring translations.

The myriad gender options on Facebook have already raised criticism: it might have been braver to remove gender completely. However, the industries dwelling on the gender assignment, now apparently diversified, would fall short of large data sets used for gender-targeted ads.

Yet cyberspace allows us to show a non-gender-incognito identity. As illustrated in Appearance, there are ways to camouflage one's visible identity elements by crafting an identity well beyond one's actual appearance, gender, age and ethnicity.

Your personal perspective on Gender

Gender emerges not as an individual attribute but something that is 'accomplished' in interaction with others. People, therefore, are *doing* gender. Reflecting on the information provided in the descriptions 'Gender as a self-fulfilling industry' and 'Gender in the digital space' what does this identity element mean to you? How do you bring it alive in digital space and in face-to-face interaction? The following questions might help the evaluation of your personal activation level on Gender.

- Do I see myself as a human being first or as a gendered individual?

- To what extent are gender aspects of my identity important?

- How conscious am I of my own gender in day-to-day business interactions, particularly when I am in meetings or gatherings comprised mainly of people of the opposite sex? Do I downplay this part of my identity or do I use it as a toolbox to get things?

- Have I, in the past, experienced discrimination on the basis of my sex, and if so, have I become very conscious of gender issues in my organisation?

The section to capture self-evaluation is at the end of the chapter.

GENERATION

The world of work in five generations

The world's workforce is diversifying. In just a few years, up to five generations will collaborate in the world of work.

Box 5.3   The Undo Generation

The Undo Generation – Generational Tensions on a High-Performance Team

The flight crew interact with the aircraft's automated flight system, using interfaces, like a computer with a keypad and a monitor (one for each pilot). The two interfaces are, of course, linked to the same system, so any information keyed in by one pilot will show up on the other pilot's monitor. Typically, before take-off, the more junior First Officer will enter the aircraft performance data and the flight plan data into the computer, using the keypad. It is then standard procedure for the Captain to check the data entered.

Recently, Captains, more senior in age, report that younger First Officers type in data too fast for them to be able to follow. In addition, they tend to be less diligent about monitoring the accuracy of their typing actions. When the Captain points out an error in the data input, the First Officer will simply correct the wrong input.

The above interaction has been labelled as an illustration of the 'undo generation': individuals that grew up with the technology that provides sufficient flexibility to 'undo' incorrect inputs or actions. This mindset is subconsciously transferred over to the interaction with an aircraft computer, without perhaps full appreciation of the potential repercussions of wrong inputs, which could potentially contribute to a fatal accident.

These examples of 'generational tensions' refer to instances where differences in perceptions, outlooks, attitudes and experience among team members belonging to different age-defined generations appear to produce 'tensions' with possible implications for flight safety.

Today, 50 per cent of the world population is below 27 years old. As of 2015 there will be five generations in the workplace:

- The traditionalists, born between 1922 and 1943. With the rise of retirement age and more flexible work approaches a small group from this generation will have an active work life in 2015 (Toossi 2012:47).[12]

- The baby boomers, born between 1944 and 1964, often characterised as workaholics with a number of career paths pursued mostly in one company. Their socialisation happened in face-to-face space and their presence on digital communication channels is still minor.

- Generation X, born between 1965 and 1977. With the invention of the WorldWideWeb in 1989,[13] they were the first generation who from their teenage days had access to digital communication. Email is still the dominant channel; however, a significant number have profiles on one or more social media sites.

- Generation Y, also known as the 'millennials', who wish to work for organisations that foster innovative thinking, develop their skills and make a positive contribution to society (The Deloitte Millenial Survey 2014).

- Generation C, also known as the 'digital natives' (Friedrich et al. 2010:2). Born after 1990, they are just about to attend university or enter the world of work, ready to transform the ways we socialise, shop, work and bring out their inner selves.

In 2025, millennials will form 75 per cent of the global workforce. Workplace implications are many, stretching well beyond the visible identity of Generation, as the above reality strip of the 'undo generation' demonstrates. True boundary crossers perceive differences in age and generation as less important. With businesses potentially paying increasing attention to Generation, leadership and communications styles have started changing, and hierarchies have started to become flatter. The workplace might promote communities of interest, passion and engagement across generation boundaries.

---

12 The data is US-based by the Bureau of Labor Statistics.
13 Tim Berners-Lee was the man who led the development of the World Wide Web (with help of course) and the definition of HTML (HyperText Markup Language) used to create web pages, HTTP (HyperText Transfer Protocol) and URLs (Universal Resource Locators). All of these developments took place between 1989 and 1991.

Attracting and keeping younger workers is one of the biggest talent challenges in the cyberconnected world of work. Consequently, people-management strategies have changed and will continue to change so that they integrate state-of-the-art working practices and are less like the pyramid structures of former workplace experiences.

THE DIGITAL NATIVES

Being connected on a 24/7 basis will be the norm in 2020 – indeed, a prerequisite for participation in society.

As digital literacy will become a prime concern for the older generations, it will be Generation C who will have to support aging parents and grandparents with their technology expertise for the handling of home management systems and technology-assisted living. The generation gap will open unprecedented business opportunities for start-ups and other ingenious entrepreneurs among the digital natives.

In parallel, the older groups will continue to lag in the intensity of their digital behaviour. Generation C will distance itself further, particularly in the development of its own pervasive culture of communication. That culture has led observers to dub this group 'the Silent Generation' (Friedrich et al. 2010:8), as digital communication channels have replaced the physical interaction embraced by prior generations.

Like the flight crew, an increasing number of people will find themselves in the world of work embedded in complex social and technological systems, facing unprecedented changes – if they still have a job then.

Your personal perspective on Generation

Obviously, the physical representation of the generation element can be changed to a certain extent these days. Specifically, a number of possible interventions for conquering the signs of aging are offered; these are covered in the description of Appearance.

This element describes the extent to which your age and the associated generation represent an integral part of your identity. Particularly, it refers to the physical aspect of the element, that is, your real age visible to others and the assumed age group ascribed to you. Equally, it refers to non-physical representation, that is, the interests, values and outlook on work people have about the generation of your age.

Independent of the generation you feel you belong to, in your preferred role of boundary-crosser you may feel your age is relatively average or 'normal' and that you have a strong ability to leverage ideas and adopt approaches from people of different age groups.

How does this visible element of your identity shape the way you understand yourself and the ways you connect with your interaction partners?

- What does it mean to me? How do I bring it to life? In digital space? In face-to-face interaction?

- What behaviours do I activate?

- In what ways do I see myself as a member of a specific generation?

- How do I interact with members of other generations?

Go to the end of the chapter to plot your self-evaluation.

ETHNICITY

The changing picture of Ethnicity

The changing picture of ethnicity over time coincides with increased mobility, induced by historical, political, economic and social reasons.

Race and ethnicity are terms often used interchangeably. Strictly speaking, they are related, respectively, to biological and sociological factors. Race refers to a person's physical appearance, such as skin colour, eye colour or hair colour. Ethnicity, on the other hand, relates to cultural factors such as nationality, culture, ancestry, language and beliefs.

In the context of the identity portfolio, the visible 'face' of ethnicity refers to any physical aspects of a person's appearance that display their ethnic background or ancestry to others. It includes tangible aspects such as names that provide insights into ethnic background, which might or might not be misleading. In any case, it provokes assumptions that, in turn, shape the perceptions of the interaction partners.

Ethnicity and its visible format can act as misleading pointers to cultural differences; for example, stereotyping, and at worst may form the basis for racial discrimination. When stereotypes such as these are allowed to influence social judgements, decisions about representatives will be based on general beliefs about the behaviours, traits and qualities associated with ethnicity instead of the actual traits of the representatives being judged. In the world of work, perceptions connected to ethnicity might discriminate at the hiring stage; other issues, such as double and shifting standards in evaluation devalue on-the-job performance (Lee, Fiske 2008:139).

In today's interconnected world, individuals may interact mainly with people from diverse ethnic backgrounds, so that they are not often made aware of any ethnically-based differences in appearance between themselves and their business colleagues and partners. Working across this boundary over a long period of time, or in a multi-ethnic environment, may reduce the awareness of these differences and they no longer shape the perceptions people have of others.

Equally, ethnicity may provide a source of pride in a distinct identity or an outward signal of difference that could be used for creativity and innovation.

The digital response

Addressing ethnicity and shedding light on potential discrimination is now reflected in apps, for example, the Everyday Racism app by All Together Now, developed in collaboration with the University of Western Sydney, Deakin University and Melbourne University. Everyday Racism is a game/education app which challenges users to live a week in the life of an Aboriginal man, a Muslim woman, an Indian student or just themselves. It gives the users the opportunity to experience what life can be for cultural and ethnic minorities in Australia.[14] They can also choose to play as themselves, where they will be able to see how discrimination plays out in society and how it affects others from a third-person perspective.

Whilst technology can be of great support in addressing societal issues such as discrimination in connection with ethnicity, a lack of access to the internet is a major element of the digital divide. Smart-phone apps allow usage even when offline, and can thus be used in remote areas with poor infrastructure and limited

---

14 http://alltogethernow.org.au/news/campaigns/everydayracism/.

access to the internet.[15] Nevertheless, research consistently identifies ethnicity, income, age and education as significant predictors of access to technology.

As idiosyncratic to the tangible elements above, the identity element of Ethnicity can also be well camouflaged in the cyberworld, should the user wish to design an identity well beyond this visible part of identity.

Your Ethnic self

This element describes the extent to which your ethnicity is an integral part of your identity. How do potential similarities or differences due to ethnic background inform the ways you establish connection with others? You might experience conscious recognition and pleasure in working across boundaries with people from different ethnic backgrounds. You might actively search for opportunities to connect with people from diverse ethnic backgrounds.

How do you bring your ethnicity to life in digital space and in face-to-face interaction? The following questions might help the evaluation of your personal activation level on Ethnicity.

- To what extent have I got the opportunity to mix with people from different ethnic backgrounds?

- To what extent do I feel proficient at working in a multi-ethnic environment?

- Do I perceive other elements of my identity as likely to be more important in initiating contact with others?

Go to the end of the chapter to plot your self-evaluation.

Academic Background

The one remaining theoretical concept is the geology model, originally based on Lévi-Strauss' structuralist approach (also see Chapter 2). In brief, Lévi-Strauss proposed the idea that the human brain systematically processes units of information in a structured way. This attempts to explain the world we live in and provides tools with which to operate in it.

---

15 Assuming that the devices can be charged.

The geology model based on LéviStrauss' structuralist approach explains to a wider business audience the ongoing transformation processes that occur, with culture as a problem-solving vehicle.

Originally, the geology model was designed for use in cross-cultural/intercultural training in order to show the complexity of culture in a structured yet open-ended way. The model placed the structures below the surface, for example, 'family' as a social construct, and illustrated their various versions at the surface, such as the nuclear family, polyandry or polygamy.

For the use of the identity portfolio the original geology was slightly adapted, now showing the intangible elements below the surface and the tangible ones above ground. The open-endedness of the geology model indicates the ever-changing nature of the elements. Technological, cultural and social boundaries are subject to permanent modification as is the geological substance of our planet.

It is important to remember to:

- understand that culture is not a closed system;

- recognise more easily the reciprocal action of elements across boundaries;

- start with mutualities within a culture or among cultures rather than with differences.

The Visible Me in Organisation Development

Outlooks on work in the cyberconnected world are undergoing significant transformation. Organisations are slowly acknowledging the structural changes occasioned by:

- the opportunities and threats technological developments present;

- the worldwide demographic shift and its ramifications for society and organisations;

- the global economic turbulences of the recent financial crisis through which large populations have been affected; and finally

- the pressing human challenges caused by these changes, not necessarily unprecedented, but certainly new in the extent of the interconnectedness in which they all happen.

People in charge of organisation development in enterprises and organisations across the world, small and large alike, are trying to come to grip with these changes to prepare for the future.

To stay abreast of the demographic, economic and technological developments, organisations must build interconnectivity, that is, the active endeavour to leverage the entire identity portfolio, and the connected appraisals of self and others that people in the light of all the changes bring to an organisation.

In organisation development today, profit and not-for-profit organisations alike still focus on the tangible aspects of identity, missing a great number of opportunities the interconnected world offers.

Regarding diversity and inclusion and with some geographic variation, Ethnicity, Gender and Generation are still top on the agenda of organisation development. In German-speaking countries, particularly, issues in relation to Gender and Generation have been singled out and made high priority by some large organisations. Diversity, for many, is still synonymous with gender, and the discussion of the introduction of a quota system with the aim of getting women into senior roles is relentless, still polarising, and resulting in heated discussions.

In contrast, there have been attempts to integrate selected tangible elements of identity into an overall development agenda, such as inclusive leadership development and the development of a culture that embraces difference.

The ability of organisations to cyberconnect is becoming increasingly important for superior performance. Cyberconnecting means establishing meaningful connections across technological, cultural and social boundaries, mirrored in organisations succeeding in today's hybrid business world. It is the conscious act of building interconnectivity. Deriving strength through interconnectivity and cultivating a culture of collaboration where all people can thrive requires the acknowledgement of both the tangible and intangible aspects of people's identity. The intangible elements of identity such as Lifelong learning, Sociability and Communication largely impact outlooks on work and the capability to cross boundaries.

The tangible elements are only the starting point; the key to success for performance through client-centricity lies in the intangible elements. They reveal volumes about people's intrinsic motivation and are thus key to unlocking individual performance. When scaled up to the organisation level by the help the tools the cyberconnected world has to offer, they represent the road to success.

Let us now turn from organisational considerations back to you as an individual by presenting the promised section on self-evaluation (see Figure 5.4).

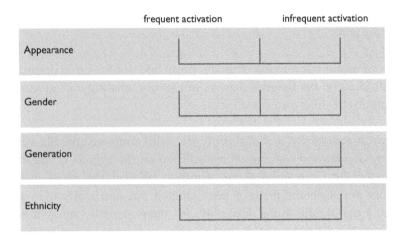

Figure 5.4   Self-evaluation for tangible identity elements

REFLECTING ON THE VISIBLE ME

- Bear in mind that you know yourself best.

- Focus on one current project, and within it, on one key business contact who is of critical importance for the success or failure of the project.

- As you read through the descriptions of the elements, reflect on the extent to which you activate the specific element when interacting with the person of choice.

- Mark 'Frequent activation' or 'Infrequent activation' on the axis provided for each element.

GUIDELINE FOR EVALUATION OF BUSINESS CONTACT

In preparation for the upcoming chapter on the 'Lens of Perception' you can conduct an evaluation across the four elements for one of your key business contacts in order to draw an identity portfolio of that person. As with the self-evaluation, the appraisal of the other should further be tested test in future interactions in order to avoid toxic assumptions.

BRIDGING THE GAP BETWEEN ONE'S OWN AND OTHERS' IDENTITY PORTFOLIOS

The self-evaluation of your identity portfolio and the appraisal of your business contact might show some gaps among selected identity elements. Bridging strategies will be discussed in detail in Chapter 7.

Chapter 6

Exploring the Extended Me
– The Eight Intangible Identity
Elements

In today's cyberconnected world of work people expect more from their working relationships with colleagues, clients and the organisations than ever before; for example, wellbeing, meaning and stimulation.

Increasingly, they also expect the organisations they work for to contribute positively to the societal and the environmental good. In short, people want a workplace where they, and others, can do more than survive – they want to flourish and grow. In a world of increasing competition for resources and best talent, we all contribute to creating the kind of environment which will attract and retain colleagues, clients and users we want to work with.

We each have a wealth of experience and insight about organisations and organisational change to bring to this inquiry. However, much of this wealth remains undiscovered in both the face-to-face and the virtual interaction of hectic day-to-day business.

The capacity for discovery, self-renewal, innovation and the expansion of possibilities is much prized in modern organisations. Such capacity can come in many forms: product or intellectual capital innovation, technological breakthroughs, exceptional personal qualities, corporate social and ecological responsibility, all through increased interconnectivity.

'Exploring the extended me' means inquiring into the details of your full identity portfolio. You will travel through some familiar although lesser explored areas, but also through unfamiliar areas known as the intangible identity elements, which can bring positive change to the ways we shape business relationships in today's cyberconnected world of work. We can think of ourselves as generative, abounding in experiences that we contribute to and gain from the world of work.

In order to build interconnectivity, organisations must foster the discovery muscle, which starts with the exploration of the intangible aspects of identity that we bring into these interactions. Curiosity is needed for this exploration in us individuals, reflected in the organisation's communication channels, and embedded in its feedback processes and systems.

The Eight Intangible Identity Elements

This chapter provides you with the opportunity to investigate systematically the ways and the extent to which the intangible elements shape your sense of identity. Some key considerations will assist you on your journey of exploration:

- how you bring the intangible elements alive in the ways you connect with people;

- to what extent you acknowledge them in the ways you innovate;

- in what ways they are reflected in the technological breakthroughs your enterprise pursues; and, among many other aspects,

- how they are shown in its corporate responsibilities.

Chapter 5 provided you with an introduction to the tangible and intangible nature of the 12 identity elements and presented a thorough introduction to the four tangible identity elements, namely, Appearance, Gender, Generation and Ethnicity. Following the same plan, Chapter 6 now concentrates on the detailed introduction of the eight intangible identity elements, which are essential for building effective, sustainable business relationships.

As presented in the geology model in Chapter 4 and shown in Chapter 5, the intangible identity elements (see Figure 6.1) are situated below the surface and are thus not immediately recognisable.

They typically weave the fabric essential to building effective work-based relationships based upon common experience and potentially shared or negotiated values.

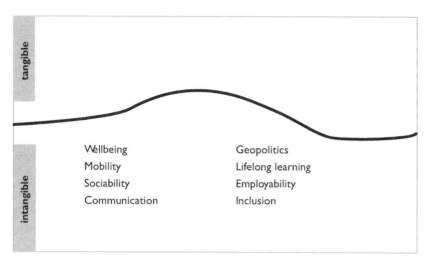

Figure 6.1   The intangible identity elements

Key characteristics of the intangible elements are that:

- they are developmental: they change and shape with our life experience;

- they require a second look: they are more difficult to detect and to determine. People are often unaware of them in their own and others' identity constructions;

- they sometimes come with a 'jetlag': when people are not directly concerned, some of the intangible elements resurface only after generations, as in the case of a conflict renewed by grandchildren or great grandchildren of the original combatants, living in a completely different geographic location.

Their conscious activation presupposes a number of requirements: a) self-awareness, b) knowledge about the other and the context and c) time. This means that the productive management of diversity needs to be learned and developed.

This chapter continues the pattern of Chapter 5, describing each of the eight intangible elements and breaking each into three component parts: explanations of the term involved, the digital component and your personal perception. Again, at the end of the chapter there is a section for self-evaluation for each of the eight intangible identity elements, which are 'Wellbeing', 'Mobility', 'Sociability', 'Communication', 'Geopolitics', 'Lifelong learning', 'Employability' and 'Inclusion'.

WELLBEING

Wellbeing and its effect on performance

Although many economies are going through tough times, the wellbeing industry has proved resilient, and some fast-moving businesses are finding success. This is the result of more people becoming aware of the wider benefits of getting fit and partly because technology is revolutionising the way they can track, record and motivate themselves.

Well before the hype of the digital age, consumers drastically reshaped their notions of health and wellness. Riding the 'aerobics wave' centring around some Hollywood stars in the 1980s, consumers made the connection between health, wellness and quality of life, and a multi-billion-dollar industry has been spawned by companies leveraging this trend in combination with apparel, vitamins and other supplies, sport centres of unparalleled size, and wellness hotels and spas.

Nevertheless, the world of cyberconnected work has caused countless health-related problems for people, ultimately affecting their employers' performance. Stress levels as a result of hyperconnectivity, meaning being connected 24/7, are unparalleled. The absence of daily physical activity, poor nutrition and smoking are major contributors to employees' poor health. For example, there is a rising tide of obesity, coronary heart disease, high blood pressure, strokes and some cancers, all of which are too often related to employees' lifestyles. Increasing levels of stress are also caused by employees' fear of the future, uncertainty of employment, pension provision and insecurity, and debt.

The consequent lack of employees' wellbeing and its impact, both physical and psychological, on their work performance, is also negatively influencing their employer's business performance through absenteeism, reduced productivity and engagement.

With the rising cost of healthcare systems and the resulting decline of paid services, the market for prevention is increasing in importance, enabling the new consumerisation of healthcare and wellbeing. With today's digital outlook the wellbeing industry will be totally transformed in just a few years.

Your digital Wellbeing

The number of wellbeing apps is increasing daily. The offering covers nearly every aspect of wellbeing, so that you can now diagnose your own symptoms, track your fertility, get fit, monitor mood swings, lose weight or track your sleep patterns. At the heart of the digital wellbeing revolution is the smart-phone or tablet. Regardless of whether you prefer a smart-phone, a tablet or a wearable, one day the device will know your body better than you do. The fundamental idea of these apps is to assist you in managing your own condition and ultimately to enable you to lead a better and healthier life.

National health services and health insurers have discovered the world of digital health. Even the retail industry is staking a claim in the new market; for example, supermarket chains offer healthy eating apps.

Doctors, physicians, coaches and trainers are increasingly interconnected with you as client or patient. Your data is being continuously monitored, and you can review the results on the logs and graph options. The expert can, for example, update you with advice on blood glucose control. The app you select will become aware of your habits and cravings, meaning it could have an autonomous dialogue with the coaches, trainers and expert systems.

Digital wellbeing requires unique boundary crossing, in that specialists who have never before worked together now need to collaborate and co-create new solutions. Academics, games and application designers and hospital specialists come together to explore the ways in which new approaches can help improve the lives of groups often marginalised through an illness, with the ultimate goal of designing apps, video games and healthcare solutions tailored to their specific needs. This multidisciplinary approach is novel and will open the doors for some ground-breaking therapeutic relationships between groups.

As of this writing, the legal and market conditions for developing digital health and wellbeing products and services need further improvement.

Your personal Wellbeing

Wellbeing as an identity element describes for you as an individual the condition of your physical, medical and psychological state. This includes fitness, health and the ability to maintain high levels of energy in the world of work. It describes the extent to which your assumed strength and fitness or a potential illness represents an integral part of your identity. How do the energy and the investment you make in looking after yourself shape the ways you understand yourself and contribute to your sense of identity?

Your Wellbeing may or may not be immediately obvious to others; finding out if you have this element of identity in common with others may initially be discovered only through dialogue.

When performing the self-evaluation exercise at the end of the chapter, consider the following:

- the ways you meet and relate easily with people who also focus on Wellbeing, whether through shared health-based activities or through shared interest;

- the extent to which these relationships may take on a competitive edge;

- the ways circumstances foster or impede your efforts;

- the potential avoidance of contact with people who are obviously unhealthy.

MOBILITY

Far, fast, flexible

Mobility ranges from the sexiness of a cosmopolitan lifestyle all the way to the conundrum of getting to places on a daily basis. Mobility also includes all things mobile, such as wearables and smart-phones, which accompany the mobile person. The reality strip below presents a less sexy part of mobility: commuting in a megacity in North Africa.

Box 6.1   Physical Mobility

08:10am Cairo time: minibuses arrive in front of the glittering building, stopping one behind the other, forming a 'bus snake', their sleek exterior design reflected in the glass front of the office buildings. As the passengers disembark, some of them chat, while others are quiet and look rather tired. They cluster on meticulously manicured lawns featuring rows of palm trees guarding the buildings and offering scarce shade in distorted palm tree shapes. The spotlessly smooth and shiny glass fronts offer spectacular scenery mirroring the morning sun's rays played back by the surrounding desert. These airconditioned minibuses were on the road for more than an hour, starting at the collection point in chaotic downtown Cairo. By the time the passengers reached the minibuses, some of them had already travelled for more than an hour, often on non-air-conditioned and crowded public buses and vans serving as collective taxis. All the passengers arrive at the same time. They enter the buildings one after the other, briefly put their mobiles aside, show their ID passes to the security control, and once at their desks, log on to the IT system, changing from passengers to employees.

The need for physical mobility as exemplified above might be the result of working for a prestigious employer, situated in a high-tech compound outside the urban centre. Whilst the commute probably causes stress, working for a celebrated brand might impact other identity elements.

'Mobility is on the increase'; 'Mobility and migration'; 'demographic changes underway'; 'growing shortages of skilled labour' – all of these are frequently used catchphrases in association with mobility.

In general terms, mobility refers to the ability to move or be moved freely and easily. Clearly, this implies a number of aspects, one of which is physical capability, which in turn has an impact on possible methods of travel from one place to another, equally applicable for leisure time and business travel.

In addition to its physical connotation, mobility also refers to the ability to move between different levels in society or employment. Certainly the workplace makes a significant contribution to the first aspect of mobility, often requiring people to move to another city or country; besides, it requires many business people to go on regular short-term assignments of varying extent, length and intensity. The resulting levels of alienation experienced in the host countries vary greatly depending on the individual and the contingencies inherent in the environment.

In an increasing number of cases relocation and short-term assignments come in combination, that is, people who live outside their place of origin are required to travel extensively on business. Finally, mobility manifests in commuter journeys. This type of mobility contributes a significant percentage of the working week hours and is mostly perceived as unproductive, tiring, stressful and certainly unsexy.

The zeros and ones of Mobility

Recently mobility has acquired a new, additional meaning, namely, all things mobile.

Making your business mobile is no longer a matter for debate. Today's mobile users, your customers and employees, expect interaction with you at their fingertips. Enterprise mobility goes beyond mobile apps; much more, it influences how you run your business.

Due to technology evolutions, low-cost bandwidth and the limitless nature of the cloud, the use of consumer devices such as iPhone, iPad, Android phones and tablets, Windows phones and tablets, and BlackBerry and on-demand services such as access to office email, sales dashboard and inventory data gave rise to the concept of IT-based mobility. This, in turn, fosters people's mobility.

A pronounced preference for mobility is often complemented by the early adoption of all things mobile such as wearables, the latest versions of tablets or smart-phones, and the most recent smart home controls. It typically connects with Lifelong learning, Sociability and Inclusion in different yet simultaneous networks.

Entire industries have been creating business opportunities for mobile people, offering products and services to ease the mobile person's life. These range from face-to-face expat products and services to technology-based aides in the form of numerous apps provided on all common platforms.

The proliferation and increasing sophistication of interaction and collaboration technology will result in less frequent travel, in particular for knowledge workers, while mobility, manifested in physical travel, will be the province of an exclusive target group and more likely tailored to the luxury segment.

YOUR PERSONAL PERSPECTIVE ON MOBILITY

The Mobility identity element describes the extent to which mobility in relation to your business and your private life shapes your identity. Mobility might be an integral part of life and associated coping strategies might be dealt with easily, since connected relationships have similar understanding of mobility-related challenges. These coping strategies represent the life cycle's state-of-the-art to such an extent that the nomad-like lifestyle is a trendsetter among friends and the wider network. Even the family is integrated along travel routes. The infrastructure is laid out for regular visitors or belongings are kept to a minimum. The communication strategy is aligned with the mobile lifestyle; a digital identity is carefully crafted for this purpose, overall aiming to disseminate lifestyle news and to stay connected. The network prefers a similar lifestyle with matching coping strategies, all of which supports learning from one another in this field.

In what ways do you believe your level of Mobility shapes your sense of identity? The section for the self-evaluation is at the end of the chapter. The following points might assist you in your reflection:

- you might consider yourself a global citizen by choice;

- you are a shaper of the mobile industry;

- you tend to think of yourself as an early adopter of all things mobile.

SOCIABILITY

Fun and necessity

Sub-cultures form on the basis of different preferences and boundaries are often redefined on unexpected terms. The vignette below from the SonaConn life case illustrates the importance of interconnectivity across identities.

Box 6.2   Red or White?

Some of the team members did not consume alcohol, independent of their religious affiliation as Sikhs, Muslims or Christians, and were made fun of by other team members who routinely consumed alcohol. The grouping into those who did and those who did not consume alcohol grew even more obvious once the non-alcohol-consumers started looking into recreational activities different from those of the alcohol consumers, who typically socialised at the bar in the evening. Alternative recreational habits included going to the gym or exploring Cairo for more educational purposes.

The identity element of Sociability is profoundly context-driven. For example, when going to a dinner, one's identity as a vegetarian may be rather more crucial than one's identity as a quantum physicist. Let us now look at the broader picture of sociability.

The essence of sociability is traditionally defined as the play-form of association, that is, the pleasurable, joyful and delightful experience that comes from people's interaction in society. Imagine the perfect social situation, when you are having fun with friends, family or colleagues, chatting, joking and enjoying the sheer delight of their company.[1] This pure pleasure of sociability is possible because we are able to detach ourselves from the real, material and concrete forms of social life that involve structures and positionings, usually related to hierarchies and inequality in social fields.

In the world of work, most human associations are entered into because of some ulterior motives; nevertheless, there is a residue of pure sociability or association for its own sake.

Sociability as an identity element is brought to life by involvement in sports and other leisure activities. It might also mean the commitment to some social work, all in alignment with one's belief and value system, and disclosed in the workplace. Although this is an intangible element of identity, it is easy to make certain aspects visible, for example by displaying artefacts connected to the specific activity or association, easing potential relationship-building efforts.

Sociability a component characteristic of extraversion, whose trait is characterised by sociability, assertiveness, emotional expressiveness and excitability. People who are high in this trait are often described as being outgoing and talkative, while those low in this trait are described as quiet and reserved.

Revolutionising Sociability

The digital world initiated a revolution in the meaning of sociability. The unparalleled growth of social networks gave it a whole new meaning, questioning the traditional meaning often confused with extraversion. Whilst social networks used to be solely virtual, astute mobile application vendors are bringing to market applications that help mobile users connect and interact with people in close proximity. This emerging market, called proximity-based mobile social networking, is expected to grow to $1.9 billion in revenues by 2016.[2] This trend not only provides new opportunities for application vendors but also has the potential to disrupt the current social networking market and the architecture of

---

1   Simmel 1949:257.
2   http://research.gigaom.com/report/proximity-based-mobile-social-networking-outlook-and-analysis/?utm_source=tech&utm_medium=editorial&utm_campaign=auto3&utm_term=795661+when-it-comes-to-new-markets-one-size-does-not-fit-all&utm_content=gigaguest.

the web. The primary filter uses geo-proximity to determine who is discoverable on the social network.[3] By enabling users to meet new people and interact with them and their locally relevant content, proximity-based social networking applications are far more engaging. This experience will drive user adoption and is thus bringing an entirely new, not yet predictable perspective to sociability.

Modes of sociability are observably changing. Face-to-face sociability has largely shifted to mobile, even in immediate geo-proximity. Kids sitting next to another on a train or in a coffee shop are texting one another, rather than using verbal communication.

Your personal perspective on Sociability

The Sociability identity element describes the extent to which the activities you engage in provide you and the group of people around you with a sense of identity; and the values that are connected to these people and activities are perceived by others and yourself.

If we abstract from wealth, position and power, if we forget status and other burdens of 'real' life, then we can playfully engage in the game of sociability, of enjoying the presence of others, or playing the conversational and relational games that make conviviality and shared experience.

In face-to-face interaction you might want to consider mentioning the activities you engage in, for example, work for the social good, sports clubs, some potential involvement in a political party or other interest group.

In the cyberconnected world of work sociability stretches well into our private space; formerly well-defined boundaries have become flawed. The format of the activities you engage in is disembodied, not linked to a specific country or even a specific place. It no longer requires the establishment of a physical place such as a campus – just think Massive Open Online Courses (MOOCs), a sports club, a charity shop or the representational office of a political party, with the attendant social groups composed of people who have been presorted along specific intellectual and economic lines. The social engagement largely happens in the virtual space expressed by the number of contacts on social media networks, or by collaborating or competing through apps. Measuring sociability has a new format.

---

3   This differs from location-based social networks such as Foursquare, which simply broadcast a user's location to existing friends.

How does this invisible element of your identity shape the way you understand yourself and the ways you connect with your interaction partners?

- What does it mean to me? How do I bring it to life? In digital space? In face-to-face interaction?

- To what extent do I support the establishment and maintenance of networks in the world of work?

- In what ways to I socialise with others in groups or organisations that are recognised in the wider community?

COMMUNICATION

Styles, channels and the impressions they create

Communication is the expression of ideas and views through different channels. Communication channels can be face-to-face or virtual, each with a multitude of ways to convey the message. In any case, communication requires a sender and a receiver.

Communication is big business: language learning, communication as a people development tool, intercultural communication for global business profit maximisation. Industries enabling this service sector are equally numerous: telecommunications, cloud platforms, software production and connected to all of these, maintenance and service. These service delivery models have either been supplemented, or are rapidly being replaced, by online and mobile communication service delivery models.

Communication also refers to languages and their use as a first, second or other language. As an invisible element the use and styles of communication are only displayed in interaction. Giving feedback by email can lead to critical situations as the example below from the SonaConn case illustrates:

Box 6.3   The Uncomfortable Email Response

ALL of the required equipment was in place. We told you THAT YOU BETTER USE TABLE AND CHAIRS instead for beanbags.

The vocabulary of the initial email largely contained words such as 'helpful, concerned, appreciate'. Also, the email author focused on the equipment that was made available for the first programme run: 'Our view is that the conference centre was spacious, well organised and pleasant. Most of the equipment required was provided, which made our job as workshop facilitators that little bit easier.'

The response message from the client contained passages highlighted in red, bold face at font size 14, which is significantly larger than the font size of 10 used in the initiating email. Additionally, parts of the answers were underlined, such as some of the numbers of items of equipment made available for the pilot programme.

The style of email text illustrated above, such as using bold face, large font size and exclamation marks, is not used in business communication from the point of view of English first-language speakers and was perceived as inappropriate, unprofessional and even shocking. Those involved and familiar with the response felt uncomfortable and assumed that they had done something wrong.

Virtual communication in general, and, as illustrated, email communication, generate first and second impressions different from your intended ones. Many people still argue that face-to-face communication can help to clarify conflicts. However, face-to-face communication is largely subject to first impressions, and in fact can lead to stereotyping. Take, for example, people working with a project manager who wears a head scarf. What appraisals would a person not accustomed to that style generate about the project manager?

Typing and tapping

'I updated my profile'; one of the consequences of enabling technology is the transformation of communication. Organisations use new and emerging technology, including social media, to communicate both to and from their internal and external stakeholders. Some organisations and individuals alike position themselves as early adopters of new communication channels whilst others adopt the role of followers. Written communication and related services in cyberspace are changing at the speed of the delivery model.

In 2012, emoticons celebrated their thirtieth birthday. The hybrid terminology of 'emotions' and 'icons' is pictorial representations of feelings. When they first appeared in cyberspace, their later fame was entirely unexpected. Indeed, they shaped the communication style in the digital space. Now used pervasively in web forums, instant messengers and online games, emoticons started out with the smiley face :-) and sad face :-(. Products and services were designed fostering their popularity, some of them even acknowledging different cultural styles as observed, for example, between Americans and Koreans.[4]

A similar popularity was achieved by some internet slang (for example, 'afk' meaning 'away from keyboard'), around which dictionaries and other support tools evolved. Communication styles are changing with the exponential growth in the volume and speed of newly available technology. Millennials want and expect detailed, regular feedback and praise for a job well done; they want feedback frequently or continually on the job. With the younger generations who are entering the world of work and the empowerment of the individual, organisations are already seeking for solutions to provide for the communication needs of the future workforce.

Your personal perspective on Communication

Communication refers to the extent to which the potential multiplicity in languages and communication styles you are exposed to shapes your sense of identity. How does this influence your behaviour in building relationships across boundaries?

The following questions might be useful for your self-evaluation:

- Is the lingua franca in use a second or third language to everybody? Are clarification and understanding standard procedures? Are continuous attention to and raised awareness of your own language use and the communication styles used by others essential?

- Is working in a second or third language necessary but perceived as difficult?

- Is most communication asynchronous, and is written communication your preferred style?

- Are social media and cloud-based services standard procedures and perceived as comfortable?

---

4   Jack et al. 2012:7242.

GEOPOLITICS

Land, sea, wind and power

Geopolitics is the study of the relationship among politics, geography, demography, economics and connected power. It refers to the shifting situation of superpowers and the effect this has on their citizens. The global megatrends of demographics and the increasing proportion of elderly people across the globe impact national welfare systems, pension funds and healthcare.

Geography and habitat influence the way people manage the cyberconnected day's routine and its ramification for the world of work. Cold climates, ice and snow, just like great heat, potential sand storms and other hazards, structure the way people manage the world of work. As will be described in detail in Chapter 9, religion and its practices organise the workday in many parts of the world.

In addition to the impact of habitat, socioeconomics inform the individual's socialisation process, for example the way nation states and regions manage multilingualism: consider the difference between growing up in a place where language and dialect switching is part of the routine relationship-building process and growing up in a place where you are constantly told that learning a second language is difficult. Even our country's history informs the way we build work-based relationships. Commonalities and differences in the business partners' national or regional histories can foster cooperation or hinder it altogether.

When generating products and services for places other than the ones people are used to, or when collaborating with people from different geopolitical conditions, this shapes their identity, the way they interact and thus the outcomes generated.

Global citizenship

The impact of geopolitics on digital identity exerts pressure on infrastructure and resources. People in developed countries have greater access to new technologies at present; at the same time, many of the innovations provide turnaround opportunities for less-developed countries to capitalise on new markets. For example, in some African countries money transfers by mobile, known as M-Pesa or mobile money, bypassed banking systems by using text messages, and phone network size trade became worth billions.

Technology has a great impact on a nation's economy, industries and markets. Whilst some governments position themselves as early adopters of technology, others will need to pull up their socks by providing Communication both to and from their citizens, ensuring access to leading thinking on emerging technologies and trends, and creating conditions for new enterprises, for example start-ups, to flourish. Countries are now virtual environments as well as real places, and increasingly their citizens are globally networked individuals.

Deriving meaning from Geopolitics

Deriving meaning from Geopolitics as an identity element describes the ways the politics, the geographic space such as country or inner city, and potentially the religion or some spiritual affiliation you experienced shaped your sense of identity and, as a result, influence the ways you establish business relationships. These aspects of life are likely to be grounded in your own upbringing and your previous experiences throughout your life. This background will affect your assumptions about people from different types of background and impact on your workplace interactions.

The following considerations might help you to evaluate your activation level of this intangible identity element:

- To what extent am I interested in exploring potential differences due to religion, climate, history and politics, and do I perceive these differences as positive?

- In what ways does cross-fertilisation based on geopolitics help me connect with partners from different backgrounds on a social and professional level?

- What are my experiences acquired on earlier projects with regard to geopolitics that allow the smooth incorporation of relationship-building processes?

Go to the end of the chapter to plot your self-evaluation.

LIFELONG LEARNING

Lifelong learning as a continuous journey

Let us reflect back on Carolyn's story in the role of communications expert and quality manager in charge of two topics packaged in workshops, 'Communicating for Impact' and 'Performing through our People'.

Box 6.4   Carolyn on Her Way to Geek

A concise note on Carolyn, who, as of this writing, is 32. To make it to retirement in the role of communications specialist, she will have to adopt some of the new skills required for the coming decades. Beyond being a social media consumer, she will have to become a social media creator, including some of the necessary page creation skills, including some basic coding knowledge. Even in a senior role, these skills will help her lead teams to implement communication projects successfully.

Lifelong learning is the fabric that changes lives, societies and economies. It showcases life-changing stories of people progressing in their career and achieving greater academic advancement.

Generally, we need to distinguish three types of learning:[5]

1.   Formal education, which includes all compulsory education, upper secondary level (basic vocational training or upper-secondary specialised school) and tertiary level (for example, higher education institutions or higher vocational education).

2.   Non-formal education, which includes activities taking place outside the formal education system. These may be, for example, courses, conferences, seminars, private courses or on-the-job training.

3.   Informal learning activities, which include activities undertaken with a specific learning goal but which take place outside of a teaching context. This type of continuing education is very diverse and may range from reading specialist literature to learning with friends or colleagues.

---

5   UNESCO, the OECD and Eurostat in CH-EAS 2013:3.

Traditionally, non-formal education would qualify as continuing education. The interconnected lifestyle with its digital footprint of today, however, includes informal learning activities in lifelong learning.

The German-speaking countries with their dual education systems and intensive apprenticeship programmes have built very close links between the education system and industry. A dual education system combines apprenticeships in a company and vocational education at a vocational school into one course. The dual-track differs from most foreign systems of vocational and professional education and training: practical training (apprenticeship) on three to four days a week at a training company is supplemented by theoretical classes (vocational and general educational subjects) on one to two days at the vocational school. While many other European countries have developed extensive vocational programmes, they have fallen short of the full commitment to apprenticeship programmes.[6]

The evidence currently available points to a tendency for the gains in initial employment that come with apprenticeship programmes to be offset in varying degrees by lessened employability later in life.

Lifelong learning going digital

Globally, the education sector is going through an unparalleled change. MOOCs have rapidly revolutionised the education landscape, to the concern of established academic organisations. Lifelong learning received yet another connotation by the addition of MOOCs, accessible to millions of people worldwide.

MOOCs turned the existing format of lifelong learning upside down, increased the speed of change in the education sector, and rattled scholars to an extent that many of them have rethought their teaching style, now more readily accepting new teaching formats such as the flipped classroom, or trusting peer-to-peer learning.

Organisations in the role of prospective employer will not care much if you come waving your MOOC completion certificate without any quality assurance of either the course content or its assessment standards. Accreditation is, therefore, now the central challenge that MOOCs must grapple with to gain credibility within academia and currency with employers. And yet, MOOCs

---

6   https://swisseducation.educa.ch/en/vocational-education-and-training-0.

are set to shake up the corporate and non-profit training worlds. They have become an integral part of the learning and development agenda, especially modern, innovative organisations. These massive and open courses not only teach people but also bring learners together, provide networking opportunities and get a buzz going.

Deriving a sense of identity from Lifelong learning

The identity element of Lifelong learning describes the extent to which your approach towards learning and further development contributes to your sense of identity, how it impacts on the way you understand/perceive yourself, and how the perception others have of you is shaped by this element of identity.

The considerations below might be helpful for the further exploration of your personal activation level on Lifelong learning:

In the workplace context and beyond, Lifelong learning has become an integral part of your journey of life. Acquiring new knowledge and learning new skills, whether through formal education, non-formal education or informal learning activities, is important to you. Openness to continuous learning is reflected in a collection of completed courses and potential academic degrees. The benefits of favourable professional development provide you with opportunities in and outside the workplace.

Lifelong learning might be so pronounced that you have a shaping role in the future of learning, covering a range of use scenarios including e-learning, educational technology and distance education, which focuses on learning with mobile devices in organisations and beyond. Using mobile tools for creating learning aides and materials has become an important part of informal learning. The data trail that the digitalisation of learning in organisation entails is an opportunity for the implementation of improvements to existing learning and development programmes. MOOCs are yet another opportunity for experimentation, whether in the role of occasional visitor or course completer. Informal learning challenges must be juggled with the day's schedule.

The self-evaluation section is at the end of the chapter.

INCLUSION

Inclusion in a shifting world

With the shift in demographics, Inclusion has reached an unmatched level of importance. As nations have acquired more wealth, many have also experienced growing inequality within their borders. The ramifications for the cyberconnected world are many: on the one hand there is an aging population remaining in the world of work, while on the other, the digital generation will soon be entering their first jobs and pursuing their careers. The level of work-related worldwide migration across sectors and hierarchies is beyond compare, resulting in potential exclusion from social interactions further to Ethnicity and other visible elements from the identity portfolio.

We are all individually and collectively responsible for the inclusion of people in the workplace and, beyond, namely in society. So are enterprises and organisations, which should reflect inclusion on their development agenda, whether through developing accessible transportation and communities, ensuring the age-appropriate healthcare and social services or providing an adequate social protection basis.

Digital Inclusion

Inclusion through social interaction happens in both the face-to-face and the cyberconnected world. Digital inclusion ensures that individuals and groups have access to, and skills to use, information and communication technologies (ICT) and are therefore able to participate in and benefit from the growing knowledge and information society. Digital inclusion requires a reduction in the disparities that remain in some geographic, ethnic and socio-economic groups. Availability, that is, access to broadband connections, is a key enabler for digital inclusion. Price is often a barrier to both adoption of internet services and ownership of a device.

Digital inclusion also assumes a commitment to enabling people to have the knowledge and any necessary tools that allow them to make use of digital resources, serving both the purpose of personal development and that of positive organisational results.

Digital inclusion in the workplace allows for greater flexibility. It is a key indicator for an organisation's digital maturity, its relationship with people, in the role of customers, employees and the stakeholder network, reflected in products and services, made available at their fingertips. Digital inclusion can unify like-minded people and can be regarded as valuable resource for promoting positive social interaction.

My sense of Inclusion

Inclusion refers to aspects of your identity relating to how and how much you are included at work in general, in networking and in the flow of information. If you are included, you are likely to feel a strong sense of confidence in the value that you have to offer to social networks in the workplace and beyond. You are likely to take pride in the extent of your networks and the number of people you include in your list of friends and business contacts. At work, you are likely to be included in meetings and to be influential in the informal aspects of the organisation, having an expectation that people will share important information and gossip with you over the coffee machine. You may wish to consider the following points:

- To what extent do business networks and their connected wealth offer greater opportunities, allowing me to manage technological, cultural and social boundaries whose doors would otherwise remain locked?

- To what extent can I participate in today's digital ongoings and in what ways does this make me feel included?

- How quickly do I signal interest and build trust with people from other cultures and professions?

EMPLOYABILITY

Employability in the cyberconnected world

The shift in demographics resulting in higher life expectancies and falling birth rates challenges new thinking on employability. The large proportion of the population which is aging and an uneven spread of large youth populations require organisations to act where policies often fail.

Employability is inextricably linked to three other identity elements: Generation, Communication and Lifelong learning. With this in mind enterprises will have to invest in programmes that lead to job creation. For reasons of future competitiveness and the inclusion of Generation C, organisations will have to focus on youth development through human capital investments, increasing brand appeal and thereby becoming an employer of choice. For example, the dual-track education system as promoted by the German-speaking countries, which combines an apprenticeship with theoretical classes (see Lifelong learning for details), fosters close collaboration between the private and the education sectors. Support for private sector firms to invest in staff training and development, for example, tax incentives, is indispensable in winning over the challenge of employability.

Many mature businesses are facing a significantly senior and aging workforce, often with only a few more years to go until retirement. The challenge is to remain agile as an organisation whilst leveraging the knowledge, skills and experience this group brings. Organisations are already offering flexible work after retirement, meeting the needs of the aging group such as retaining financial security and enjoying social benefits of team-working, usually across generations. Employability can create a strong sense of identity, connected to the belief about the extent to which the role and the organisation are valued in the broader community.

Novel leadership understanding, leading geographically dispersed but cyberconnected teams, requires new skill development more diverse than ever before.

Digital entrepreneurs and Employability for future generations

The technological advances of recent years offer novel work opportunities. Many of the much-celebrated digital generation are, however, just consumers of social media hype. Their willingness to put personal information into public domains and their attitude towards privacy cedes control of their identity to others. The disclosure of potentially unsuitable content may put their Employability at risk. The need for digital literacy programmes has become ever more important in order to enable them to take control of their online identity and avoid the lack of qualified digital creators. These programmes have to focus on digital literacy, in the sense of digital making rather than digital consumption. Interests, passions and pastimes as a gateway to digital making activities inspire young people to become creators, not just users of digital technologies.

In light of socioeconomic changes and the rise of individualism, employability for Generation Y and, in future, C means holding several jobs and working wherever and whenever. Whilst many regions in the so-called developed world are struggling to develop the required numbers of digital creators, skilled and innovative digital entrepreneurs will emerge throughout the developing world in massive numbers. The rise of these entrepreneurs has the potential to significantly disrupt traditional Western business models, and they have the highly connected audience that can benefit from their new ideas. Skill development will have to keep pace with the exponential growth of new tech.

Your personal perspective on Employability

Employability is connected to your belief about the extent to which your role and organisation are valued in the broader community. Thus, you are likely to remain very conscious of the brand appeal of your organisation and the status of the role you perform. You are likely to be proactive in telling others about the work you do and the experience/skills that this has given you and you may also be quick to ask about and show respect for this area of identity in others. It might motivate you to work hard and make deeper connections with those who share your working context. This is an intangible identity element, so it will be necessary for you to share experiences and opinions with others to discover whether they also activate this identity element:

- Freelancers, employees and entrepreneurs alike: to what extent do you draw respect and recognition from the work you do and the organisations you work for?

- To what extent do you enjoy and get positive energy from your working life?

- In what ways does this identity element provide you with a strong driver for you to win business and build a professional network?

- How strongly do you act as an ambassador for your organisation and your work?

Winning the Organisation Development Challenge

Some companies create and innovate technology; others use and adopt it; but in the cyberage, both must closely interconnect tech with human behaviour. Face-to-face and cyberinteractions are at the heart of effective work-based relationships; their interplay informs achievements at organisational level.

In turn, to build effective business relations, organisations must foster the discovery muscle – curiosity combined with skills – in individuals.

Exploring refers to the focus people bring to activating key aspects of their identity portfolio, when involved in critical work-based relationships – in other words the key aspects of who they are that enable them to build interconnectivity with others. In addition to the 'tangible' elements of the identity portfolio – Appearance, Gender, Generation and Ethnicity – that have been traditionally focused on in thinking about diversity, there are 'intangible' elements – Wellbeing, Mobility, Sociability, Communication, Geopolitics, Lifelong learning, Inclusion and Employability – that are less obvious but even more critical in establishing connections across boundaries. The activation of these elements with particular people in particular contexts constructs the 'diversity' between them, and can be adapted and developed to build stronger links.

Building interconnectivity requires boundary-spanning capabilities. These are a set of skills that enable people to apply the full identity portfolio in themselves and to activate it in others through exploration and dialogue. This in turn needs a mindset of curiosity and interest in people. Building interconnectivity is not merely an individual responsibility, but also requires an organisational environment that fosters the willingness to explore, indeed, to build the discovery muscle.

Beyond boundary-spanning capabilities, building interconnectivity requires boundary awareness. Boundary awareness includes the knowledge of global trends and their impacts on people, carefully factored into decision-making processes. Traditional organisational boundaries such as functional and hierarchical silos will increasingly take on less defined dimensions, requiring people in the world of work to incorporate knowledge of global trends and impacts into their decision-making processes. For example, the heightened global competition for people, business and resources as a result of the shift in economic power means that decision-makers in organisations will need to be increasingly aware of emerging international trends and strategies.

There is no formula for developing a mindset for building interconnectivity. Whereas in the past it was enough to develop only a relatively small elite group of expats for international assignments, the need now is to prepare people throughout the organisation and beyond, to span boundaries not only globally but also within the same region and affiliate.

People respond to different aspects of the many journeys to interconnectivity in their unique ways. In addition to their individual reactions, what makes this group distinctive is the challenges they have encountered and the opportunities for learning they have experienced. They are a distinct category of people with a unique outlook on life. It is certainly true that they gain rich perspectives from different cultures, languages, values and the overall exposure of geopolitical affairs. But this traditional passport-based view misses the greater expertise that a new generation is developing as boundary-spanners in the role of ambassadors of interconnectivity. However, policy-induced barriers to mobility such as the loss of pension entitlements, differences in national regulations of professional qualifications, inaccessibility of certain jobs and housing market frictions exist at the cost of the individual. The persistence of education, employment and housing market regulations, welfare states and fiscal systems increase the personal cost of mobility. This might be at the expense of international experience and learning and thus limit identity-developing experiences.

Mobility in the traditional sense and all things mobile go hand in hand. Ever-increasing interconnectedness drives the need for enterprise collaboration and mobility, providing people with real-time information anywhere anytime, aiming at higher efficiency and productivity. The result is the consumeration of IT in the form of Bring Your Own Device (BYOD).[7] This in turn is the point for organisations to build interconnectivity, that is, the need for the development and implementation of a sound mobility strategy in alignment with the development of people's identity portfolios.

Key issues to consider on the journey to interconnectivity typically complement a number of identity elements:

- Mobility: To what extent has mobility been developed as a key success factor in your organisation development agenda? What are its pillars? In what way do you mobilise people to enjoy geographical, social and technological mobility?

- Inclusion and Wellbeing: In what ways does your organisation tackle the transition from the traditional approach of expatriate management to including cosmopolitan experts, migrants and short assignment staff on local contracts?

---

7   This causes organisations to consider important aspects of data security and employee privacy, which, as explained in Chapter 1, is beyond the scope of this book.

- Lifelong learning: What strategies does your organisation pursue to leverage people's tacit knowledge of geographical, social and technological mobility, aiming to increase the organisation's cross-boundary productivity?

- Communication: To what extent does the organisation's back-end enterprise data assist mobile employees in getting critical information that speeds up decision-making processes and increases the efficiency of the employee?

- Employability: How does your organisation support the consumeration of IT-based mobility, enabling people to become smart users by making use of a well-defined BYOD policy, and aiming to drive employee satisfaction by simultaneously reducing operation expenditure?

- Sociability: What effective communication processes does the organisation offer to increase collaboration between the organisation's stakeholders, that is, external and internal clients, whilst they at the office or on the move?

- Geopolitics and Lifelong learning: To what extent does the organisation offer mobile learning solutions that provide access anytime anywhere to help increase learning efficiency, collaboration and productivity of the employee?

We can think of these organisations as 'generative' – fertile environments where people and ideas flourish, where life-giving properties of connectivity, inspiration and innovation and renewal across generations are nurtured and cultivated.

EXPLORING THE EXTENDED ME

As suggested in Chapter 5 for the tangible elements of your identity portfolio, at the end of this chapter there is a section for self-evaluation of the intangible elements (see Figure 6.2). Once having completed the chart for self-evaluation, you can use it to draw an identity portfolio for selected key business partners. Again, for potential gaps in the identity profiles carry on to Chapter 7 for some helpful bridging strategies.

	frequent activation	infrequent activation
Wellbeing		
Mobility		
Sociability		
Communication		
Lifelong learning		
Geopolitics		
Employability		
Inclusion		

Figure 6.2   Self-evaluation for intangible identity elements

Chapter 7

Breaking through the Stereotype Game – The Lens of Perception

Seamless Collaboration in the Cyberconnected World of Work

Having explored The Lens of Multiple Identity we now focus on The Lens of Perception (see Figure 7.1).

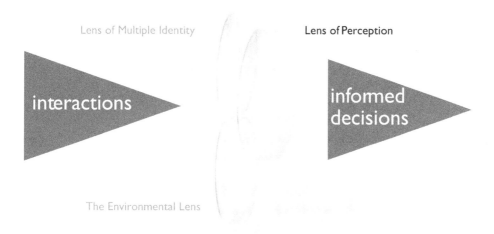

Lens of Multiple Identity

Lens of Perception

interactions

informed decisions

The Environmental Lens

Figure 7.1   The Lens of Perception

The anticipated outcome of the application of The Three Lenses of Diversity is informed decisions solidly based on meaningful interpretations in order to build effective cross-boundary relationships and as a consequence to achieve better business results.

The process aims at the observations collected from interactions filtered through each lens to come to meaningful interpretations without jumping to conclusions.

Embedding seamless collaboration requires a cultural shift within the organisation to change the way it looks at both its people, internal and external, and its business processes. As part of this cultural shift, people's understanding of diversity, the approaches towards collaboration, and finally, the relationship between the business and IT will change.

Seamless collaboration requires the successful application of relationship-building skills and bridging strategies in personal interactions, further reflected in the use of technology.

Misperception of the 'other' often keeps us from establishing winning relationships and thus anticipated business outcomes.

Enterprises always push to enhance the way their employees communicate with each other. The reasoning is simple: better communication leads to faster and higher-quality work, which, in turn, leads to increased productivity. They see social technology changing the way users interact and collaborate with each other, and they naturally want to harness that propensity for communication and collaboration within the organisation. The starting point for seamless collaboration lies in the success of the interaction of individuals, impacting team collaboration and scaled up to organisation level. Irrespective of whether the nature of the collaboration channel is face-to-face or virtual, the perception of the 'other' is at the heart of its quality. The Lens of Perception helps you filter potential stereotypes which result in self-fulfilling prophecies. See Table 7.1 for an outline of the key meanings and benefits of The Lens of Perception. The Belonging and Othering model serves as a bridging strategy.

Table 7.1   Key meaning and key benefit of The Lens of Perception

Key meaning		Key benefit
The Lens of Perception refers to the ways we see others as well as the ways we are seen by others in these interactions. This process applies to individuals and groups equally.	$\longrightarrow$	The Lens of Perception will help bring your own potential prejudices to the surface and thus help you to become more flexible in a changing interconnected business world.

Seamless collaboration today can involve millions of stakeholders and their diverse needs and expectations. To achieve this, organisations must move beyond standalone social and collaboration channels. They must begin to directly embed those channels into their core business processes, tightly based upon people's social and collaboration needs, enabling them to break through and move beyond organisation boundaries.

But many are still looking at it the wrong way. The one-size-fits-all approach pushes preconceived solutions into organisations and market places, putting the culture 'in need' in a bear hug, attempting to overwhelm and to bend it around the existing solution.

Traditionally, widely-used IT systems have come from American tech companies that expanded into international markets. Historically, most internet-driven technology has radiated outward from Silicon Valley, scaled internationally on the basis of projection bias and false consensus bias, along the line of, 'If people like it here, they'll like it everywhere.'

Streamlined interactions with consumers, predominantly concerning transactions and speaking to people's extrinsic motivation only, can be and have proved to be extremely successful – end consumers readily accept being treated in this way. However, organisation settings require a culture–technology fit in order to meet the relationship nature of interactions, for internal and external stakeholders, speaking to people's intrinsic motivation.

The one-size-fits-all approach will fail to buy in the next billion technology users, located all over the world in cultures and economies with diverse needs and expectations, compared to North American and European early adopters from the twentieth century.

The winners in the next wave of applications and services will be those who best balance the product, marketing and strategic tension between standardisation and localisation. Collaboration requires the development of bridging skills supported by a culture whose channels and business process have collaboration instilled in their core.

The following real-life example elaborates the key issues of perception, essential to mirror an organisation's channel and processes.

ACTION – TRANSACTION – INTERACTION

In the introduction we revisited the meaning of The Lens of Perception and the key benefit of its application. Let us now see it in action using the real-life case of the mobile health and safety project by MyMemLab and A1Guard.

Before looking at the implications of The Lens of Perception, we need to investigate the use and activation level of the multiple identities of the two key people on the project: the managing director of the MyMemLab start-up and the learning and development director of A1Guard. For this purpose, they completed the cyberIdentity Development Tool (cyberIDT), focusing solely on the implementation of the mobile health and safety project. A comparison of the two profiles in Figure 7.2 shows the following results.[1]

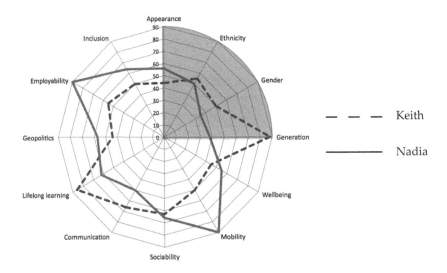

Figure 7.2   MyMemLab and A1Guard identity element profiles

Research suggests that all 12 elements are key to successful interactions and sustainable relationships. However, with only a finite amount of attention to distribute among the 12 elements you cannot score high on all of them, as is seen with Nadia, the managing director of MyMemLab, and Keith, the learning and development director of A1Guard.

---

1   Results are generated from the cyberIDT questionnaire. Question scores for each Identity Element are added together and presented as percentage illustrated as a spider diagram. The dark quadrant covers the tangible and the white quadrants are the intangible identity elements.

The spider diagram shows activation levels of the identity elements for Nadia and Keith: Nadia's two most frequently activated elements are Mobility and Employability; Keith's two most frequently activated identity elements are Generation and Lifelong learning.

Potential stereotypes and self-fulfilling prophecies the two key people might have associated with their identity elements might surface in their face-to-face and virtual interaction. 'Belonging' and 'Othering' come into play in the relationship space between the two key people involved in the interaction, as indicated in the diagram shown above.

The spider diagram shows the activation level for each of the 12 identity elements in percentage terms. The two elements showing the biggest gaps, Generation and Mobility, and the two elements showing the smallest gaps, Ethnicity and Sociability, are discussed below.

THE BARRIERS TO EFFECTIVE INTERACTION

Self-views, appraisals, and in general, stereotypes guide our cognition process in an information-overloaded world. Detecting the cognition process in one-to-one interaction requires reflection and awareness. Scaling the cognition process up to the organisation level helps to uncover potential biases embedded in the organisation culture. At any level, the uncovering process requires attention to detail.

Table 7.2   **Potential barriers to effective interaction**

Differing identity elements	Keith	Nadia
Generation	Highly aware of own age and age difference with business partner, experience due to age does not equip him with required level of expertise in mobile organisation development.	Now 38, connects well with baby boomers, her own generation (X), and Generation Y and C. Used to working with people across age groups and enjoys the experience.
Mobility	Travels for business purposes, when required and not avoidable, leisure travel to popular holiday destinations.	Well-travelled person, multilingual, has lived internationally, current mobility challenges add to stress level, at the same time give competitive edge on geographically diverse and culturally-loaded needs and expectations.

Differing activation levels of selected identity elements in interactions can have a detrimental impact on the relationship-building process and thus have a negative effect on project performance. Identifying the particular barriers that separate one business partner from the 'other' is essential in order to build a bridging strategy. Let us, therefore, start looking at the activation levels of the two interaction partners, Nadia and Keith (see Table 7.2).

On Mobility: mutual perceptions dynamic

Figure 7.3 highlights the connection between our personal preferences and our first and longer-term impressions of other people. Our preferences are coded in the socialisation process and experiences collected over time with the leading question:

'What is it about my coding that makes me see the other person the way I do?'

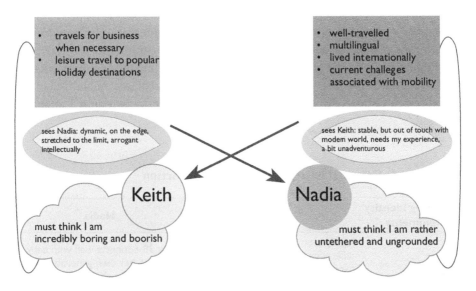

Figure 7.3   Mutual perceptions dynamic

The initial reaction can be modified over time through awareness, openness and specifically delivery, that is, proof and reliability. Practically speaking, what is needed for the project? Activities such as non-business communication and any displayed behaviours that help build trust.

The text in the 'eyes' represents the assumptions each party may reach on the basis of the Mobility element. The text in the thought bubbles is the next step: being aware of how each might be seen by the other party.[2]

THE WINNERS TO EFFECTIVE INTERACTION

Keith and Nadia bring to their interaction a number of elements of their identity portfolios with a similar or the same activation level. This similarity in activation levels should enable them to build commonality quickly on these aspects of interaction, helping them overcome the barriers illustrated above more easily (see Table 7.3).

Table 7.3   **Potential winners for effective interaction**

	Keith	**Nadia**
Sociability	Enjoys a good meal and a beer with friends and colleagues, used to play rugby and still enjoys watching a good game. His appreciation of socialising opens the door so that other elements of his identity can come into play.	Does a lot of sports whenever possible and likes to eat, also enjoys a good glass of wine. Enjoys networking for purely social reasons and uses this influence to get things done on projects.
Ethnicity	Is proficient at working in a multi-ethnic environment, typically avoids opinions and judgments based on stereotypes, different ethnic backgrounds are not relevant to him in a business context.	Radiates pride in her ethnic identity, is always ready to provide an opportunity to explore different personal histories, actively inquires into another person's history.

Potential blind spots might be leveraged by the raised activation level of another identity element, for example, Mobility. See more details in the section 'Bridging barriers through Belonging and Othering'.

DEVELOPING RELATIONSHIP-BUILDING SKILLS

Relationship-building skills consist of two sets of skills:

- cognitive skills, including observation skills and awareness gained through observation; and

---

2   I am indebted to Elisabeth Cassels-Brown and her work on Mutual Perception Dynamic delivered on the Intercultural Training course at the Vienna University of Economics and Business.

- collaboration skills, specifically, behaviours associated with relationship-building skills, including listening, and questioning and assertion skills.

Relationship-building skills are essential for successfully bridging boundaries. One purpose of relationship-building skills is the capability to break through the stereotype game.

Stereotypes as a result of the general cognitive process of categorising serve to simplify and systematise the abundance and complexity of the information received from the environment. Variance bias, known to psychologists as out-group homogeneity bias, describes the understanding that we see fine-grained differences in groups we identify with, but underestimate variance in distant cultures. Examples of this are: there are Americans who think that New Yorkers and Californians are dramatically different, but then talk about 'Indians' as if they can be seen as a unified whole. This is a two-way bias. To many Indians, 'Americans all love Big Macs', but India 'is a land of many languages and many cultures'. There are Germans who think that people from Hamburg are cold and distant while Bavarians are warm and companionable, but talk about the 'Spanish' in terms of one homogenous group.

Variance bias leads to the systematic underestimation of opportunities outside the mainstream taste. This provides spaces for local competitors to flourish and grow and may explain why the multinationals successful in many emerging markets are those that have been there for a very long time. They often have a proliferation of brands and variants, and importantly, they have learned over time to recognise and cater to this diversity. Even multinationals, often perceived as diverse companies, stumble into the stereotype trap. Unconscious biases discourage people from climbing the next step on the career ladder, creating the most inclusive teams or building a relationship vital to success in an organisation change programme as illustrated above.

Expected behaviour can come alive[3] in people's interactions. Nadia and Keith could well fall into the trap of generating self-fulfilling prophecies (see Table 7.4).

---

3   Based on Interpreting Interpersonal Behaviour: The Effects of Expectancy by Jones 1986:43.

Table 7.4   Potential self-fulfilling prophecies

Nadia:	Overly explains issues on the assumption that Keith lacks necessary knowledge, confirmed by ambiguous responses
Keith:	Nadia is arrogant intellectually; Keith turns off because he is unnerved by Nadia's behaviour; as a result he does not contribute his actual knowledge, that is, industry expertise

The nano-behaviours displayed in people's interaction require attention with the aim of avoiding their extrapolation to organisation level.

Smashing stereotypes actively addresses unconscious bias (not just towards business contacts 'unlike us' but also positive bias towards those who are 'like us') and provides tips and tools on how to identify and address them. This initial step, necessary to further develop relationship-building skills, takes into account the geology model of the 12 identity elements, the tangible elements of diversity of its people: Appearance, Gender, Generation and Ethnicity; as well as the intangible elements: Wellbeing, Mobility, Communication, Sociability, Geopolitics, Lifelong learning, Employability, Inclusion and the whole portfolio of facades that are hard to detect, that each of us has and that makes us who we are.

Seamless collaboration

Different tactics for dealing with obvious external differences and hidden internal elements are fundamental to overcoming barriers to business success. This extends from the development of interpersonal skills on the basis of self-motivation through to support mechanisms provided by the organisation.

Among the most common of these support mechanisms are extrinsic and intrinsic motivation. We will now consider the appropriacy and effectiveness of these forms of motivation.

Extrinsic versus intrinsic motivation

Bridging strategies cover face-to-face and virtual space. In fact, they need to complement one another in tackling people's emotions, incorporating intrinsic and extrinsic motivation.

The term for extrinsic motivation is derived from 'external', that is, motivation coming from the outside. For example, you motivate your 16-year-old to wash your car in return for EUR 20.00. This approach rests on the assumption that the child will deliver the service against the reward. In this case, the real motivation is the end result of EUR 20.00.

Obviously, external motivation stimulation is not sustainable long term, especially if the reward system or scoring mechanism lacks newness and variety. In the longer run, people and users will get bored by motivation factors solely based on external sources. With this in mind, let us look at intrinsic motivation.

The term is derived from 'internal', that is, motivation from within. Intrinsic motivation stimuli speak to people's subconscious motivational elements, such as their understanding of power and status, their sense of achievement and recognition and, finally, their value system, all embedded in their composition of multiple identity construction.

One value of intrinsic motivation is its effectiveness in convincing people to invest the effort necessary to build awareness and further develop the skills required for their jobs, such as observation. We will now discuss the usefulness of this particular skill in smashing stereotypes.

Smashing stereotypes by observing

Observation is a cognitive skill widely used in everyday settings, ranging through a variety of activities from sitting in a street café watching passers-by to engaging in investigative professions. Clearly, café settings and investigation settings represent two extremes. Observation skills presented in this section aim at people in organisations working across boundaries who wish to develop relationship–building skills for success in business.

Participant observation has been presented as a vital tool for organisation development strategy, in particular with the aim of uncovering implicit organisation issues that need further work. In addition to the technique's use as an analysis tool it is an essential skill which should be integrated in the learning and development agenda of organisations.

Observation is getting information about objects, events, moves, behaviours and phenomena by using one or more senses. Types of observation include scientific observation, natural observation, direct and indirect observation, participant and non-participant observation, structured and unstructured observation, and controlled and non-controlled observation.

For the purpose of breaking through stereotypes, there is no need to become an expert in field research. Instead, it is vital to develop the necessary skill set to detect potential stereotypes of one's own and others, detect self-fulfilling prophecies, and as a result, prevent pitfalls.

This section is designed for business people tasked with the hybrid role of simultaneously having to do business and coach their employees – that is, those whose aim is to develop their own observation skills and potentially, those of others. Let us start with an overview of the benefits and challenges (see Table 7.5).

Table 7.5   Benefits and challenges of behaviour observation

Benefits	Challenges
• most direct measure of behaviour • provides immediate information • easy to carry out, saves time • used in natural or experimental settings	• meaningful aspects can be overlooked • potential form is interpretation • complex to analyse • requires some in-depth training

The outcome of observation is an abundance of data, which implies the potential to overlook meaningful details, lost in data richness and interpretation. Leveraging the full potential of observation requires some in-depth training. Nonetheless, starting small and setting appropriate goals provides immediate insights and allows you to make instant progress.

The synthesis of your hybrid role of businessperson and observer supports the nature of creating a natural setting, and, as a result, overcomes the potential issue of creating an artificial situation that the observer's presence typically causes. The hybrid role gives you the opportunity to build explicit awareness of people's behaviour, specifically, little details of how people do things such as how closely they stand, how they nod or what intonation they use.

Building memory is an essential asset complementing observation. It is not good enough just to observe; you need to record your observations. Business interactions will allow for only a few selected methods such as the occasional note or taking a random picture. In the course of the preparation for the interaction, for example a meeting, include a checklist of the things to observe. When reflecting on the interaction, compile an observation guide to assist you (see Table 7.6).

What are you observing?

Table 7.6   Examples of nano-behaviours to observe

In yourself	In your client
• physical sensation • your internal monologue • body language • congruity/genuineness • emotions	• non-verbal communication: facial expression, eye accessing cues • body language: posture, position changes, hand gestures, head nodding, rigidity/looseness • proxemics: use of space • para-verbal communication: tone of voice, volume, pitch, intensity, non-word utterances

In today's fast-moving business world, we are always under pressure to act now, rather than spend time reasoning things through and reflecting on the actual occurrences.

Not only can this lead us to a wrong conclusion, but it can also cause conflict with other people, who may have drawn quite different conclusions on the same matter. Especially in a fast business environment, you need to make sure your actions and decisions are founded on reality.

In Chapter 4 we explored the quality of decision-making processes on the basis of the differentiation between observation and interpretation. The Three Lenses provide the necessary aid for recognising this substantial difference, preventing the decision-maker from making quick and often toxic assumptions and finally, jumping to conclusions.

Let us now focus on the core steps between observation and interpretation (see Figure 7.4). Developing a first set of observation skills is just like building up new muscles, this time without any physical exercise. Observation helps you understand the difference between 'what people say they do' and 'what they really do'.

The best way forward is to start with yourself. Always start small and note your progress. Select one item from the list of what to observe, for example, body language, and focus on just one aspect. After you have gained some experience, carry on to Step 1. Table 7.7 outlines the three steps to observation.

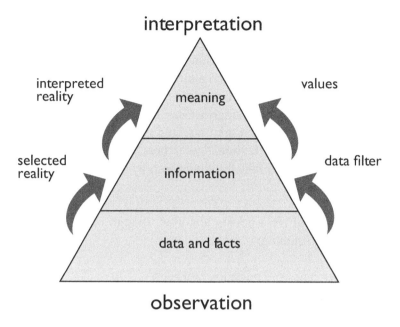

Figure 7.4   Observation versus interpretation[4]

Table 7.7   The three steps to observation

Step 1	**Select one individual to observe.**
	Clearly, this should be the key business partner leading you to success.
Step 2	**Select one activity to observe.**
	Revisit the list above and focus on one small activity easily accessible in the next direct interaction.
	Example: eye accessing cues. Watching eye movements allows you to discover how someone is processing information. If you know this, you can adjust your questions and what you are doing to suit their processing. This helps create greater rapport.
Step 3	**Observe and test observation**.
	After the observation, where possible, spend ten to 15 minutes drawing sketches and making notes to document your actual observations.
	The observed activity is a result of an individual decision process. This means it is subject to change depending on the situation. Therefore in describing a person's behaviour it is important also to describe the situation in which the behaviour occurred.
	Observations are rarely absolutely objective. The description based on the observation is almost always flavoured by at least a touch of subjectivity. The more aware of this fact you are, the more reliable and valid your information, and finally, the meaning.

---

4   Based on the ladder of inference in combination with the knowledge pyramid.

Smashing stereotypes by listening

Listening is an important collaboration skill. We all know that listening is important. So why do we find it such a difficult skill? One contributing factor is that 'ordinarily (if communicating in their native language), people speak 120 to 180 words per minute, though we can listen at three to four times that rate, namely, up to 800 words a minute.' This significant gap in 'brainpower' can make it difficult to pay attention. Researchers from a US university wanted to learn what people are actually thinking about when they are supposed to be actively listening.[5]

- 20 per cent were paying attention, though only 12 per cent were actively listening;

- 20 per cent were pursuing fantasies;

- 20 per cent were reminiscing;

- The remaining 40 per cent were daydreaming, worrying, pondering religious thoughts, or thinking about lunch.

Easily observable external barriers are, for example, noise; physical distraction such as that the room is too hot or too cold; the speaker's inexpressive voice; mismatch between non-verbal and verbal communication, misuse of jargon/ technical terms; the speaker's appearance and stereotypes related to this.

The most common internal barrier is the one of 'silent arguing'. Most people do not listen with the intent to understand, but with the intent to reply. With all the external and internal barriers in mind, what can you do to deal better with those barriers?

The three levels of listening are head (facts), heart (feelings) and feet (intentions) (see Table 7.8). Learning to listen at all three levels gives us a far more complete understanding of what other people say about their identities.

---

5   Atwater 1992.

Table 7.8   The three levels of listening

Step 1	**Thinking / Facts**
	• What sort of words are chosen?
	• What data has been used?
	• What logic and analysis has been applied?
	• What judgements and opinions have been made?
Step 2	**Feelings / Emotions**
	• How are they feeling right now?
	• How did they feel at that time?
Step 3	**Intentions and Assumptions**
	• What do they intend to do about it?
	• What is their level of commitment to this action?
	• What assumptions are you hearing? (observation versus interpretation)

Smashing stereotypes by questioning and asserting

Effective questioning is a critical component to building trust in a relationship. Different types of questions provide you with different qualities or types of information (see Table 7.9).

Table 7.9   The three types of questions

Situation 'What?'	• What is happening?
	• When does this occur?
	• What's going on?
	• What do you believe you can change?
	• What would you like to change?
	• What do you believe you cannot change?
Motivation 'Why?'	• Why is this important?
	• What is most important to you? *and/or* How is that important to you?
	• What led you to make that decision? *and/or* What were the factors in your decision?
	• How do you feel about that?
	• How confident are you? *and/or* What obstacles are there?
Implication 'What if?'	• What would happen if X occurred?
	• If you do (or don't do) X, what could happen?
	• What would be the impact of X?
	• What's the worst thing that could happen?
	• What is the consequence of X?

Assertion is expressing your thoughts and feelings to another person. Assertion skills, which consist of four components listed in Table 7.10 below, are crucial for influencing that person's behaviour.

Table 7.10   The four components of assertion

Releasing	• temporarily suspend your agenda • be open-minded; consider other views • don't interrupt; be patient
Attending	• orient your body towards the other • maintain appropriate eye contact • be sensitive to incongruence in the speaker's verbal and nonverbal communication
Amplifying	• encourage the other to continue • inquire – ask questions • find common ground
Summarising	• paraphrase and link perspectives • contrast or differ constructively • note the speaker's feelings

Observation, listening, questioning and assertion are essential skills for spanning social, technological and cultural boundaries. They are the precursor to displayed behaviours needed to build effect cross-boundary work relationships.

Bridging Strategies

Bridging strategies are the key to effective cross-boundary relationships. They are an integral part of relationship-building skills. Developing relationship-building skills is essential for two reasons:

- seamless collaboration in the cyberconnected world of work requires a supporting culture, whose channels and processes mirror the relationship orientation;

- mobility needs relationship-building skills for its implementation across silos and boundaries.

BRIDGING BARRIERS THROUGH BELONGING AND OTHERING

Over centuries the intercultural field has largely dwelled on the 'other'. Initially setting out to meet the needs of the work of the Peace Corps and some missionaries, the intercultural field soon became an industry to serve the interests of enterprises for the maximisation of profit generated from international business. The result was the over-emphasis of difference.

The more recent multiple identity construction approach now allows a focus on commonalities by simultaneously acknowledging difference. The connected concept is known as Belonging and Othering. Traditionally, Belonging is typically thought of as a positive phenomenon, whilst Othering is thought of as negative.

As stated in Chapter 4, however, when taken to the extreme Belonging can have counter-productive effects on the relationship-building process. The negative effect of being 'besties', or overly pronounced Belonging, would be groupthink. On the other hand, the negative effect for the hot zone of a relationship, that is, Othering, would be the absence of any common ground.

The purpose of Belonging and Othering is to build bridging strategies in a potential conflict situation. Belonging and Othering in the function of bridging strategy requires the development of relationship-building skills. The proposed set comprises observation skills, active listening skills, and questioning and assertion skills. The process captures two ways to move from Othering to Belonging and vice versa:

- Belonging through difference; and

- Othering through sameness.

The objective of the two directions is to:

- leverage different activation levels of identity elements brought into the interaction;

- create Belonging in order to establish some common ground; and

- generate Othering with the overall objective of breaking through groupthink.

Overall, the process is:

- multidimensional and partly contradictory;

- asymmetrically power-loaded: it strongly depends on existing power differentials brought out by the interaction partner and their willingness to overcome them;

- dialogical: Belonging needs Othering, and vice versa, to create meaning.

In the MyMemLab life case, Nadia and Keith might hit it off on the basis of the Ethnicity and Sociability identity elements, based on similar self-views and appraisals despite other differing tangible identity elements. Othering might come into play on the basis of different activation levels of Generation and Mobility.

Because ethnicity, associated self-views, values and appraisals are not likely to cause any conflict between the key partners, they might overlook its opportunity and challenges for the mobile learning project. Streamlined views and the resulting lack of awareness cause the risk of ignoring the various needs of users due to different ethnic backgrounds.

In the specific case of the interaction between Nadia and Keith, Nadia's activation level of Mobility will come in as a bridging strategy to end users, assuming that she manages to convey the importance of the message to Keith. Finally, they both need to achieve the implementation of the necessary customisation.

Let us now capture the bridging strategies for leveraging the diversity generated in interaction:

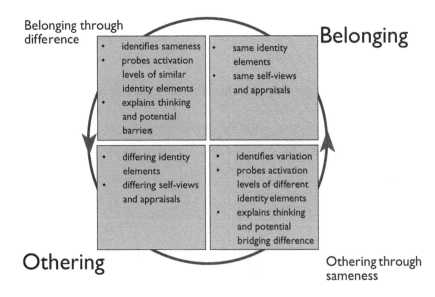

Figure 7.5   The process – Belonging and Othering

As illustrated in Chapter 4, the starting point of the dialogical process is the extreme ends of Belonging and Othering (see Figure 7.5). For the purpose of generating successful business outcomes the process comprises four distinct steps, each of which is supplemented with helpful tools (see Table 7.11).

Table 7.11   The four-step process of Belonging and Othering

Step	Tool
Step 1: Identification of key people Identifying key people I need to build a relationship with for business reasons.	**Relationship mapping** A relationship map shows the importance of each relationship and the extent to which I feel comfortable relating to and communicating with that person.[6]
Step 2: Identification of identity elements Identifying my own and others' identity elements for the purpose of surfacing self-views and appraisals beyond first, potentially misleading impressions. For understanding the potential overlaps or particular barriers that connect or separate me from the 'other': • identify sameness; • identify variation.	**The Lens of Multiple Identity** The Lens of Multiple Identity, its geology model with its vocabulary and meaning of tangible and intangible identity elements.
Step 3: Exploration of activation levels Exploring the activation level of my own identity elements and activated elements of my interaction partner: • probe activation levels of similar identity elements; • probe activation levels of differing identity elements; • seek other's views.	**Relationship-building skills** Relationship-building skills such as observation skills, active listening skills, and questioning and assertion skills.
Step 4: Application of bridging strategies Applying bridging strategies to create: • Belonging through difference. Applying leveraging strategies to create • Othering through sameness. By • explaining thinking; • addressing potential ways of bridging; • addressing potential barriers in a culture-sensitive way.	**Belonging and Othering, The Environmental Lens** Relationship-building skills as listed above; The Environmental Lens: see 'scapes' for context-bound appraisals.

---

6   Relationship mapping tools are widely available online.

For the application of bridging strategies Nadia can utilise Belonging by downplaying her Mobility element where she observes that this is necessary, such as in direct interaction with Keith, but bringing it out for the benefit of the project. Both can utilise Othering by seeking views outside their comfort zone, that is, outside their common understanding of Ethnicity. This element will be extraordinarily helpful in exploring and meeting diverse user needs.

Understanding the cognition process in one-to-one, in one-to-many and in many-to-many interaction requires awareness and reflection. Knowing the identity elements, developing the boundary-spanning skills and, finally, applying the bridging strategies guarantee seamless collaboration.

Winning the Organisation Development Challenge

The previous section presented the skills and bridging strategies necessary to break through the stereotype game in order to win over key business people in direct interactions. We now look at the further development of the individual, which requires an environment that encourages the individual to prosper and grow – a culture of interconnectivity.

Benefits:

- nourishes the ability to build constructive business relationships across personal and digital boundaries of differing identities;

- fosters collaboration in and between groups of people with diverse cultural, social, organisational or hierarchical backgrounds;

- closes the gap between current cultures, that is, shifts from a potentially biased-driven to a desired collaboration culture.

Change models have filled the management literature. The following section presents two selected approaches that prepare people for welcoming transition and readiness for change, enabling them to build a culture of interconnectivity. See Figure 7.6 for the change approach through individual accountability scaled from the individual to the team, and finally, to the organisation.

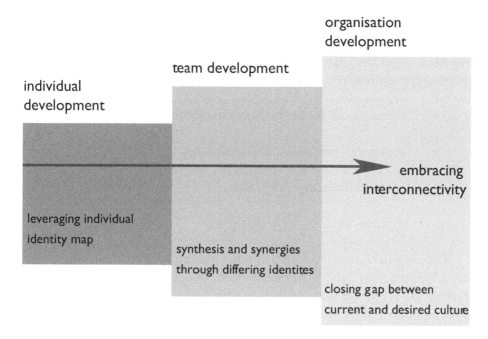

Figure 7.6   Organisation development through individual accountability

This section discusses two ways to tackle the issue of overcoming preconceived views in order to improve organisation performance.

The first approach develops people to become change agents, involving them in shaping the future built on trust and collaboration. Typically, the approach is delivered face-to-face, complemented by online or mobile learning modules.

The second approach focuses on bridging barriers by the use of gamification in mobile learning and development, that is, the selected use of game elements in a non-game environment.

MOBILISING A CULTURE OF COLLABORATION AND ENGAGEMENT

A collaboration culture is a culture that is characterised by participation, commitment and personal responsibility on the individual level mirrored in the organisation culture.[7] Change in organisations has many faces. This section

---

7   An approach in favour of the view that a culture is something that an organisation is, as opposed to the view that a culture is something an organisation just has (Smircich 1983). The characteristics

discusses the mobilisation approach[8] to implement a culture of collaboration and engagement. See Figure 7.7 that illustrates how the mobilisation approach generates maximum output with minimal external input. The mobilisation approach:

- empowers all people in the organisation;

- engages all people in a dialogue; and

- overcomes preconceived views

in order to improve organisation performance.

The approach rests on the internal multiplication of learning and development. This type of dissemination, also known as the 'Train The Trainer' (TTT) approach, requires only a few stakeholders in order to reach a large number of employees. For example, the approach prepares a few leaders to pass on the relationship-building skills described above to their team.

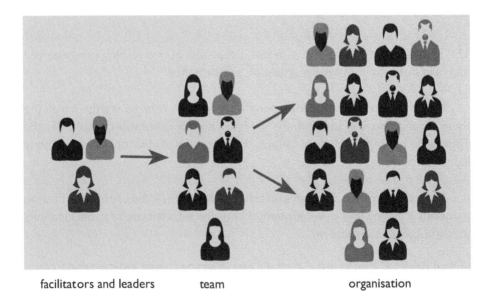

facilitators and leaders   team   organisation

Figure 7.7   Impacting your organisation with minimal external input

---

of an 'is' culture are depicted as follows: a) how meaning that emerges from social interaction is negotiated and shared; and b) how senior managers play an integral part in the continuous process of creation, although they are not able to control it. See Chapter 2 for details.

8   With kind permission of the Scandinavian Employeeship Institute, SESI.

The approach ultimately leads to the mobilisation of all employees, helping them to redefine their roles, becoming accountable for optimising performance and liberating new energy.

The benefits of the mobilisation approach are as follows:

- The learning transfer starts as early as Day One of the programme, when the selected stakeholders, usually leaders, need to adopt the role of facilitators and multipliers of the message.

- The knowledge transfer will be secured when the external consultants leave the organisation.

- The leaders will be made directly accountable for the process of creating the collaboration culture.

- The collaboration culture will be immediately embedded and sustained within the organisation.

- The TTT approach incorporates the cross-boundary component as leaders of various levels engage in a dialogue across cultural and organisational boundaries.

With the introduction of this type of change initiative there are a number of risks:

- Time consumption: leaders tend to be unwilling to commit to additional responsibilities by taking on the role of facilitator and coach.

- Definition of pilot: careful evaluation of the starting point in the organisation is needed, including region, hierarchical level and reputation of selected department in the organisation.

- Existing approaches: integration of existing processes, frameworks, and models and the buy-in of their owners and ambassadors.

Successful management of risks produces a great role model for further dissemination throughout the organisation for the mobilisation of a collaboration culture. Further into the roll-out it creates a company dialogue that helps both the leaders and their teams to have a common understanding of the future vision, values and standards. The newly created effective communication channels between people give each individual, not only the management, the feeling that their identities, self-views and appraisals contribute to the development of their own future as well as the future of the enterprise. Finally, it positions the organisation as a healthy and innovative employer of choice.

Successful risk management consists of:

- Clarification of overall direction; for example, identification and development of relationship-building skills and timely feedback processes, made available digitally, all suitable for international roll-out and integration into a regular executive global learning portfolio.

- Thorough needs assessment to ensure the achievement of anticipated outcomes through people, using, for example, semi-structured interviews or focus groups.

- Alignment with existing frameworks, approaches and technology, such as a competency model successfully in use across the organisation, and social and collaboration channels for the use of disseminating the message.

- Evaluation of the pilot workshop for potential necessary adaptations for further roll-out of the programme.

The programme envisaged should reflect the current situation within the organisation, taking into account the present and future organisational challenges and also those of the wider environment, such as international processes and connected cross-boundary work, reporting lines and responsibilities. Selected virtual change elements need to create authentic interdependence with their face-to-face counterparts in order to meet the next generation of digital collaboration culture requirements. The integration of virtual and face-to-face in a planned, pedagogically valuable way needs leadership, proper planning, administrator support, budget capacity and staff training.[9]

Table 7.12 outlines the requirements the learning partner should meet for a change programme of this type.

---

9   http://www.teachthought.com/trends/flipped-classroom-trends/10-conditions-for-achieving-success-with-blended-learning/.

The up-to-date delivery capabilities mentioned above will of necessity involve new technologies which revolutionise the way people collaborate and connect; they change information management processes as well as work-style innovations in a continually evolving workforce. The app industry has boomed into a multi-billion-dollar industry with millions of products available to end consumers. The nature of this young industry remains very fragmented; some have made it to the status of large players who have experienced multiple successes, whilst most others have disappeared. The organisation development industry is now starting to feature mobile applications for the use of human behaviour change and development.

Table 7.12   Learning partner requirements

Global orientation	Look for a partner/provider with experience in delivering global, intercultural leadership/change programmes and in managing the unique challenges this entails.
Team diversity	Inquire into the diversity the partner team brings to the cooperation. The team is the role model mirroring its credibility by its own diversity.
Delivery capabilities	Ensure the face-to-face and digital delivery capabilities of the change partner across regions, sustained across hierarchical, functional, regional and social boundaries.

BRIDGING BARRIERS THROUGH GAMIFICATION

Stereotypes (with variance bias as a sub-form) and self-fulfilling prophecies lead to the systematic underestimation of opportunities and advancement, hampering organisation performance. A more recent trend in organisation is the use of gamification to reconcile conflicting interests. The term 'gamification' refers to transferring the features of game elements and game design to non-game contexts. It describes the process of game thinking and game mechanics to engage users and solve problems (Zichermann 2011).

Gamification has seen both terrific hype and terrific backlash over the past few years. By 2015, over 40 per cent of Forbes Global 1,000 companies surveyed will use gamification as the primary mechanism to transform business operations.[10]

---

10 http://www.forbes.com/sites/gartnergroup/2013/01/21/the-gamification-of-business/.

This fairly recent business approach, owing its roots to the entertainment industry, is constantly pushing its boundaries over normally accepted solutions. With this in mind, the overall purpose of gamification in the business world is to motivate and engage an audience to achieve a desired outcome by positively influencing an anticipated behaviour change beneficial to the organisation output. Specifically, it can be used in applications and processes to improve:

- user engagement, such as increased customer loyalty through higher effectiveness of customer service;

- return on investment (ROI), by increasing sales of product groups and connected profits;

- data quality, by improving participation in community platforms; and

- effectiveness in training and development.

Gamification can help make the workplace more engaging and productive because it changes the rules of engagement and as a result inspires employees to change behaviours. However, it brings with it a number of risks:

- Gamified applications have spilled over from the game stores into organisations. Playing a game to win a cuddly toy is usually an act of free will and fun; but playing a game to keep one's job is a different thing altogether.

- They often become more of a time sink than a timesaver.

- They lack a clear objective in alignment with the overall strategy.

- The rules of the gamified application are not aligned with the rules which shaped the organisation's culture.

- They become a self-fulfilling prophecy generating behaviours detrimental to the enterprise performance.

The building blocks of gamified applications come in many shapes and sizes. One game's form of resistance is chance, while another's is competition and yet another's is collaboration.[11]

---

11 Dignan 2011:110.

Many well-known applications can be understood as games. Loyalty programmes work on the basis of extrinsic motivation drivers displayed by the use of points, badges, leaderboards, prizes and progress bars. Airline miles and shopping loyalty cards as primitive forms of play aim for winning more points for personal gain or status, for example, a gold or platinum card, and some tangible rewards connected to that status.

Table 7.13   Extrinsic and intrinsic motivation drivers

Extrinsic motivation drivers	Intrinsic motivation drivers
• points	• status and power
• leaderboards	• authority
• badges	• mastery
• prizes	• belonging
• progress bars	• pride
	• fun

A number of applications combine extrinsic and intrinsic motivation drivers (see Table 7.13). Business networks like LinkedIn can be understood as games, triggering networkers' intrinsic motivation such as their sense of power, achievement, status and recognition. Networkers commit to the rules of the game by adding new contacts, posting news and making contributions to professional groups. They thereby perform the required tasks to achieve a certain outcome displayed by the number of network contacts, the number of profile visitors and the progress bar on the contribution level.

Strava is a smart-phone running and cycling GPS tracker, taking performance analytics to the next level with a wide catalogue of 'records' for climbs, descents and other challenges. It ranks a user's performance and compares it over specific courses to thousands of other users. The gamified application has been hugely successful. Nevertheless, critics view it as a paradox, describing it as the most anti-social form of social media, feeding egoistic behaviour.[12]

Whilst competition-based ranking can be highly successful in communities where participants seek this type of advancement, self-realisation, purpose or meaning, it can be devastating in other settings such as managing performance in organisations.

---

12 http://reviews.mtbr.com/the-angry-singlespeeder-why-strava-sucks.

Just at the end of 2013 Microsoft abolished 'stack ranking', their employee-evaluation process that has been roundly criticised by many current and former Microsoft employees. Leaders were forced to rate every single member of the team on a bell curve from excellent to poor, even if the whole team had performed excellently.[13] This competition-based gamified performance management is one of the reasons for Microsoft's inability to foster high-performing teams, a major cause of its 'lost decade'.[14]

Whilst not all stack ranking approaches are detrimental to the anticipated outcome, this one raises some key issues:

- Inward looking: in this approach there is no involvement of the clients, whereas in reality external stakeholders should be involved in a feedback process. At the end of the day, the client determines the value of the company.

- Rules of competition: the rules of competition are detrimental to working across boundaries, or far worse, they create boundaries and, as a result, isolation and a slower learning curve over time (Dignan 2011), hampering business success.

- Wrong behaviours: people seek only contacts beneficial to their personal curve, not the overall objective. Accomplishments are often discredited to the extent of exclusion and, finally, redundancy.

In the cyberage, organisations that seek to develop a collaboration culture should precede the anticipated change with a gamified application. Gamified change initiatives need to feature a range of activities, for example, timely feedback processes, the 'other' view, meaningful discussions and knowledge exchange. The selection of game mechanics fostering collaboration requires thorough investigation of people's intrinsic motivation drivers such as their self-views, appraisals, values and sense of Belonging. The target users' buy-in into the design process is invaluable and, at the same time, provides the design team with essential information on potential cultural differences in the adoption and use of gamified collaboration, cooperation and co-creation.

---

13 In addition, the ratings feed compensation.
14 http://blogs.hbr.org/2013/11/dont-rate-your-employees-on-a-curve/.

The appropriate design, per application per organisation, based on the existing or the anticipated organisation culture or end user requirements, can ensure the success of gamification applications in the long run. Continuous monitoring of user engagement on a regular basis so as to modify and evolve game mechanics over a period of time will assist with better game design and thereby contribute to the success of gamification applications. Successful gamified applications based on the customer culture or end user requirements can drive real business goals and revenues, thereby enhancing the brand name. Only the co-creation of the digital making process ensures an organisation culture – people fit result.

Cyberconnecting through Human-to-Human Interaction

To recapitulate, leveraging a strategic position in the cyberage requires most organisations to tackle the challenge of transition and change.

Seamless collaboration in human-to-human interaction requires the successful development and application of relationship-building skills and bridging strategies, reflected in the use of technology in human–cyber interaction.

The starting point for seamless collaboration lies in the success of the interaction of individuals, impacting team collaboration and scaled up to organisation level. Irrespective of whether the nature of the collaboration channel is face-to-face or virtual, the perception of the 'other' is at the heart of its quality. Breaking through stereotypes opens new opportunities. The Lens of Perception in action filters potential stereotypes and resulting self-fulfilling prophecies, uncovering potential blind spots that hamper change readiness.

The real-life example of Nadia's and Keith's interaction illustrates the need to look into the details of the ramifications of identity constructions in order to boost performance. Introspection and reflectedness in combination with selected tools are essential to move from unreflected action to meaningful interaction. Effective tools are observation skills, listening skills, and questioning and assertion skills. In combination with the ability to differentiate observation from interpretation, they are a cracker set for success. True relationship-building happens through the balance of Belonging and Othering as a bridging strategy for overcoming potential barriers.

Stereotypes (with variance bias as a sub-form) and self-fulfilling prophecies lead to the systematic underestimation of opportunities and advancement, hampering organisation performance outside the mainstream taste. Organisations have to think about strategies that enable people to break through the stereotype game for the overall purpose of performance improvement.

The closing section of this chapter describes two successful ways to meet the implementation challenge advancing from individual development to organisation development. The mobilisation approach, also known as the TTT approach, enables organisations to roll out complex change needs. The impact on the organisation is maximum with minimal input of external resources.

With the unprecedented number of mobile devices, organisations around the globe are increasingly looking into mobile organisation development. Whilst the relatively recent approach of gamification is not a universal remedy, it offers elements vital to organisation development, given that its mechanics are aligned with the future culture characterised by collaboration and cooperation.

Chapter 8

Completing the Roadmap to Interconnectivity – The Environmental Lens

Building interconnectivity requires a close look at the bigger picture, that is, the environment, in which the interactions are happening. Having discovered The Lens of Multiple Identity and The Lens of Perception, the question arises where to start the journey to building interconnectivity.

This chapter proposes to investigate the origins of why and where the organisation development initiative sparked. The investigation itself, in particular if you 'inherit' the organisation development initiative, might present a revelation and a door opener for further exploration. The next section covers the competencies required from you and the people around you to build interconnectivity in a meaningful way. For mastering the human-centric approach to technology innovation and its successful adoptions it is paramount to involve all the key stakeholders right from the start, not only in the role of feedback providers, but in the role of co-creators. Immersion is key to co-creation in order to tackle the current and future global challenges that concern us all. The final section of this chapter provides you with an introduction to co-creation, based on the example of the development of a mobility strategy for A1 Guard, provided by MyMemLab.

The framework 'The Three Lenses of Diversity' is the roadmap for building interconnectivity. Interconnectivity stands for connecting reciprocally. In the interconnectivity building process, the identity portfolio of key decision-makers and stakeholders comes into play. It impacts perception, both self-views and appraisals, which in turn influences the ways we see the places around us, the physical place and the digital space, both subject to rapid change.

Some of these change drivers are likely to have significant impact on identities. The impact of social media, the development of increasingly dense networks of information and rapid developments in mobile communications technology will continue to transform the ways in which people interact both locally and globally. The world of work is exposed to some overarching themes, which have had and will have significant influence on our identity maps in the coming years: hyperconnectivity and the associated blurring between public and private identities, and the increasing social plurality changing the environment in which we interact. Therefore we need to pay close attention to the environment in which interactions of critical importance take place, be this a megacity such as Cairo or New Delhi, a social media network where we leave our digital trace for the generations to come, or the subsidiary of a client firm in a rural neighbourhood in relatively close distance to the enterprise headquarters where we work.

Two key questions might be of assistance in navigating the potentially uncharted space in the cyberconnected environment and in geo-proximity:

- What are the enablers provided by the environment that assist building effective work-based relationships, for example the infrastructure, such as a reliable internet connection?

- What are the barriers induced by the environment that impact effective relationship-building efforts, for example, an unfavourable immigration situation causing long queues even for business travelers?

Before entering an interaction, one should think about its strategic component, that is, the implications inherent to the environment.

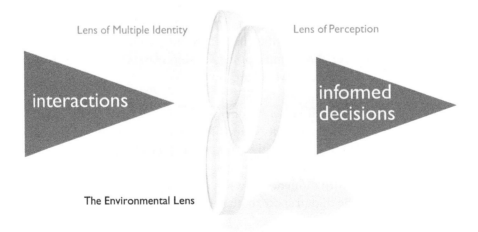

Figure 8.1   The Environmental Lens

You might be leading a multimillion infrastructure project in charge of thousands of people, or introducing an innovation programme transforming the enterprise from a tech follower to a true tech leader. In any role and for any situation of strategic importance, it is vital to analyse the implications the environment brings to the actual interaction, prior to its happening.

The key meaning and key benefit of The Environmental Lens (see Figure 8.1) are summarised in Table 8.1.

Table 8.1   Key meaning and key benefit of The Environmental Lens

Key meaning	Key benefit
The Environmental Lens helps us to examine the environments in which the interaction takes place. These may be the organisation, the geopolitics of its location, the media and communication, and the technological and financial configuration within which the interaction is embedded.	The Environmental Lens will uncover symptoms of what happens at a broader level in the organisation, its markets and environments across boundaries. • Acting upon the contingencies delivered by the environment, by actively incorporating the diverse people needs caused by the environment • Balancing localisation against standardisation, reflected in products and services

The benefits of acknowledging environmental contingencies include:

- Recognising and understanding the environment's complexity and its impact on human and tech interaction. This includes the contingencies of the physical places, such as a culture of the values and norms of a megacity as opposed to those of a lush countryside impacting the interaction.

- Organising the abundant information resulting from the recognition process in order to make better strategic decisions, bundled and made operable by the five scapes.

- Acting upon the implications the environment has on the individual in order to build effective relationships across social, technological and cultural boundaries.

Where to Start the Interconnectivity Building Process

To recap, we have moved from The Lens of Multiple Identity to The Lens of Perception and have now arrived at The Environmental Lens. The steps in the strategic interconnectivity-building process moved from individuals and their identity constructions to their self-views and appraisals. The missing ingredient to make The Three Lenses of Diversity function as a framework or a roadmap is The Environmental Lens, presented in Chapter 4 and now explored in full detail.

For successful mastery of future organisation development challenges, you can equally well start with the application of The Environmental Lens and follow through with the application of the other two lenses.

Here are three considerations to help you decide where to start the roadmap:

1. Personal preferences: you may tend to conceive the big picture first ('What's happening in the immediate and more remote environment?') and then deal with details, or you may rather start with people ('What are they about?') and then detect where they interact and what implications the environment has for them and their interactions.

2. Framing the transformation initiative: each change programme has a starting point, which could be an informal spark or a structured process. Depending upon this starting point, any one of The Three Lenses might be an appropriate entry to the roadmap. For example, when addressing a bias issue that hampers organisation performance, you might want to consider applying The Lens of Perception first.

3. The perceived impact of the people's diversity as opposed to the strength of the environmental contingencies: for example, a relatively homogenous group of middle-aged male German technicians need to work on a large-scale construction project in Southeast Asia, involving multi-stakeholder connections. The contingencies from the environment might have more impact, so it would be essential to analyse them before the rather homogeneous identity profile of the group of technicians.

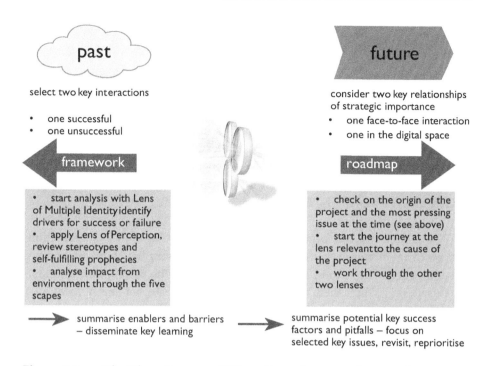

Figure 8.2   The Three Lenses of Diversity as framework or roadmap

So far, we have mostly referred to The Three Lenses of Diversity as a framework. As such it can serve:

- your personal reflection, thus increasing awareness and personal development to build effective business relationships;

- reflection with peers and other stakeholders, for both successful interactions and those that require a different approach for future success in business.

For the application on key interactions in future projects, The Three Lenses of Diversity can be used as a roadmap to outline potential difficult situations and their successful mastery.

Thus The Three Lenses of Diversity has double value, as a framework for reflecting on past interactions and as a roadmap for future projects (see Figure 8.2).

From Cairo to Cyberspace

The two key live cases SonaConn and MyMemLab, which have been accompanying us throughout the book, will also lead us through The Environmental Lens. In each case there is a high level of interconnectivity, yet they are unique in their own ways. One is a multimillion project primarily in the physical space; the other is much smaller in financial terms, but offering an unprecedented interconnectivity between human-to-human and human-to-tech interactions. They will assist in illustrating the application of the five scapes, the core tool of The Environmental Lens.

The habitats in which organisations operate and cross-boundary interactions take place are increasingly complex to capture and describe. These interactions are embedded within the complex interweaving of the geopolitics of today's organisations (which themselves are so often spread over many locations), the media landscape, and the technological and financial configurations. The habitats configurated in the five scapes provide a helpful structure to grasp the environment in which interactions happen. Again, their boundaries are seamless: a precise distinction between them is difficult to draw.

The five scapes highlight how the environment potentially shapes and influences the 12 identity elements. This can easily be experienced through immersion or by observation. An example of immersion would be adopting a selected element of Appearance by wearing a headscarf in communities where it is normally not worn, while an example of observation would be witnessing the role of fathers and the management and the implications of paternity leave across Europe. Identity switching illustrates most explicitly the ways in which the environment impacts selected aspects of our identity map. Equally, it helps us understand some of the pressures it puts on business contacts, such as the media, tech and finance.

THE ENVIRONMENTAL LENS – SONACONN

We have had a number of glimpses of Carolyn's challenges. So far, their presentations were in connection with Gender and Generation. Let us now look in full at the environmental contingencies where all of this happened.

The complexity with which interactions happen in today's cyberconnected world is organised by the use of the Ethnoscapes, Mediascapes, Technoscapes, Ideoscapes and Financescapes. Building on the introduction in Chapter 4, we continue with the illustration relevant for today's cyberconnected world of work. As boundaries in life are seamless, so are the boundaries of the scapes. For that reason, in the subsequent application on the SonaConn case selected scapes are meaningfully combined. That is, the Ethnoscapes and Ideoscapes are analysed in combination, the Mediascapes and the Technoscapes, and finally, the Financescapes are treated as an entity. The following story illustrates the interplay between infrastructure, technology and local migration.

Box 8.1   SMS: Buses Leaving Now!

The senior managers worked on a brief reflexive exercise. It was quiet in the room. At 3:30pm smart-phones started beeping, vibrating, or a brief 'allah' ringtone went off.

Everyone immediately attended to the smart-phones. Some said, 'the mini-buses are leaving at 3:45. Top management have just sent a message.' The senior managers got up and rushed out the door to get on the mini-buses that take employees back into downtown.

On that day the internet had been down since the morning.

Switching to short text messages due to internet downtime in order to send employees home illustrates the impact the environment has on a high-tech organisation. Let us now continue step by step.

Ethnoscapes

Ethnoscapes are the macro-perspective of The Lens of Multiple Identity. Whilst The Lens of Multiple Identity describes the various identities we have simultaneously, Ethnoscapes capture the helicopter view of identity brought alive in migration as a consequence of the economic downturn, which will potentially give rise to greater social and economic polarisation between increasingly wealthy and ever more impoverished groups. Equally, it is a result of global business activities with ample job opportunities, high employment rates, and high salaries and wages, which in turn, causes a steady increase in mobility. Global migration and its people flow create the formation of shifting group identities.

Specifically, in the course of permanent or multiple temporary migrations, people often need to respond to questions such as: 'Do you feel Malaysian or Canadian?' Rather than having a single identity, people have several overlapping identities, which shift in emphasis in different life stages and environments. As discussed in Chapter 5 and 6, a person can have many identities simultaneously, although one identity might be more important under particular circumstances. In a new place a person may find their identity as a specialist in one technical field most important, while at home they might identify as a caring parent.

Ideoscapes

Ideoscapes are a concentration of images, highly political and often directly linked to state ideologies and their power interests or counter-ideologies of movements. Ideoscapes centre on the ideologies of a leading body; they might include freedom, welfare rights, sovereignty and democracy and those that oppose it. They have great influence on any interaction related to short-term or long-term migration. Specifically, democracy and associated rights represent a strong pull factor for migration.

In the world of work, ideoscapes as a concentration of politics, ideologies and power interests translate from state ideologies to organisational and corporate cultures. People cross boundaries by moving between functions, business units, headquarters and subsidiaries, from operational to corporate. These kinds of interactions necessitate physical mobility in terms of commutes, regional or international assignments, and flexibility of mindset to master the switching between majority and minority cultures, characteristic in different places of the organisation. This migration requires successful navigation through the changing rhetoric and understanding of the politics, interests and ideologies of:

- the corporate culture, that is, the 'has' culture valued by dominant members; or

- the organisational culture, that is, the 'is' culture whose meaning emerges from social interaction through the activation of selected elements of the people's identity portfolios.

Global or local migration and its people flow contribute to the continuous reconfiguration of this negotiation process. Therefore, the boundary between physical mobility and the necessary flexibility of the mindset is seamless. On the SonaConn project, identity-shaping contingencies uncovered through the Ethnoscapes and Ideoscapes were:

**Box 8.2   SonaConn – Ethnoscapes and Ideoscapes
                   as Identity-Shaping Forces**

- **Migration flow**

Temporary from Europe to Egypt and the Middle East and North Africa (MENA); pull factor for the temporary migration was the employment opportunity for the consultants working for or associated with the European consulting firm, some in the role of freelancers, the benefits and the overall status that comes with a highly recognised assignment in the tech sector in this region.

- **The landscapes of group identity**

The construction of identities on the basis of reductionism, which we may call 'singular affiliation', which is the assumption that any person pre-eminently belongs, for all practical purposes, to one collectivity only, no more and no less, such as 'the Brits' or 'the Egyptians', although at times up to 14 national identities were involved.

- **Global citizen mindset**

The temporary migration and its continuous shift between the local and global contributed significantly to the 'global citizen' understanding of the stakeholders and the production of an 'elite' that rides the wave of globalisation, occupying influential positions or roles in the important spheres of social life; typically these are incumbents: leaders and decision-makers, policy makers. Elites are thus 'makers' or 'shakers': groups whose 'cultural capital' positions them above their fellow citizens and whose decisions crucially shape what happens in the wider society.

- **The local migration**

Commuters shift identity between the organisation's overt values of the company site in a highly guarded business park, a green spot in the desert and those of the outside world. They switch between the corporate identity with its own logic outside the city and their private identities in urban places, disseminating global headquarter values for further local production.

- **Political unrest**

The great political unrest in the region, which peaked at times, threatened the project overall, the recruitment of consultants for the project and its delivery. People safety was a serious subject throughout the project, shaping the temporary political identity of some of the team.

Mediascapes

From newspapers and magazines through film and broadcasting, all media have been contending with the effect of digitalisation. The emergence of a new digital media world has provided the public with new formats of media consumption at an unparalleled speed of dissemination of information. On the rise are new forms of businesses which were previously impossible and are now rather unexpectedly in the information business.

Image-centred strips of reality are produced and shared by micromessages, photos, clips, videos and short blogs. The spread of social media and the increase in online presence are key factors which permit people to become active shapers of mediascapes as opposed to taking on the role of mere consumers. This has been expressed in recent uprisings which organise protest, shape the narrative and put pressure on the international community. Implications for the individual include hyperconnectivity and having several online identities.

Technoscapes

The proliferation, synthesis and exploitation of data have redefined the global configuration of technology. Whereas technologies were once orchestrated through political agendas and large-scale economies, they now bring about new types of cultural interactions and exchanges through the power of technology, which can happen at unprecedented speeds. The growing quantity of personal and financial data generated online raises questions over who 'owns' and can access the data and, in general, means that there is more opportunity for criminal exploitation and cybercrime.

The new configuration of technology has led people to become accustomed to switching seamlessly between the internet and the physical world, and using social media to conduct their lives in a way which dissolves the divide between online and offline identities. Living in a digital world may lead to greater fusion with the like-minded with simultaneous separation from those who are unable to use this technology.

Technoscapes also includes learning technology and the ability to provide people with new learning experiences digitally through synchronous online interaction, fostering Lifeong learning.

Box 8.3   SonaConn – Mediascapes and Technoscapes as Identity-Shaping Forces

• **The time-space compression**

'Thinking' the other location generates 'time-space compression', a sense of dramatically reducing distance in your imagination in order to be able to plan the unplannable. The strategy of using both synchronous and non-synchronous ways of communication, emails and concalls, video-chats and webinars supported the case.

• **Media and design**

The client's feedback was that 'they expected something more state-of-the-art featuring some of the latest multi-media tools'. Ready-made booklets with a glossy touch were standard and participants expected these to be delivered with the programme. Specifications on structure and layout were provided.

• **Hyperconnectivity**

There was simultaneous availability of multiple media next to face-to-face interaction: 24-hour news on recent political escalation in the Middle East, ubiquitous use of smart-phones in meetings and during conversations, texting and writing emails. Social media started facilitating political movements.*

• **Proliferation of communication technologies**

The poor infrastructure of landlines prompted national and international telecommunication firms to offer new products and services. Competition for the mobile end user resulted in the battle of the next wave of high-speed mobile technologies to replace the network in place.

* The usage has been thought to be very influential, for example, in the mobilisation of dissent in Egypt, and raised the international profile of these events.

Financescapes

Financescapes capture the financial context of the interaction. They describe the disposition of global capital and financial flow, rapidly moving and available to stakeholders through currency markets, stock exchanges and commodity speculations. Financescapes are cross-boundary movements of loans, equities, direct and indirect investments, and currencies that transcend the power of the nation state. They are the global flows of finance in which uncontrolled and rapid movements of capital can destabilise national economies. When things go wrong, costly bailouts by the state, that is, the taxpayer, can be expected for financial speculators.

Conversely, the global flow of capital can contribute to the wealth of an organisation. Technology as such is very closely tied to financial markets, largely determining the speed at which money moves in the global arena.

The emergence of 'around-the-world' 24/7 financial markets where major cross-boundary financial transactions are made in cyberspace represents a familiar example of the economic face of globalisation. Individuals and their participation are embedded in the global financescapes, by generating or losing revenue in financial products; in any case, the management of their finances is entirely online, or their payments are entirely mobile.

Box 8.4   SonaConn – Financescapes as Identity-Shaping Forces

• **Population is power**

The country's demography makes the battle over the market place specifically fierce. Cash-rich competitors from other Middle East countries are entering the market in the anticipation of significant market share.

• **The tech–finance centre**

The Ministry of Telecommunications and all other telecommunication providers are thus fierce competitors and are situated in the direct neighbourhood of the high-tech business compound. Their financial power is demonstrated by means of a Silicon Valley just outside a megacity. Through high turnover of the workforce among the tech organisations in the compound and close personal, including family and networks, the exchange of information about 'what the other is up to' is high.

• **Who is in – who is out**

Identity creation is generated through clearly visible identity tags displaying Belonging to 'the haves'. Employees also wear the tags outside work to display Belonging. The tags provide permission to pass the tight security controls in and out of the heavily guarded compound, a green spot in the desert.

If Carolyn had known more about the project context, whose texture is made up of politics, media and tech, it would have been easier to respond to comments, objections, offences and even to compliments, all experienced in direct interactions throughout the course of the project.

THE ENVIRONMENTAL LENS – MYMEMLAB

Whilst The Environmental Lens applied on the SonaConn project highlights some of the key influencers on interactions in hindsight, Nadia and Keith can use the application of the roadmap to consider the impact the environment on their fairly new collaboration and the implications it has on the final product. In addition, building on the introduction of The Environmental Lens in Chapter 4 based on the MyMemLab case, the analysis below adds aspects from the landscape and their impact on Nadia and Keith and others that have not been mentioned yet. Specifically,

- How might the context, in particular the immediate physical places and the digital space, inform their own and other identity portfolios?

- How might the environmental contingencies impact relationship-building efforts? This includes the work relationship between Nadia and Keith, the wider stakeholder network, and also the identification of future key relationships important to foster.

Nadia, Keith and their teams will gain valuable insights from the analysis through the five scapes. Understanding and acting upon the contextual issues impacting their own and client interactions will help them develop and build a winning mobile application. The clients will benefit thereby from a unique and effective learning experience, assisting them in adopting the necessary behaviours to increase safety in the workplace. Aspects to consider are captured in Table 8.2 below.

Table 8.2   Analysis of the scapes in relation to the MyMemLab–A1Guard project

Ethnoscapes	• The identity maps of people concerned with the mobile learning programme: Keith and Nadia's peers, their current clients, their future users. • Their identity profiles, such as age, gender, learning experiences (specifically mobile learning) and preferred communication styles, but also their experience in a shifting world of short-term and long-term migration and its ramification on their approach to all things mobile. • Of specific importance for the success of this programme is the analysis of end user learning needs and expectations, all culturally loaded across boundaries.

Table 8.2   Continued

Mediascapes	•	The communication channels through which to market the newly published learning app, easing its adoption.
	•	Suitable social media in alignment with the organisation culture to facilitate links between like-minded individuals to create niche communities of interest.
	•	The approach of switching seamlessly between the physical and the online world.
Technoscapes	•	The human–tech interface and, specifically, the analysis of people's 'mobile fluency'.
	•	Easier identification of user behaviour through data triangulation from multiple anonymised data sets, each giving an additional piece of information, potentially available from applications the future user groups already use.[1]
	•	The design and delivery of the application (or, initially, the prototype), and its integration into existing enterprise applications to meet future needs.
Ideoscapes	•	The opportunity to create the resources for a proper needs analysis through immersion. The potential to initiate a co-creation process, involving future users into the design process.
	•	The option to shift from traditional learning to a contemporary way of learning on a topic that is typically viewed as less stimulating and thus bears the risk of potential resistance.
	•	Preferred ways of cooperation, which might be collaboration or competition reflected in the game mechanism, reflecting the organisation culture of the involved client organisations and AIGuard's proposed way to disseminate learning
Financescapes	•	The return on Investment (ROI) for AIGuard and the related opportunity to become a bigger player in the industry.
	•	Some of the global capital, of which MyMemLab aims to win a small share, enabled through the success and the subsequent improved attractiveness to potential investors.
	•	The business model and, as a subset, the store account model AIGuard and MyMemLab set up for the successful cooperation.

The analysis using the scapes enables A1Guard and MyMemLab decision-makers to make informed decisions on proactive business perspectives concerning how to generate business value through the partner and clients by earning their trust. Applying the skills illustrated in Chapter 7 such as observation, active listening, questioning and asserting, Keith, Nadia and their team gain valuable insights for building a winning application, clients adopt quickly and easily.

---

1   In alignment with the clients' privacy policies.

ROADMAP QUESTIONS

In summary of the SonaConn and MyMemLab cases, the questions below are useful for the application of each scape. When applying The Environmental Lens to your current or upcoming challenge, in what ways do these items affect relationship-building efforts?

- How does the environment, for example, megacity or country-side, impressive headquarters building or small subsidiary office, top-floor conference room as opposed to open plan co-working space for start-ups, inform your own and others' identity portfolios?

- What identity issues are likely to arise, embedded in and resulting from the physical flow/migrational mobility of people?

- Which elements of the identity map might your business partner activate in response to some of the challenges from migration?

- To what degree are you or your partners constantly connected to the outside world through the media and actively establishing identities through social media?

- To what degree do technology and switching between the physical and the online world shape your identity map? Think, for example, of internet connectivity or social media.

- What is the political situation in the country? How does this impact on any of your business relationships?

- What is the climate like where most of your workplace interactions take place?

- In what ways do different levels of financial affluence between you and your partners impact effective business relationship-building efforts?

- What other environmental factors impact relationship-building efforts?

Boundary-Spanning Competencies

Boundaries in today's cyberconnected world of work increasingly intersect. Seizing opportunities in this paradigm requires approaches and efforts which reflect this seamlessness. The mobilisation approach described in Chapter 7, which seeks to reframe boundaries and to create a shared identity among stakeholders with usually conflicting interests, is becoming increasingly popular for the approach of the co-creation of sustainable outcomes. It is based on the participation, engagement and personal responsibility of the individual mirrored in the final product or service.

Co-creation[2] originally describes the cooperation of society and business. As increasing numbers of Western companies look towards emerging and developing markets for future profits, they discover that locally operating social entrepreneurs possess the technical skills, local relationships and knowledge about social, cultural and technological challenges that are critical to developing and working in new markets. Recent innovation calls foster the collaboration between profit and not-for-profit organisations and demonstrate how some companies are turning to non-government organisations (NGOs) as critical problem-solvers and partners. Shared-value partnerships are a major new opportunity for the private sector and the NGO of the future to create greater impact.

The innovation partners bring specialised knowledge of specific target populations, which helps companies better design and tailor their products to those markets. The co-creation is certainly not restricted to two partners but can well expand into the inclusion of the people affected and concerned in the target population. In today's cyberconnected world this addresses the future users of all things mobile across the globe.

The nature of knowledge, skills and behaviours is changing; in the world of cyberconnected co-creation, digital literacy, the capability that equips an individual living, learning and working in a digital world is one key ingredient for the successful collaboration with partners across social, technological and cultural boundaries.

---

2   The concept of co-creation was first introduced by Herstatt and Von Hippel in their 1992 publication 'Developing New Product Concepts via the Lead User Method: A Case Study in a "Low Tech" Field'. They describe the process of joint development of new product or service concepts with manufacturer personnel. It is based on the successful application of a Lead User market research method carried out by Cornelius Herstatt at Hilti AG, a major European manufacturer of products and materials used in construction.

Spanning Social, Technological and Cultural Boundaries

Building interconnectivity across boundaries necessitates boundary-spanning capabilities. This practice aims to establish relationships by interaction partners temporarily altering the emphasis they put on selected identities from their identity portfolio. The shift in the importance of coexisting identities must happen in the awareness of the key partner's perception of self and the boundaries within which the interaction happens.

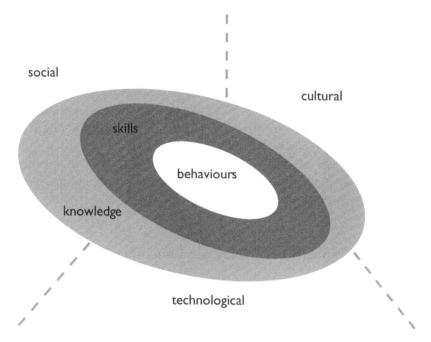

Figure 8.3   Boundary-spanning competencies

For successful practice the necessary boundary-spanning capabilities are as shown in Figure 8.3.

- Knowledge is the information one has in specific content areas.[3] For building interconnectivity in particular, it presents the body of information about boundaries, applied directly to the performance of the interaction where it happens. This includes knowledge about socioeconomic drivers, technology trends and cultural approaches, usually acquired through continuous education or training.

---

3   Spencer, Spencer 1993:10.

- Skills are the competence to work with and through other people, and the exercise of judgement. Under this heading can be included the sensitivity to particular situations and flexibility in adopting the most appropriate style. They include analytic thinking such as processing knowledge and data, determining cause and effect, organising data and plans, and conceptual thinking such as recognising patterns in complex data.[4] For building interconnectivity in particular, observation and listening skills, questioning and asserting skills qualify. See Chapter 7 for details.

- Behaviours refer to the way one acts towards others or responds to the environment through the application of the above skills, thus making a difference in outcome and performance. These behaviours are observable sets of actions and ideally generate quantifiable outcomes which would result, for example, in the inclusion of minority user and participant groups. See Chapter 7, section 'Bridging Barriers through Belonging and Othering', for details.

If you are in a position which requires you to span boundaries, the points to look into are shown in Table 8.3.

Table 8.3   Spanning social, technological and cultural boundaries

	Social	Technological	Cultural
Knowledge	Socioeconomic drivers and the global competition for people, business and resources

Incorporation of knowledge about global trends and demographic developments and impact on decision-making processes

Understanding of systematic interaction of policies and trends | Identification of most innovative design, development and deployment of technologies, bringing new perspectives to address industry, regional and global issues

Adoption of knowledge of technology trends and strategies that have significant impact on business and society

Mastery of a carefully selected body of tech expertise necessary to lead and work with tech and non-tech people | Familiarity with dominant and lesser-known approaches to diversity

Expertise in intercultural approaches and their pros and cons

International dimensions of traditional domestic policies

Investigation of methods and tools for successful global roll-outs |

---

4   Spencer, Spencer 1993:11.

Skills	Observation, listening, questioning and asserting skills
	Skills are the bridging element between knowledge and behaviour. They are essential to bring behaviours alive. For full details revisit Chapter 7

Behaviours			
	Selecting appropriate resources specifically with a view to boundary-spanning capabilities	Using language and communication style that enables understanding between tech and non-tech people	Role-modelling culturally appropriate behaviours
	Building high levels of trust; the higher the trust, the less time and expense it takes to successfully span boundaries	Role-modelling the view that technology is a strategic asset, rather than overhead, for competitive advantage	Leading collaboration by more deeply focusing on human relationships and identity
	Examining the readiness diverse stakeholders bring for several iterations of (technology) programme adaptations	Building synergistic relationships among IT, R&D and business development (sales)	Redesigning and customising to fit different learning and development preferences across the globe
		Providing digital literacy enablers for people to make full use of technology	Enabling action-learning in teams and groups with maximum diversity

Bridging strategies	
	Identification of sameness and difference and balancing Belonging and Othering all through the process for establishing effective business relationships across boundaries

As portrayed in Chapter 7, knowledge, skills and behaviours are an integral part of lifelong learning. Building interconnectivity, therefore, builds on a long-term perspective. Boundaries between social, technological and cultural competencies are seamless. In reality, they widely overlap. While the list is by no means exhaustive, the categorisation allows for easier review. Further details are highlighted in Chapter 9.

Developing a Co-Creation Mobility Strategy

Enterprises and organisations today are experiencing increasing mobility of executives, employees and customers. In response to the increased mobile interaction with internal and external people, organisations wishing to leverage the opportunities available through mobile technologies are faced with the daunting task of identifying the impact on infrastructure, implementing the right solutions and deciding where and when they should invest to evolve their business. The roadmap to interconnectivity helps develop a strategy for the organisation's infrastructure that supports mobility and achieves business goals in alignment with people's diverse needs and their perception of the world around them.

The solutions need to be able to leverage existing information systems to improve productivity by the simultaneous buy-in of people's needs and expectations such as the various device platforms employees want to use, for example, iOS, Android, Windows and BlackBerry operating systems.

Specifically, this illustrates the indispensable need to collaborate across technological, social and cultural boundaries. The deep-seated diversity characteristic of cross-boundary collaboration can be unfolded with the help of The Three Lenses of Diversity: stakeholders' multiple identity constructions, captured by tangible and intangible elements, people's self-views and appraisals of others, and finally, the demographic, economic and technological configurations inherent in the environment. Within this multitude of boundaries, there is asymmetry, expressed by vertical or hierarchical, and horizontal or functional asymmetry.

Co-creation, originating in the cooperation between social entrepreneurs and business, mostly for the purpose of creating social impact in developing markets now expands to the development process of all things mobile, products and services alike. In addition to developing products and services, the respective organisations are developed through interaction, which transforms them and their co-creating employees and leaders through new visions, management practices, skills and structures.

In the above case the situation includes the stakeholders shown in Figure 8.4:

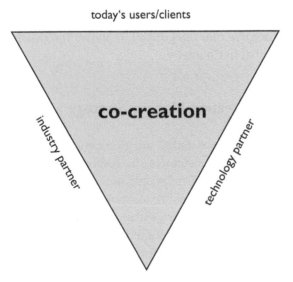

Figure 8.4   The mobility strategy co-creation partners

The co-creation process would typically feature the steps shown in Figure 8.5:

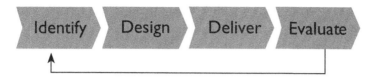

Figure 8.5   The mobility strategy co-creation process

IDENTIFY

Identification contains the co-creation strategy and the needs analysis or diagnostics.

Co-creation Strategy

MyMemLab work with the A1Guard organisation's key stakeholders to develop a mobile learning strategy. The industry client seeks to link high-level business objectives with learning strategies, determine how best to integrate mobile, and create a specific plan of action to design, develop and implement the identified mobile solution. MyMemLab work with A1Guard to create the strategy that achieves their business objectives.

Diagnostics

MyMemLab assess the mobile learning environment within A1Guard's market segment. They also guide them to understand how mobile learning can support their overall business strategies and goals.

MyMemLab conduct surveys for A1Guard on how best to deliver the requisite knowledge to the target audience. Once identified, MyMemLab survey their target audience to make sure that the enterprise's mobile learning strategy aligns with the future users' learning preferences, work approach and familiarity with all things mobile.

In particular, the co-creation happens in the course of direct interaction with the future users for the identification of the detailed needs meaningful in the region where the application is mostly used and will therefore be culturally relevant. Through immersion into today's and future user groups and their work, they uncover the root causes for the need and the overall purpose of the mobile application.

DESIGN

The co-creation partners design the content; in so doing, the future users become not just recipients but co-creators.

MyMemLab expand on the proof of concept by building a test model of the mobile solution. This prototype allows for live testing to confirm that it meets A1Guard's vision, can integrate with their other systems, and meets their business requirements, but it does not include all features – just enough for testing. The final mobile application will be full-featured.

The proof of concept is a cost-effective way of testing key features and the user experience (UX) at the front end of the project so that time and resources are used effectively to create key features for A1Guard and their end users. The proof of concept could consist of features such as a test of a successful learning outcome, a simple port of content management system (CMS) or learning content management system (LCMS) content to a mobile delivery system.

DELIVER

Based on the learning cycle from Steps 1 and 2, MyMemLab develop applications in iOS, Android, Windows Mobile and Web, based on latest technologies like Ruby on Rails, Node.js, AngularJS and other technologies, including maintenance. Services include their integration into existing enterprise applications' project management based on PMI or agile methods such as SCRUM.

EVALUATE

MyMemLab assist A1Guard in identifying key metrics that support business objectives and determine how those metrics can be captured and assessed. MyMemLab evaluate the impact on performance by collecting data during and after the use of the mobile application. The data collection is accomplished using a variety of techniques:

- field techniques: by collection of observable behaviours and interpretation of learning progress summarised in management report;

- digital techniques: by the use of analytics tools, their analysis and illustration of learning progress.

The correlation serves to calculate the ROI of the mobile learning initiative, and thus evaluates the alignment of the initiative with the A1Guard business objectives. Key insights feed into the next cycle of co-creation strategy development, needs identification, delivery and evaluation. Chapter 9 gives some in-depth coverage on UX from the field.

From Practice to Application

Before we suggest a way to put the context and the practice into application, let us summarise Part II. Prior to investigating 'What's next' we shall recap Chapters 4 through 8.

Chapter 4 focuses on the human-centric perspective by developing interactions from transactions to relationships by the use of The Three Lenses of Diversity. As today's clients and consumers are more than transactions, we need to acknowledge the individual's diversity. Digital enables us to understand, connect and deliver to them in more relevant and personalised ways, speaking to their individual needs, even in large numbers.

The Lens of Multiple Identity serves as the umbrella for the next two chapters: Chapter 5 introduces the tangible aspects of people's diversity in order to meet their needs and expectations, whereas Chapter 6 explores the less visible part of people's coexisting identities, which often is the fabric for successful sustainable relationships.

Chapter 7 presents The Lens of Perception in action, showing how the perception of the 'other' is at the heart of the quality of effective work relationships and offering ways to break through stereotypes in order to open new opportunities and uncover potential blind spots that hamper change readiness.

Chapter 8 closes Part II of the book: The Practice, by giving an in-depth view of The Environmental Lens, and by suggesting the thorough analysis of the landscapes impacting relationships in the analogue and the digital space.

The Three Lenses of Diversity are the roadmap to interconnectivity. You can start the discovery journey with the outlooks The Lens of Multiple Identity has to offer or with The Environmental Lens, and then work through the implications The Lens of Perception offers. Whichever route you select, The Three Lenses of Diversity provide a sustainable method for organising thinking to tackle current and future social, technological and cultural challenges, whilst the subjects for application presented in Part III are exposed to rapid change.

PART III
The Application

Chapter 9

Creating Value
from Embracing Tech

Part III, broadly speaking, covers the question of 'What next?' Having covered the theoretical background, the toolbox and the framework for the in-depth exploration of the process of building interconnectivity, it is time to move on to the current realities of mobile learning and organisation development in the cyberconnected world. Products and services generated in the cyberconnected world are changing ever more quickly; nevertheless the importance of the underlying human-to-human interactions in the generation of products and services in the cyberconnected world of work will continue to grow.

In your role of decision-maker in the organisation and, as a consequence, shaper of its development you are most likely facing some strategic decisions on the future of your company. Whether IT still lives a dusty existence in the basement of your organisation or you are a key shaper of the sector, this chapter captures intercultural, technological and hierarchical boundary-crossing aspects as part of the design and implementation process of your organisation development initiatives.

Like the book as a whole, Chapter 9 moves from human-to-human interaction to the interactions embedded in the cyberconnected world of work. Leveraging interconnections between technology and people is critical for any organisation's existence today. Technology works best when its products and services connect people in meaningful experiences and inspire exploration and discovery.

The chapter offers the following:

- The illustration of effective technological, cultural and social boundary-spanning by the use of real-life examples.

- The modelling of two selected approaches from real-life examples; one is human-to-human interaction in the tech sector; the other is human-to-tech interaction.

- The importance of needs assessment and its reflection in superior organisation performance.

Every Business is a Digital Business

Successful companies no longer separate business from technology but use their close interaction effectively to the extent of full integration. The examples below illustrate the transformation of businesses now and in the future:

- The inability to make a simple purchase, such as kilo of tomatoes in a supermarket, due to check-out desks remaining closed during a major power failure.

- Data storage centres moving closer to urban centres in order to increase speed to serve clients better, or building their own power station because power is a serious cost factor and yet the future of cloud services.

- The availability of increasingly inexpensive devices allowing the participation of formerly excluded populations in the cyberconnected world, power supplies provided.[1]

- The NOMO (no mobile device) phobia many people are facing, leaving them unable to move without their mobile device nearby; and WiFi as a basic need at the bottom of the Maslow's needs pyramid, triggering innovative illustrations of century old human needs models as shown in Figure 9.1.

---

1   For example, Project Loon looks to use a global network of high-altitude balloons to connect people in rural and remote areas who have no internet access at all. The balloons float in the stratosphere, twice as high as airplanes and the weather. In the stratosphere, there are many layers of wind, and each layer of wind varies in direction and speed. Loon balloons go where they're needed by rising or descending into a layer of wind blowing in the desired direction of travel. People can connect to the balloon network using a special internet antenna attached to their building. The signal bounces from this antenna up to the balloon network, and then down to the global internet on Earth. See http://www.google.com/loon/ for details.

Figure 9.1   WiFi as a basic human need[2]

The examples selected point to technology trends and their ramifications point to the mobility technology evolution, which has traditionally been consumer-driven rather than enterprise-driven. Apple has certainly changed the nature of consumer products and, as a result, influenced consumer behaviour and expectations on devices well beyond the Apple range.

The use of consumer devices such as iPhone, iPad, Android, Windows phones and tablets, and on-demand services such as access to office email, inventory data, sales data and big data processed for further use gave rise to the concept of IT consumerisation.

Digital maturity is still relatively low in many industries. To remain competitive, improve customer experience and achieve profitability, enterprises need to fully embrace digital transformation at all levels. Key areas to focus are:

---

2   Based on Maslow's pyramid of needs; the source of the WiFi addition is unknown.

- Integration across channels to enable external and internal clients to shift seamlessly between channels and more easily manage an ever-changing set of user interfaces and connection points.

- Maximisation of social media to market offerings, push products and services and gain real-time client/user insights.

- Recognition of the benefits made available through analytics techniques to provide value across multiple boundaries between business units such as R&D, risk management and customer services.

Today, people in the role of customers, employees and the wider network expect interaction with your organisation at their fingertips. Building interconnectivity creates the necessary interconnections across social, technological and cultural boundaries. It further entails progression from layer to layer:

- human-to-human;

- human-to-device;
  and through the two above;

- human-to-cyber.

The interplay of these interactions opens the door to intriguing application opportunities, which in turn requires unique boundary-crossing because specialists who have never worked together before now need to collaborate and co-create new solutions. Academics, application designers and coders, legal and subject matter specialists need to come together to explore the ways in which new approaches contribute to enterprises and organisation performance through superior products and services. The degree of this multidisciplinary approach is novel and opens doors for some ground-breaking innovation, yet presents some unprecedented challenges to boundary-spanning.

As such, the unparalleled acceleration of technological development impacts research and application opportunities for anthropologists, who increasingly contribute to the tech field. As discussed in Chapter 2 the origins of ethnography lie in early expeditions to lands and cultures unknown by adventuring geographers, missionaries, pioneers, traders, businessmen and social scientists. The documents they left behind describe the new 'ways of life' from the communities they had encountered. Just over a hundred years later, ethnographers find themselves in a world without hidden unexplored physical locations and tribal peoples.

Instead, they are immersed in cultural communities and questions to investigate a variety of motivations from recent technology trends, researched upon the availability of digital sources. Today's ethnographers study communities of identity, social network communities, new media and social reproduction, health and safety behaviours in a mobile world, entrepreneurial practices in IT start-ups, and countless other topics, hoping to gain insight into who we are, where we are going and what it means to be human.

Technology, overall, has unquestionably changed our culture in a myriad of ways in the last 30 years. Information and communications technology (ICT), in particular, has transformed society. Not only has ICT ushered in the information age, but ICT-based technologies have also been instrumental in enabling research, development and growth of technologies in many other fields such as applied science, engineering, health and transport. As such it creates novel opportunities: it gives rise to new markets and challenges existing institutions.

The following section presents the two real-life cases introduced in Chapter 1 with a view to illustrating the much-needed multidisciplinary approach and the ways it connects people, enabled by technology. These cases span from the analogue field, embedded in the high-tech sector, all the way to the cyberconnected world of work, specifically of its making. Yet each focuses on the people who create interconnectivity.

Human Interaction in the World of Zeroes and Ones

What exactly is an anthropologist doing on a military site or in a big data centre?

The first real-life case, SonaConn, introduced in Chapter 1, is a large and complex programme in the expert area of change management in the telecommunication industry in Egypt. As a telecom provider, the enterprise provides digital transformation to millions of organisations and end users, connecting them globally.

The UK-based corporation called for this worldwide implementation of performance drivers (PDs) designed to support managers in developing skills to grow the business across the globe. The skill development process was specifically designed for the challenges faced in the Middle East and North Africa (MENA) market, then under severe attack from new competitors entering this prosperous market.

Although the client's industry is a digital one, the core elements of the programme were delivered in a face-to-face format by a programme consisting of large group events and smaller, highly interactive workshops held on dispersed locations in and outside Cairo. Due to the nature of the delivery format this real-life case thus qualifies as 'traditional'. In addition to the face-to-face delivery mode of the programme, most of the information necessary for the needs analysis upon which the design rested came from face-to-face interviews with key stakeholders and focus group results. Both the needs analysis period and the delivery period required the team to stay on site in Cairo or regularly travel back and forth to their mainly European home destinations, and, as a result, qualifies as multi-sited research.

The previously mentioned start-up MyMemLab is the other real-life case provider. They develop, design and implement mobile development solutions, often using selected elements from gamification, helping to deliver global organisation performance benefits. They are a truly virtual organisation, using shared office spaces in three different European cities; their small team of five to seven experts spread around the world lives a modern nomad lifestyle. MyMemLab are a cloud-based firm, making use of all things virtual. The company aims to become a key player in the mobile learning industry.

HUMAN-TO-HUMAN INTERACTION IN TECH

The nature of the first real-life case, that is, the large and complex project for the purpose of PD implementation in the telecommunication industry in Egypt, required the approach of multi-site research. The key stakeholder groups consisted of:

- the organisation development team in the Cairo headquarters;

- the consultant and facilitator team of the British consulting firm; and

- a group of approximately 1,600 senior and middle managers in the role of participants.

Whilst the nature of the organisation development programme was largely 'analogue', the representatives of the key stakeholder groups were scattered around Europe and MENA region, requiring research in multiple sites.

Known as multi-sited research, this approach offers the opportunity to remove the ethnographer or team of ethnographers from the strong traditional connection to just one group of subjects among whom fieldwork is done and instead to place them within and between groups and locations. Multi-sited research responds to the challenge of combining multi-sited work with the need for in-depth analysis, allowing for a more considered study of social worlds, even the more analogue space.

Whilst this research approach brings with it a number of logistical challenges, it is also necessary to pay close attention to the ambiguities of fieldwork ethics it entails. The multi-sited engagements imply not only interaction with informants across a number of dispersed sites, but also fieldwork by telephone and email, collecting data eclectically from a disparate array of sources, attending carefully to popular cultures, and reading newspapers and official documents. Skills of synthesis may become more important than ever.

In reality, field research never falls simply and neatly into the analogue, or the mulit-sited, or the digital category, but finds its place on a continuum, creating increasing complexity with regard to requirements for the field researcher while involving participation, these days often mass participation, by the client.

THE TOOLBOX

On the SonaConn project, data sources were numerous and geographically dispersed. Multi-site research specifically included the various company sites in Cairo, including sales shops, multi-channel partner shops, offices and call-centres. Beyond the work locations in the Cairo neighbourhood, other sites played a key role in the course of the data collection, such as international airports, home locations of the team working on the project, and of course, the headquarters of the British consulting firm in England.

Whilst the data of this complex project were one of the core sources for the development of the framework of The Three Lenses of Diversity (see Chapter 3 for details), the insights and learning it yielded were among the sources of the model 'Spanning boundaries to meet diverse user needs'.

Let us go step-by-step, first viewing the research flow and specifically the ways the outcomes of the needs analysis from the anthropology toolbox progressed into a complex programme design. The chart below (Figure 9.2) provides an overview of the flow. The collected data were reviewed with the help of tools from cultural anthropology, which included identifying patterns, labelling significant iterations and merging findings into a few selected pilot workshops for the purposes of testing the sense-making process in face-to-face delivery with participants. Findings were continuously evaluated throughout the process.

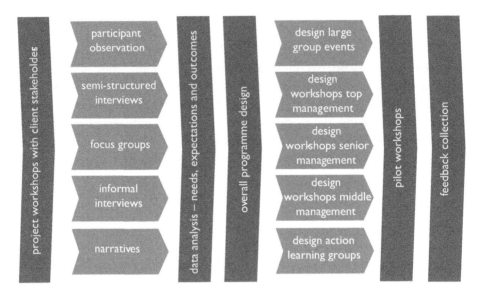

Figure 9.2   Flow for needs analysis

Data,[3] specifically from this complex project for first order findings, included the following: participant observation from 31 days' presence of researcher in Cairo; 27 semi-structured interviews conducted with a range of key stakeholders throughout the needs analysis phase in and outside Cairo; informal interviews with senior management all situated in the Egyptian headquarters; feedback sessions from focus groups; and numerous stories from team members, participants and individuals related but external to the project.[4]

As described in detail in Chapter 2 many of the methods from the anthropology toolbox have made it into the research practice of organisations, specifically, in product development and consumer behaviour. From the list above, most likely, participant observation is lesser known and thus little used in the business world.

---

3   The project and its qualitative data research for the programme architecture started before the events in Egypt in 2011, which obviously have changed the local situation. Nevertheless, the findings on the implications for boundary-spanning still apply.

4   See research details in Chapter 3.

Let us now explore the key insights from the needs analysis outcomes delivered by the anthropology toolbox, which eventually progressed into a complex programme design that met the needs of a diverse participant group in a challenging environment.

In a nutshell, the key success factors of the complex programme were:

- it was delivered on time across geographic and cultural boundaries;

- it met the diverse needs and expectations of participants and key decision-makers;

- the thorough needs analysis led to the model 'Spanning boundaries to meet diverse needs', helpful for future use in international roll-outs.

THE THREE LENSES OF DIVERSITY IN ACTION

The project challenges were many. Had Carolyn and others had The Three Lenses before the project began, some of these challenges could have been predicted and then avoided or more easily dealt with. Table 9.1 below summarises the insights Carolyn derived during their work on the project.

The diverse stakeholder group and the complexity inherent in the many physical sites were as follows:

Stakeholders concerned:

- programme participants;

- decision-makers at SonaConn headquarters and affiliates;

- consulting team, facilitation team and decision-makers at UK headquarters.

Multi-sites were:

- MENA and Cairo sites: client headquarters, affiliate sites, residential sites;

- SonaConn headquarters in UK;

- temporary accommodation in MENA for consulting team;

- international home locations of facilitator team.

The Three Lenses of Diversity helped to organise the challenges. At the same time, the process also showed some boundary-spanning aspects.

Table 9.1   Project challenges organised by the help of The Lens of Multiple Identity

The Lens of Multiple Identity	Challenge	Solution
Appearance	• Different clothing style in public and private identities for men and women	• Regionally appropriate clothing style for consulting team during business day and spare time, guidelines provided by regionally experienced team members
Gender	• Etiquette regarding physical proximity • Female Western leaders working with Middle East predominantly male teams	• Sensitive seating arrangements in workshop rooms • Male and female consultants on team
Generation	• Female leaders and female subject matter experts (see Carolyn) often younger than male Middle East leaders	• Consultants and subject leaders representing different generations
Ethnicity	• Predominantly ethnically homogenous group of participants, but no Arabs on facilitator/consultant team	• Diverse mix of team from across the globe, reflecting many different ethnic backgrounds
Wellbeing and Mobility	• Great stress levels from commuting in Cairo, MENA and internationally • Frequent flight delays, leading to lack of sleep, exhaustion and increase in work-related nervousness • Concern for personal safety	• Change in programme schedule, for example, start on Sunday at lunch time • Change of flight routes and airlines where possible • Choice of hotel with security guards
Sociability	• Alcohol consumption by some of the consulting team	• Consumption of alcohol only in hotel bar where permitted for Westerners • Sub-groups among consulting team formed based on alternative recreational habits, for example, sports or sight-seeing

Communication	• Different communication styles, indirect versus direct communication, lots of simultaneous communication	• Multi-lingual team: some of the team reads, writes and speaks some Arabic, unexpected from Westerners, which serves as an ice-breaker
Geopolitics	• Great temperature difference, up to 30 degrees between indoors and outdoors • History between Great Britain and Middle East	• Regionally appropriate clothing in terms of climatic conditions (many layers) although outdoors up to 50 degrees • Omitting topic altogether and focusing on history of nation states represented on the diverse team
Lifelong learning	• Different learning approaches (discussed in detail in next section)	• Tailoring towards etiquette, content, approaches (see below) • Linking theme among all stakeholders • Incredible willingness to learn helped overcome challenge
Inclusion and Employability	• Staying updated with latest leadership and management approaches and technology trends and developments	• Common theme as a result of management development programme • Integral part of lifelong learning – need to remain employable • Set-up of programme (large group events) enabled all three managerial levels to mingle

Table 9.2   Project challenges organised by the help of The Lens of Perception

Othering	Belonging
• Stereotypes associated with 'typical Westerners', in particular, typical British behaviour disseminated through media and impressions from tourists such as binge drinking, 'half-naked' male and female tourists • Women in facilitator role: younger, more educated women mainly from European countries teaching senior Arabs • Perception about what people in economically developing countries could afford – hesitation to come across as a 'rich Westerner'	• 'Westerners' did not reinforce stereotypes – positive surprises due to diversity within the consultant team; feedback on consultants'/facilitator's diverse mix very positive • Dress appropriately, don't drink alcohol, some speak Arabic • Role models for young female professionals; senior male consultants on team to fulfil expectations • Gradual release of details about travel and lifestyle that accelerated when common ground was found

Table 9.2 provides an overview of challenges organised by using The Lens of Perception. The column labelled 'Othering' captures the differences that created distance, while the column labelled 'Belonging' shows ways of reaching the necessary levels of sameness.

In our summary of The Environmental Lens in Chapter 8 we discussed the demographic, geopolitical and media landscape in which the project took place, with the help of the five scapes:

- the challenges in connection with great heat, sandstorms and infrastructure issues;

- the political conflict in the immediate environment putting the project resourcing and, at times, its delivery, at risk; and

- the superior digital connectedness inherent in the environment, which triggered the project in the first place.

The needs analysis shows that some significant boundary-spanning is required when designing a high-impact programme across technological, social and cultural boundaries. These are the level of etiquette, the level of content and the level of preferred learning styles, as illustrated in Figure 9.3 opposite. Whilst the degree of subtlety or refinement is key to meeting diverse participants' needs, it is the degree of refinement or the quality of the relationship between the interaction partners of the two organisations that enables the degree of programme refinement.

The quality of the relationship between the interaction partners can largely be enhanced through the application of The Three Lenses of Diversity, just as the degree of programme refinement can be defined through the application of the anthropology toolbox.

The first level of boundary-spanning is called Etiquette. On the programme discussed, for example, it referred to the scheduling of breaks at times for prayer, that is, closely related to the movement of the sun.[5] One of many

---

5   For background, the structure of the working day is usually organised around two out of altogether five Muslim prayers, namely dhuhr (noon) and 'asr (late afternoon). They provide a glimpse into the great complexity involved in how prayer organises the business day, sometimes causing abrupt interruptions. Dhuhr is the time for prayer when the sun starts to decline, and 'asr is when the shadow of a thing is twice its own length. As indicated, the timing of the prayer breaks is closely related to the movement of the sun, resulting in a continuous

incidents observed that greatly impacted the interaction among participants and even more so the interaction between participants and team members was the perception of time and time management. Specifically, this found expression in the handling of breaks, comprising several forms such as comfort breaks, lunch breaks and in particular prayer breaks.

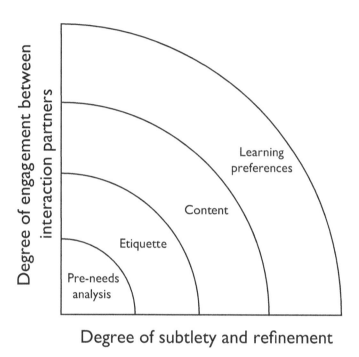

Figure 9.3   Spanning boundaries to meet diverse needs

It also referred to the adaptation of role-playing activities and simulations in accordance with overall touch behaviour and proximity behaviour acceptable in the region. Proximity and touch behaviour becomes critical when conducting activities that includes holding on to each other, such as a communication exercise known as 'leading the blind'. In this activity, one person is supposed to lead a colleague wearing a blindfold around the room. As a consequence of the behaviours described above, facilitators invited participants to team up with a person of the same sex.

change of their times throughout the year, which impacts on the working day. Prayer, the second pillar in Islam, is a fundamental part of Muslim life. It is the physical demonstration of devoutness that expresses unity regardless of where the believer is on this planet. Sites become connected by belief.

The second level of boundary-spanning is called Content Alignment. On the SonaConn project in MENA region, the method of role-playing was met with tremendous resistance. Verbal feedback was, for example, 'we don't want to make fools of ourselves' or 'this isn't any fun'. This feedback was consistent among the first few groups, which finally resulted in dropping the method of role-playing altogether due to the perceived potential loss of face. This feedback demonstrates the interconnectedness between etiquette and content. Content Alignment is the level that aligns content and context in order to meet the programme objective in alignment with the overall business strategy. This level of alignment requires a higher level of engagement from both learning partners.

The third level of boundary-spanning is called Learning Preferences. Overall, the purpose of tailoring to learning preferences is to ensure that the learning is grounded for the individual through the careful selection of appropriate activities and facilitation styles.

The vignette below describes a photo gallery adapted to regional requirements in combination with the approach of storytelling, inviting participants to bring forward their own stories or vision.

Box 9.1   Photo Gallery in Combination with Storytelling

The gallery method aimed to set up an interactive session to introduce the topic of leadership communication. The set-up invited participants to browse through the exhibition-like gallery presenting photos of 49 leaders from business and politics well-known in Europe, America and the Middle East, for example, Mohamed El-Baradei, Bill Clinton, Anita Roddick and Sheikh Hamad bin Khalifa al-Tani. An exploration round of the photo gallery was followed by a discussion with some lead questions drawing on the idiosyncrasies of 'great communicators', held partly in table group discussions and partly in plenary. Following a clarification of 'who's who', mostly about personalities from Western politics and business, participants tended to identify the same small number of 'great communicators' over a large number of sessions.

Noticeably, the lead questions on communication opened up a lively discussion, strongly linking communication with leadership. These discussions were usually held in the local Arabic dialect. In plenary discussion participants presented stories about the individuals' achievements, typically pointing to the specific's person's indispensable contribution to the region and its people. Contributions would cover both political and social efforts, such as those delivered by Bill Clinton and Rania al Abdullah (Queen Rania of Jordan). Significantly, all identified individuals were attributed with special leadership skills. The diverse mix of Western and regional personalities in the gallery invited the participants to share rich stories on communication and leadership.

Box 9.2 Key Learning from the Anthropology Toolbox

- Content and its relevance to participants' specific situations are critical for high-impact learning.

- A combination of method and content is critical when tailoring content to context as participants put their unique footprint on the content.

- Suitability of methods used to present content needs to be viewed through the Etiquette level.

- Learning preferences are linked to organisational and industry culture rather than national culture.

- Learning activities can be redesigned to fit different learning preferences.

In summary, we have reviewed an extensive piece of modern cross-boundary social science fieldwork, requiring some substantial multi-site research approaches. The insights provided by the needs analysis of the large and complex management and leadership development programme come from the use of the anthropology toolbox. The tools are the helpers to identify diverse participants' needs and to tailor the programme across boundaries, specifically, boundaries-related etiquette, the programme content and the specific learning preferences, designed for people who work in technology as enabler in MENA region.

Whilst most of the interactions described above happened in face-to-face space, we need to bear in mind that undertaking them enables the digital transformation to millions of organisations and end users, connecting them globally.

We now move to the next multidisciplinary field, in which human interaction creates connections with technology. In this world, the quality of the relationships between human and tech is key to organisation performance.

Creating Interconnectivity: Human–Tech Interaction

In our daily business routines we are experiencing an unparalleled interconnectedness. We connect with people virtually. We successfully complete complex projects with peers of different technical backgrounds across time zones. We close business deals of great strategic importance for our own organisation, the client and many connected stakeholders.

New ways of interacting with a variety of devices such as computers, tablets and smart-phones making it easier for non-tech people to work with machines on complex tasks are yet another reality in the world of today's work. As with many other aspects of technology, smart-phones have been the forerunner. Ever-increasing interconnectedness drives the need for enterprise collaboration and mobility, providing people anywhere anytime with real-time information, aiming at higher efficiency and productivity. The result is the consumeration of IT in the form of Bring Your Own Device (BYOD), which causes organisations to consider important aspects of data security, employee privacy, employment laws and regulations, and on top of it all, a sound mobility strategy. Most important of all is the excellent user experience (UX) for the successful adoption and dissemination of the application.

THE CYBERFIELD: CREATING EXCELLENT USER EXPERIENCE (UX)

Enterprise collaboration and mobility is key for boosting organisational performance across functional, hierarchical and cultural boundaries. Modern interconnected organisations achieve this through excellent UX of their mobile learning programmes, accelerating learning retention, adopting anticipated behaviour change or changing the organisational culture.

The development of a dislike of adopting new tech is common and often a result of poor usability. This might be as basic as the screen size available to mobile users; this is now being addressed in part by the sheer number of devices with 4-inch screen, or 7-inch tablets. People still carry the original iPad with them on shopping trips to look up bargains, sparing them the reduced user-friendly interfaces more traditional mobile phones entail.

Needs finding is probably the most important part of any human–mobile interaction design arsenal, commonly known as UX. Without it, the design team could spend months designing a solution that completely misses the point, eating up a considerable portion of the project resources.

Multidisciplinary teams bring novel insights into the early stages of the needs analysis. Among them, anthropologists have grasped the importance of technology and actively shape this market driver for differentiation to deliver tangible results in the design process for products and services for all things mobile. The following real-life example illustrates the contributions from the discipline's toolbox.

Succeeding with Mobile Learning presents the development of tailored mobile learning initiatives for A1Guard, a key player in the health and safety industry. For this purpose of design, development and implementation, A1Guard contracted with MyMemLab, an expert consultancy in the mobile learning industry.

A1Guard is one of the key players in the health and safety industry. As part of their broad portfolio of services to the predominantly business to business (B2B) client base, they provide training, learning and development solutions in the health and safety area. The content of their service targets the knowledge needed by highly specialised response teams, but also covers more general health and safety knowledge for industry clients' workforces. In order to stay competitive they now aim to transform some of their learning programmes from the traditional paradigm of classroom learning and practical workshops to mobile learning services, specifically apps, seizing opportunities such as:

- gaining competitive advantage over other players in the industry by offering innovative products and services;

- learning more about A1Guard customers, their behaviours and specifically their learning progress;

- developing informed learners and users;

- increasing reputation and community participation;

- turning users into brand ambassadors;

- inducing further consumption of other A1Guard services.

Creating an excellent UX is key for embracing technology in organisations. Organisations have to ensure that their mobile learning and development apps and applications stand out from the crowd in terms of providing a tailored, effective and efficient learning experience for their staff, that they involve people's emotions, and as a result drive the change anticipated in people's behaviour – both internal and external clients.

MyMemLab suggested a proper needs assessment of the mobile learning environment within A1Guard's market segment. They also conducted a thorough quantitative and qualitative analysis of how A1Guard could best deliver the requisite knowledge to the diverse target audience to ensure alignment with their learning preferences, their work approach and their familiarity with all things mobile. For the latter, they relied on specialist tools from the anthropology toolbox.

Based upon formal feedback, the A1Guard learning and development director and his team were surprised at how much they learned about the future users, especially considering:

- the identity portfolio of the audience;

- the way they understood learning; and

- the extended use of the learning tool beyond the traditional learning environment, that is, in the field.

WHAT LIES AT THE HEART OF GOOD USER EXPERIENCE (UX)?

Whilst the measurement of quantitative data has become common in the specialist area of UX in educational game design, the measurement of qualitative data is still rare. Qualitative data research concentrates on the user reactions and emotions of potential design elements, particularly how people feel about an element and, even more importantly, why they feel what they feel. These key questions can be properly investigated by the use of the tools from the anthropology toolbox. Specifically, user diaries, participant observation and in-depth interviews are indispensable aids for creating excellent UX. The three steps are:

- Step 1: Understanding the user's traditional space, what work routines look like, what displayed behaviours are, and how users act, interact and react.

- Step 2: Understanding how people respond to application mock-ups[6] and prototypes, what feelings they show, what their narrative of their emotions and motivation is.

- Step 3: Testing the application with end users in their environment, what the displayed reactions are, and what observable displays of motivation and behaviour change there are.

Understanding the users' sense of the world is paramount for the developer team to start asking the right questions. A diverse team of social researchers and technologists is considered to be the best way forward.

THE TOOLBOX

User Diaries or User Logs

The User Log is a type of diary that the future users keep over a defined period in order to record their experience and their impressions in their daily contexts. Details as to what, when and how the recording should be done will be agreed upon with the client. These diaries can be created through handwritten notes, photo-shots or the use of apps. Depending on the digital literacy of the diary loggers, we suggest that future users make use of digital aids, for example, selected user-friendly apps, for ease in the recording process and for assistance with the subsequent data analysis and the connected sense-making process conducted by the researcher. For A1Guard the findings from the User Logs were used to set up the next step, that is, participation observation.

Participant observation

As portrayed earlier, participant observation describes the process of gathering data about the daily routines of users, in which the anthropologist takes on a role in the social situation under observation. It is about taking the user's understanding of how the world works and using the experience to model a broader understanding in order to theorise about what these experiences mean. For the A1Guard research this meant taking on the role of participant in classroom training and in the simulation of emergency response situations, risk levels permitting.

---

6   A mock-up is a full-sized scale model of a structure, used for demonstration, study or testing.

Box 9.3   Step-by-Step Analysis of the Future User Group with the Help of The Three Lenses of Diversity

Step 1 **The Lens of Multiple Identity**

The needs assessment at AI Guard showed that a significant proportion of the industry workforce users were males in their 40s who were experiencing first age-related wellbeing issues.

Their lifelong learning approach was mainly traditional classroom context, perceived as fun, and for the purpose of building camaraderie and for overall socialising. Many of the future users needed further training as a consequence of a career change.

The Lens of Perception

Learning on mobile devices was new to the selected test user group; they associated smart-phones with their teenage kids and the hours they spend on social media networks and playing games.

The Environmental Lens

Their work habitat ranged from high-tech office buildings to emergency scenes. In any case, extreme conditions such as great heat or cold were symptomatic. Therefore, devices needed to be operable under these circumstances, and/or they require gadgets delivered with them in order to handle the device safely.

Step 2 **Based on the first insights of Step 1: Select future users to observe**

The goal is to observe only a few individuals and the successes, breakdowns, and latent opportunities that occur when devices are used, not used or could be used to support the chosen activity. Get permission to participate in an assignment. It is important to coordinate with the future users to select a time that will be rich for observations.

Select an activity to observe

On the assumption that you design an interface for a task that doesn't yet exist on a device, it is essential to observe users doing the task as they do it now, for example, learning as in classroom facilitation.

For the AI Guard assignment this meant participating in the traditional learning setting; the use of mobile applications and handling of devices was trialled.

Step 3 Observe!

> During the observation, in addition to taking notes, use digital photographs or sketches to document activities, where permitted. These photos and sketches are meant to document the actual observations.
>
> On the A1Guard assignment the research team spent some 10 to 15 minutes after the observations interviewing the future users about the activity observed.

Summarise the findings of Steps 1, 2 and 3 straight after the observations. Reflect on them with the research team and develop a set of first ideas of opportunities for design innovation. This stage is not about finding solutions yet: the focus is only on user needs and goals. An example of a need might be 'When Pavel gets off the truck he has to wear safety gloves. Sometimes Pavel has to look up material specifications on the smart-phone or tablet. When he does this, he must be wearing gloves.'

Based on these findings, follow up with in-depth interviews.

In-depth interviews

In-depth interviews consist of a list of questions and topics to be covered in the interview. Despite the structure there is a quality of free flow, which allows the anthropologist to follow new leads and to discover potential learning needs among the user group. It involves going back and forth to users, not just to hear their narrative but also to listen to their re-interpretation and to revise their narrative.

In the example of A1Guard, the researchers followed up the insights distilled from the identity portfolio by the use of in-depth interviews. For example, they addressed the age-related wellbeing issues. They asked important questions such as: 'How can we make the interface itself easier for this specific user group?' As a result, A1Guard decided to have interfaces developed that avoided unnecessary overstrain for eyes.

Clearly, overstraining eyes impacts one's concentration levels, and, as result, impairs retention levels and thus the learning outcome, which in turn impacts the anticipated behaviour change in risk situations.

Tech is more about people and their diverse needs than about the product. It is easy to be awed by advances in technology that bring us unprecedented access to powerful tools and resources. The framework of The Three Lenses of Diversity is the foundation for the identification of diverse user needs, their readiness to adopt new tech and the environment in which they will apply it (see Figure 9.4). It serves as a roadmap to gain deeper knowledge about the user group.

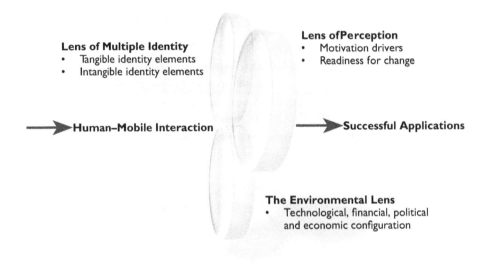

Lens of Multiple Identity
- Tangible identity elements
- Intangible identity elements

Lens of Perception
- Motivation drivers
- Readiness for change

➤**Human–Mobile Interaction**

➤**Successful Applications**

The Environmental Lens
- Technological, financial, political and economic configuration

Figure 9.4   Identifying diverse user needs

Academic Background

When transformation is introduced in organisations it tends to raise resistance, anxiety and, unknown outcomes. Although each approach presented below has been used for years or centuries or is even innate to mankind, each in its unique application is special to decision-makers in their industries. Decision-makers in the mobile application industries are still unfamiliar with most of the anthropology toolbox, specifically with participant observation, as were decision-makers in the telecoms industry with storytelling.

Participant observation has been covered throughout this book; we will simply summarise its benefits and challenges at the end of this section. The remaining concept now is storytelling, and more specifically, organisational business storytelling.

ORGANISATIONAL BUSINESS STORYTELLING

When did you last listen to a story or read an exciting blog? What stories develop in your head when you look at a stunning picture on an image-sharing site? What do you picture when you read the following story?

Box 9.4   An Indian Story

There is an Indian story – at least I heard it as an Indian story – about an Englishman who, having been told that the world rested on a platform which rested on the back of an elephant which rested in turn on the back of a turtle, asked … What did the turtle rest on? Another turtle. And that turtle? 'Ah, Sahib, after that it is turtles all the way down.'*

* Geertz 1973:29.

Storytelling has long been a feature of human societies, groups and organisations. We told each other stories long before we could read and write. Stories are narratives with characters, plots and twists which are full of meaning. While some stories may be pure fiction, others are inspired by real events. Stories entertain, inform, advise, warn and educate. They often pass moral judgements on events, casting their characters in roles as hero, villain, fool and victim. They are capable of stimulating strong emotions of enthusiasm, courage, loyalty and belonging, as well as sympathy, support, determination and empathy.

Organisational storytelling strongly builds on social science studies such as cultural anthropology and is often referred to 'Narrative Knowledge'. Stories serve as vehicles for enhancing organisational communication, performance and learning, as well as the management of change. There can be little doubt that, in the hands of imaginative leaders and educators, stories are powerful devices for creating and managing meaning.

Overall, when storytelling is skilful and authentic, it can be used to lead downwards, upwards and sideways in a variety of organisational hierarchical settings. It can be used to achieve a variety of purposes, including sparking action, communicating who you are, transmitting the brand, identifying the business strategy, sharing knowledge, getting collaboration, transmitting values, taming the grapevine, leading people into the future or shaping the behaviours necessary for success.

Stories can open windows into the cultural, political and emotional lives of organisations, allowing individuals to express deep and sometimes hidden or conflicting emotions. Organisational learning hence takes place in a number of ways:

- by placing oneself at the centre of the story making sense of these experiences, whether challenging or successful;

- by studying the stories that people tell about each other and about the organisation as a whole;

- by noting the ability to create stories for group cohesion or for relieving excessive stress and tension; and

- by expressing in a non-threatening way views and feelings which may be unacceptable in straight talk.

By collecting stories in a particular organisation, by listening and comparing different accounts, by investigating how narratives are constructed around specific events, by examining which events in an organisation's history generate stories and which ones fail to do so, we gain access to deeper organisational realities, closely linked to their members' experiences.

The success of social media platforms rests on storytelling, by recounting one's experiences in story-like or image-based forms and by following others' stories. Organisational storytelling has become an increasingly popular learning method, which allows eliciting the culture of an organisation and recording otherwise tacit knowledge about the organisation. In the cyberconnected world of work this includes company wikis, intranets, blogs or microblogging services such as Twitter.

PARTICIPANT OBSERVATION

Participant observation has been dealt with before in Chapter 2. All that is needed now is a summary of its benefits and challenges. The benefits are as follows:

- it immerses the project team in participants' and users' lives and enables a relationship to develop with research participants over the period of study;

- it captures behaviour in the different contexts of everyday life and helps to reveal unarticulated needs;

- it places a human face on data through real-life stories that people can relate to and remember;

- it allows emotional behaviour to be captured;

- by carrying out research on the everyday life environments of participants, it helps to identify discrepancies between what people say they do and what they actually do.

The challenges are as follows:

- the outcome is uncontrollable, and this uncertainty creates anxiety among decision-makers in organisation;

- the research question must be developed based on the individual situation rather being pre-fabricated;

- the necessary open-endedness often hampers buyer decisions by organisation change makers.

Embracing Digital Transformation

Building interconnectivity in today's cyberconnected world, in the attempt to embrace digital transformation, requires the acknowledgment and inclusion of diverse people's needs. The companies in both life cases create and innovate technology for others to use and adopt. Both creators and adopters must closely interconnect tech with human behaviour. Face-to-face and cyber-interactions are at the heart of effective work-based relationships.

This in turn necessitates transformation initiatives to span boundaries across technological, cultural and social silos. As illustrated in Chapter 7 on the mobilisation approach, this happens best through people and their engagement. Value-adding client-centric products and services are usually the result of accountability and co-creation.

Many of the business models in place are still too rooted back in the industrial age. They promote 'great' leaders, are largely silo-dominated and connected revenue generation models such as hours times money are not sustainable.

Embracing digital transformation requires boundary-spanning capabilities, developed by everyone in the enterprise or organisation, such as:

- boundary-spanning facilitation to create direction, alignment and commitment across boundaries in service of superior performance;

- enabling collaboration by more deeply focusing on human relationships and identity – moving from 'human doing' to 'human being';

- design thinking for a sustainable future in a cyberconnected world through the holistic form of understanding, analysis and issue solving and, as a result, shaping the emerging notion of human-centred design.

Chapter 10

Focusing on the Human Perspective within the Big Data Hype

Chapter 9 concentrates solely on the application of The Three Lenses of Diversity in service of organisation development. Specifically, technology-induced implementation developed in co-creation with anthropological practices is discussed with the aim of engaging diverse user groups. It describes how the anthropological toolbox provides the basis for a thorough needs analysis, which allows diverse people's needs to be met, in turn creating superior interconnectivity.

Chapter 10 covers the value people's multiple identities have and illustrates the emerging need for a more human-centred design of applications, achieved through the application of The Three Lenses of Diversity. The second part of the chapter focuses on the challenges ahead of organisation development in the cyberconnected world of work, revisiting co-creation in service of superior organisation performance by putting the human first. The third part of the chapter summarises the unique offering of this book and its benefits for achieving superior performance in today's and the future world of work.

Big Data – Big Hype

Big data stands for the massive amount of large data sets generated by the technology available at our fingertips, aggregated and made easily accessible. In the midst of the recent hype about big data, we need to recognise the personal, psychological, social and commercial value of the identities that people more or less voluntarily contribute to this hype. The growth in the collection and use of personal data can have benefits for individuals, organisations and government, by offering greater insights through data analysis and the development of more targeted and effective services. Identities can unify people and can be regarded as a valuable resource for promoting positive social interaction.

Nevertheless, this growth in the amount of available data has the potential for criminal exploitation or misuse. As big data predictions become more accurate, society may use them to punish people for predicted behaviours and associated crimes that they have not yet committed (Mayer-Schoeneberger, Cukier 2013:192) but that have been assigned to them based on algorithms. Even under the premise of the ethical and meaningful use of databases, there are famous examples of big data predictions that have gone terribly wrong. At the time this book was being written, Facebook hilariously debunked a Princeton study claiming that it would lose 80 per cent of its users by 2015–2017. In turn, Facebook data scientists turned the study's silly 'correlation equals causation' methodology of tracking Google search volume against Princeton, to show the university would lose all of its students by 2021.[1]

Enterprises and organisations have been mining large datasets with increasingly sophisticated tools for decades, but too often the business impact of these explorations has been relatively small-scale. Their initial aim was simply to prove the value of data mining and discovery. Whilst formerly, close-enough predictions were good-enough predictions, enterprises and organisations want more than that now. Big data can discover patterns and correlations in data that offer novel and invaluable insights, but it cannot provide insights as to why something is happening. With this lack of the ability to illustrate causation, big data needs a refreshed view of decision-making, anticipated outcomes, purpose and value to clients.

Qualitative research is about observing individual people, investigating their behaviours in specific situations such as working through an online course. It complements quantitative data (known as big data), which simply measures hard facts such as speed, acceleration or turning. Both types of data are necessary to make informed decisions about potential for the design of learning initiatives that assist people in adopting positive behaviour change.

Small data is the best method for mapping unknown territory. When organisations want to know what they do not already know, they need small data because it gives something that big data explicitly hardly offers: inspiration.

---

1   http://techcrunch.com/2014/01/23/facebook-losing-users-princeton-losing-credibility/.

SMALL DATA – THE NEXT BIG THING

> *Where is the information? Lost in the data.*
> *Where is the data? Lost in the #@&%! database! (Celko 1999)*

No doubt, 2013 was the year of big data. However, small data now cuts through the hype of big data, yielding improved quality of information contained in the data by uncovering the causality of people's behaviour. For illustration, we will use an example from the education sector, namely the course completion rates of Massive Open Online Courses (MOOCs).

Studies show that investors pumped $3.6 billion into big data start-ups[2] and simultaneously shaped mature industries. For example, the advertising industry: website owners can now more precisely understand who their clients are and better estimate the characteristics of website visitors through patterns revealed by big data. Media companies such as WordPress learn about people's age, gender, income, lifestyle characteristics and interests. All of this presents essential information for real-time advertising and the underlying trading industry competing for the most adequate slots in the shortest possible time.

The healthcare industry is also clamouring for access to the massive quantities of information produced by and about people and their interactions in connection with their wellbeing issues. Hospital and pharmacy data, smart-phones, tablets and wearables that end consumers use to track, for example, pulse, skin temperature or sugar levels can be analysed for previously invisible correlations and patterns, which in turn allows for better procedures or provides indications for necessary behaviour change. In aggregate, the data institutes what works best, and at the individual level also aims to improve quality of life.

As mentioned above, another example would be the education sector, which is undergoing an unparalleled change. MOOCs have rapidly revolutionised the education landscape, to the concern of the established academic organisations. MOOCs attract millions of students, enabling providers to analyse user data and to experiment with different features.

The amount of data collected on platforms like Coursera, iversity or Standford Online is unmatched. Analysts see every mouse click and keystroke. They know if a user clicks one answer and then selects another, or fast-forwards through part of a video.

---

2 http://smalldatagroup.com 11 December 2013.

They are using that data to explore how to customise and enhance students' learning experiences through mining the large datasets available at their fingertips with increasingly sophisticated tools.

THE HUMAN-CENTRIC APPROACH

However, the anticipated business impact of these explorations, namely the increase of course completion rates, has been relatively small-scale.

The shortcomings of this effort remind us of some important issues:

- big data is not clean; and

- data is not the same as information.

These facts take us to some important questions:

- What do people who generate all this data really do?

- What are the causes of their behaviour?

In response to these questions, focusing on just a few individuals can be extraordinarily valuable. Recognising the value of small data helps us better understand customer needs today, transforming transactions into relationships.

Box 10.1   Small Data Putting a Human Face on Big Data

Small data is the close look at small samples. Small data is individuals in their environment doing everyday stuff that is meaningful to them. Small data comes from the application of research techniques from the social sciences, in particular from anthropology, such as participant observation and in-depth interviews, whose findings, once written up, are known as ethnography.

What exactly can ethnography deliver for the sense-making process of big data? The insights data analysts can take away to customise the learning experience and raise course completion rates are:

- The first thing to understand is that the ethnographer *immerses [him or herself] in the students' lives,* developing a relationship with the students over the period of study. The researcher learns about the context where the student learns and the potential barriers this environment brings. For example, in areas with low internet access, is the student facing any physical risk when trying to reach the WiFi-equipped place of study?

- Ethnography places *a human face on data* through real-life stories. It allows the capturing of emotional behaviour. The ethnographer can capture displayed behaviours during online sessions, which helps to reveal unarticulated needs. Can the student actually work a keyboard? Why does the student click away from the course page? Does the student understand the site navigation? What external causes make them take a break?

- By carrying out research into the everyday life environments of participants, it helps to identify discrepancies between *what people say they do* and *what they actually do.* Observing and interviewing based upon the observations helps to uncover the causality of displayed behaviours.

Small data insights are essential for creating meaning out of patterns in big data.

Data is simply a record of events that took place: what happened where and when, and who was involved. Big data is an outcome of an ongoing process; in reality, it is never raw. Qualitative work puts it into perspective and provides us with insights about what people's motivation drivers really are. Thus, ethnographic significance should be integrated as a complement in collaboration with statistical significance.

INSIGHTS FROM THE THREE LENSES OF DIVERSITY

The strategic framework, The Three Lenses of Diversity, provides substantial insights into otherwise submerged issues such users' intangible identity elements, their approach to the adoption of learning and the challenges the environment potentially brings. Innate to the application of the anthropology toolbox, the issues emerge during research through coding and sense-making of the findings. Table 10.1 below summarises some of the pressing issues.

Table 10.1   Insights from The Three Lenses of Diversity

The Lens of Multiple Identity	Big data processing easily recognises many of the identity elements of large, mostly anonymous user group identity maps. Widely available analytics tools provide statistics on, for example, gender, generation, ethnicity and level of income. In what way do tangible elements such Gender and Ethnicity impact course completion rates? In contrast, many aspects of the identity maps remain unexplored. A user's wellbeing raises a number of important questions in connection with anticipated completion rates. Which wellbeing issues help or hamper access to participation in a MOOC? Specifically, Wellbeing consists of: <ul><li>Physical aspects such as the capability to work with a computer, e. g. motor skills; and</li><li>Non-physical aspects such as work–life balance which provide the necessary resources for the completion of a course.</li></ul>
The Lens of Perception	In what way do issues connected with self-views and appraisal impact performance? <ul><li>The change from face-to-face to virtual learning approaches;</li><li>The capability to create a sense of commonness with fellow students online in order to overcome the feeling of isolation (Belonging);</li><li>The contribution to a culture of engagement: Can I speak up? What impact does my contribution have? Will people laugh at me? Can I give and receive peer feedback? Is my English or Spanish (or whatever the language of the MOOC is) good enough?;</li><li>The approach to planning and organising the workload, which is typically culturally loaded;</li><li>The lack of role models among faculty to mirror the diversity among learners: most hero tutors are white male Westerners – what message does that disseminate?</li></ul>
The Environmental Lens	All of the five scapes come into play in the course of the analysis of the unsatisfactory completion rates of MOOCs. <ul><li>Students in places with a less-developed infrastructure face difficulties with internet access, which are often connected with;</li><li>Power interests expressed by politics leading into a web of safety and infrastructure challenges affecting individual situations, for example not being able to get to a learning place equipped with WiFi safely;</li><li>The need for sharing one computer or device with a group of people due to socioeconomic circumstances and the stress levels in connection with these circumstances; and</li><li>The socioeconomic disparities from the environment hamper the democratisation of education through MOOCs, once lauded as the purveyors of equality.</li></ul>

Brand leaders and decision-makers of the marketing, healthcare and education industries and beyond need to realise that data is only as valuable as the insights they can extract from it. Only the context and the meaning contributed from qualitative research transform data into information and finally into knowledge that will help them understand customer needs so they can design better products and services to give them the necessary competitive edge.

Anthropologists – The New Rock Stars

Anthropologists are receiving unparalleled attention at the intersection between the human perspective and technology in its current use and further development. At a time of heated debate on the value of humanities, major companies are hiring anthropologists like never before.

ARMCHAIR AND PITH HELMET GO MOBILE

Just 100 years ago ethnographers tramped through bushes and jungles to research exotic people and cultures; their research typically resulted in a monograph, a comprehensive study of a culture at a particular place and time captured in writing. The days of the imperialist pith helmet and leather-embroidered notebooks provided with a glass inkwell and pen are long gone.

Within just the last few years anthropologists and ethnographers have begun not only to research digital communities, but also actively to shape the domain, to the extent that nowadays they are celebrated as the next generation of rock stars, for example, in the role of data scientist, for the critical sense-making process of big data. IT is driving much of the transformation of our changing world. Every industry is now software-driven; as such, every company must adopt IT as one of its core competencies.

Forward-looking anthropologists are recognising IT as a strategic asset with which they can renew vital aspects of their research; how enterprises and organisations shape, redesign and produce things, how they create and manage new commercial transactions, and how they are beginning to collaborate at unprecedented levels both internally and with customers and suppliers. Digital efforts are the key to how companies innovate and expand their business.

For value generation in the big data world, enterprises need data scientists. The data scientist's role has been labelled as one of the 'sexiest jobs' of current and future times, and anthropologists are in the pool. Although the sexiness might be overstated, it raises two questions: what are the responsibilities of a data scientist, in particular, one with a social science background, and how do organisations benefit from them?

It is important to understand that data scientists are more than just re-branded business analysts. Their competencies comprise distinctive knowledge, a set of skills and behaviours, which distinguish them from their quantitative counterparts. These highly educated experts operate at the frontier of analytics with data sets so large and complex that less-skilled analysts using traditional tools cannot make sense of them. In their role of scientist, they test theories by exploring and running experiments with data. They also design the intricate models, algorithms and visualisations that help organisation developers distil insights from huge volumes of messy data. For the latter they need to be good communicators, as they need to educate and influence decision-makers in the value-creation process from big data. Now that senior decision-makers see the potential value that data scientists can bring to the business, expectations are high. The skill set needed is diverse. Yet rock stars at the peak of their popularity are often subject to crisis. Clearly, finding one person who can fill all these expectations and more will be difficult.

CROSS-BOUNDARY INTEGRATION

To deliver on those expectations, data scientists are going to have to work in new ways and with new colleagues, and demonstrate that they can 'move things'. Since it is nearly impossible to find all the skills and competencies needed in one person, organisations seek to create problem-solving teams consisting of a mix of quantitative and qualitative scientists. Ideally, this type of team understands diverse client needs and expectations in order to develop data-derived new products, services and features, aiming to win and retain clients and end users. To get these large-scale benefits, data scientists need to get out of their isolated corners and collaborate across boundaries. The synthesis of boundary-spanning skills among the team increases the market share and boosts performance.

The Upside-Down World of Organisation Development

Organisation development today lies in the hands of many different stakeholders in the organisation. Today's most innovative organisations leverage the feedback of internal and external people for the purpose of their development. Key to people inclusion are:

- the culture of the organisation and the extent of its participatory approach;

- the channels made available and their successful integration towards interconnecting with internal and external stakeholders.

In the industrial age it was the 'great leaders' who were given credit for leading and supporting the improvement of an organisation's visioning, empowerment and problem-solving, in brief, its overall performance and effectiveness. Today it is still the senior functions that are charged with organisation development, such as the Strategy Chief, the Head of Business Development, the Chief Technical Officer or the Human Resource Director. Innovative organisations understand that organisation development is charged by the creativity, engagement and resourcefulness of their internal and external stakeholders, powered through the meaningful integration of modern technology.

Independent of the understanding and approach towards organisations' development, today's enterprises are exposed to a number of drivers that impact their performance and effectiveness improvement efforts. These are as follows:

- The decline of higher education grows the importance of lifelong learning: the rise of tuition fees as a consequence of the economic downturn, the economic necessity for students to work parallel jobs, the increase of adjunct faculty, and above all, the overall decline of standards cause organisations to increasingly take over responsibilities of which formal education was formerly in charge.

- Both the increasing social plurality reflected inside and outside the organisation and the rise of individualism within call for greater collaboration skills among people so that organisations can operate and create value within and from the current and future global challenges.

- The increasing speed and connectivity of IT systems has resulted in increasingly connected stakeholders and accelerated action as a consequence of the faster dissemination of information through social media, all of which demands technologically advanced interactions with organisations. In turn, organisations need to give people a voice.

These drivers impact change and thereby expectations. Understanding the world of employees, clients or users is synonymous with acknowledging their coexisting, overlapping and often contradictory identities, their views of the world and the environment around them. This understanding, in turn, addresses the emerging need for a more human-centred design in all aspects of organisation development. Human-centred design can only be achieved by making end users into co-creators.

CO-CREATION AS TREASURE HUNT IN ORGANISATION DEVELOPMENT

In Chapter 8, we illustrated co-creation as a form of collaboration producing technology-induced yet human-centred solutions for organisations to leverage opportunities to successfully connect with internal and external stakeholders. Illustrated by the MyMemLab case, we discussed the co-creation process, consisting of the following steps: identification, design, delivery and evaluation, for whose success boundary-spanning competencies are indispensable.

In the cyberconnected world of work defined by rapid change, the search for solutions to societal and environmental challenges has become complex. Whilst market systems have become interconnected and supply chains have turned into supply webs, traditional approaches captured in public policy and industry norms are not changing at the speed needed to meet those challenges. As a result, there are increasingly inadequate tools to govern our societies.

Co-creation brings together specialists who have never before worked together to collaborate and generate new solutions, addressing pressing global challenges. Academics, social entrepreneurs, industry specialists, and games and application designers come together to explore the ways in which new approaches can help improve the lives of groups who are often marginalised when their identity maps do not correspond with the appraisal of the majority culture, for example, illness and poverty.

Figure 10.1   Organisation development through co-creation

The co-creation triangle shown in Figure 10.1, first introduced in Chapter 8, illustrates the partner organisations plus the recipients turned co-creators.

Future user groups come in many different roles: potential customers in emerging and developing markets for future profit generation or multiplicators in the change-making process for the social good.

Organisation development through co-created innovation has its specific focus on:

- the holistic form of understanding, analysis and problem-solving;

- the emerging notion of human-centred design brought into our consciousness; and

- the use of design methodologies that address all of our important inquiries.

Through participation and immersion in the field and dialogue with future users, recipients become active co-creators shaping the solution to their own needs, expectations and cultural expertise.

To date, most conventional design methodologies consider the needs of humans as an input but not as the purpose of the design, much less involving them in the process. Besides the superior quality of the product or service achieved through co-creation, the process has significant impact on organisation development of the enterprises and organisations involved:

Innovation

Co-creation transcends traditional boundaries to build transformative partnerships that truly create new value, driven by original, groundbreaking ideas. Although innovation does not necessarily involve something entirely new, it may consist of new products, processes or collaboration models.

What is innovative:

- The origin of the cultural immersion adventure: through cooperation with a UK-based tech partner to design a technology-induced learning programme for the local micro-entrepreneurs, a need for funding arose. In cooperation, the partners identified the tours as an income source; they changed the format from occasional event upon inquiry to unique offering tailored to the needs and expectations for changemakers, NGO representatives and anyone interested in local social issues rather than the beaten path of glitzy tourism.

- Increased engagement of local partners: the result is increased awareness of the mechanisms of local social issues.

- Generation of new jobs in Europe and Asia: translators, tour guides, helpers, marketing people.

- Opportunity to attract new clients: tourists who wish to learn about the value chain of products which arrive in Europe, for example, clothing.

- Revenue generation for the social good: local micro-entrepreneurs benefit directly and can tell their story.

**Box 10.2   Social Entrepreneurs Turning Field
                    Trip Specialists**

A social entrepreneur mainly operating in a remote rural area in Cambodia, whose mission is to eradicate poverty, promote progress and social development via financial inclusion and microfinance, just started offering a cultural immersion adventure trip. This sustainable type of tourism is designed for Western tourists interested in development work who wish to contribute to the social good. This unique cultural immersion is off the typical tourist track, as travellers get the opportunity to witness all levels of the value chain, from the bright lights of the capital city Phnom Penh to the rural communities in the beautiful countryside. They visit the communities that are working together to tackle social issues and engage with micro-entrepreneurs who have overcome poverty and thereby the risk of exploitation.

Social and market impact

Co-creation has a powerful influence on society – positively and directly impacting the lives of people or their environment. The outcome has clear potential for scale and replication, to transform industries and markets. Ideally, it simultaneously demonstrates the creation of economic value and competitive advantage for the for-profit partners involved in the collaboration. From a business perspective, social entrepreneurs typically focus on market failures. They create products, services and solutions for people who are not served by traditional markets, which in collaboration presents a great opportunity for both types of organisations. More market impact is as follows:

- marketing channels through tech partners in market places unreachable for the social entrepreneurs; and

- funding and promotion channels entirely unexplored to date, such as crowdfunding, used for reach and for community-building.

Sustainability

Sustainability in the co-creation model is manifold. There should be a clear plan for reaching long-term goals and for securing financial backing. For the long-term perspective of the collaboration this goes beyond the current financing of the work, and should present a plan to finance it in the future. In co-creation, sustainability means that:

- the businesses run without the reliance on philanthropic donations or aid for core funding;

- projects represent a high stake such as a new market, as they often spark in the place of the root cause;

- cost savings or a clear competitive advantage ensures the highest commitment of the involved organisations over time.

INTERACTION MODEL

The quality of the interaction established between the partnering organisations is key to the success of the co-creation venture. How does it go beyond a traditional partnership? In what ways does the interaction transform the partnering organisations and their employees and leaders with a view to creating a new vision, new management and collaboration practices, new skills and new organisational structures?

Potential benefits from the interaction model include the ability to:

- turn traditional business logic upside-down;

- hold the cost of the solution to an absolute minimum;

- operate on a shoestring budget; and

- work with an extreme 'client-focus'.

Besides bringing value to organisation development, co-creation shapes the thinking that helps us build our global and sustainable future as a species. Above all, co-creation is much faster than traditional ways of identifying promising new products and services, and is less costly as well. Even in the early days of co-creation, the cost of Hilti's Lead User process was found to be approximately 50 per cent below that of the product concept generation methods previously used by European manufacturer of products and materials used in construction. Also, the elapsed time from start to final agreement was approximately half that of the conventional approach[3] (Herstatt, Von Hippel 1992:13).

THE CHANGING PERSPECTIVE OF PEOPLE DEVELOPMENT

As products and services, markets and thereby organisations become more complex, the value of people's specialised knowledge, skills and displayed behaviours increases. In light of the drivers impacting performance and effectiveness improvement efforts, namely the decline of higher education, the increase of social plurality and unprecedented technology developments, organisations need to review existing and more traditional formats of people development. The boundaries between formal and non-formal education, and highly individual learning and development initiatives have become increasingly blurred and will intersect even more.

Lifelong learning as an identity element will likely gain importance, reshaping and impacting people's own identity maps and thereby informing relationship-building efforts. One integral component of lifelong learning is the discovery process of learning and development offerings.

---

3   See Chapter 8 for the origins of co-creation.

More recent formats of lifelong learning include open learning, such as open source, open science, open data, open access, open education – MOOCs have been discussed at length as one offering. This will challenge people to take control of their own education and continuous development, to determine their own personal learning objectives, to contribute to the development of the curriculum, to reflect on their progress, to learn new digital skills and to take a leadership or participant role in the virtual classroom. It typically provides people with the opportunity to connect with colleagues from different countries and professions and to better understand where areas of interests overlap and where unexpected distinctions exist.

At the same time formal functions in organisation development should support people's discovery journeys, exploring the appropriate ways forward, other channels are of equal significance. Organisational storytelling has become an increasingly popular learning method which allows elicitation of the culture of an organisation and recording of otherwise tacit knowledge about the organisation. In the cyberconnected world of work this includes company wikis, intranets, blogs, or microblogging services such as Twitter. For some, when carefully selected and tailored, gamification can be a boost for stakeholder engagement.

The digital icing on the cake of people's identity portfolio is continuously becoming a key ingredient for identity expression. Digital literacy is essential to enable people to make full use of computing and the internet to express their identities, and to connect with social media, services and information. A key issue for future organisation performance will be to ensure adequate levels of technological literacy across all stakeholder groups. As hyper-connectivity increases, people need to have a well-developed level of technological literacy to be able to express their identity online effectively and to manage different aspects of their online presence safely. To enable this, communications technology and computer skills must be taught to a quality standard with a well-informed perspective on what level of skills will be needed in the future. Ensuring these skills are taught properly will also be critical for the workplace, as IT proficiency will be of growing importance for employers. In practice, the benefits will not be realised without a substantial investment in the education of a trained workforce.

Table 10.2 below presents the impacts the drivers have on organisation development and offers actions companies can take to meet the challenges posed by the drivers.

Table 10.2   Actions to meet the challenges posed by drivers impacting organisation performance

Drivers	Actions
The decline of higher education	The need for organisations to invest in continuous development: skills such as the competence to work with and through other people, including sensitivity to particular situations and flexibility in adopting the most appropriate style. They include analytic thinking such as processing knowledge and data, determining cause and effect, organising data and plans, conceptual thinking and communication skills. With the proliferation of devices, progressive organisations will invest in people's digital literacy, empowering them to curate their online identities and protect themselves by understanding how personal information online can be cross-referenced and used.
The increase in social plurality and the rise in indivualism	The provision of a more person-centred approach to diversity and inclusion in order to succeed in today's cyberconnected world. As people are more frequently working for several organisations for reasons of self-actualisation or economic need, it is increasingly important for organisations to become attractive employers; this can be displayed by accommodation, appreciation and respect for diverse needs. There is an increase in the significance of task-focused collaboration, clear goals, rules and required skills, with simultaneous recognition of reduced loyalty due to multiple workplaces.
The increasing speed and connectivity of IT systems	The transition from traditional to mobile learning development, with the recognition and legitimisation of the need for human contact. With face-to-face management development programmes set to become a luxurious segment offering, the need for the appropriate balance between offerings is paramount. With a view to the multitude of online offerings organisation development is adopting the role of researcher, coach and integrator ensuring the needs for people development in alignment with the achievement of the organisation's superior performance.

The trend towards continuous online development and, for example, people's MOOC performance is subject to availability to online recruiters, taking advantage of the kind of information that big data allows. These are fine distinctions not only on content assimilation, but also participation, contribution to and status within associated online communities. We need to bear in mind that these new possibilities, used by recruiters and managers to efficiently and objectively get the best talent, can foster existing inequities.

OUR PROTAGONISTS: CAROLYN, NADIA AND KEITH

Meanwhile, Carolyn, Nadia and Keith have been carrying on with their working lives. With a view to the challenges ahead of their employers, what ramifications should they expect?

Nadia, the managing director of MyMemLab, is in luck: she is prepared for the future and the identity issue. She is one of the few women in tech who can both shape and benefit from the industry securing her economic future. Her current lifestyle portrays the lifestyle for many to come, working in more than one job, having to build effective work relationships with many different people across boundaries and being digitally literate will secure her future.

Keith is also in a fortunate position. He will retire soon and will be one of the last of those who can live comfortably off their pensions. Although he comes from a 'have not' background he managed to buy a small property and climb the property ladder pre-financial crisis old-style. This secures him a relatively comfortable lifestyle for the decades to come. For personal interest and use, he will retain some minimum digital literacy to stay up-to-date for his remaining working years and in the future to stay connected.

Finally, Carolyn will have to pull up her socks. Despite the growing importance of people development in organisations as a result of the decline of higher education, she will have to stay up-to-date with changes, in particular those in technology. As delivery channels for people development are rapidly changing, she needs to acquire the necessary digital skills to contribute to the design of the curriculums and to take a leadership role in the virtual facilitation room.

Conclusion

CYBERCONNECTING – WEDDING SEEMINGLY OPPOSING DISCIPLINES

As presented in Chapter 1, the building blocks of this book are IT, Diversity as a process and business anthropology. Succeeding in times filled with contradictions, uncertainty and unprecedented developments pushes the growing dependence on the synthesis of these disciplines. Leveraging opportunities from big data, co-creation and lifelong learning as subsets of organisation development require the wedding of seemingly opposing disciplines for success. Experts affiliated with the quantitative or qualitative disciplines need to complement one another, in brief, they need to become besties.

Old suspicions of 'the other', for example that qualitative research methods such as interviews and observations are wobbly or lacking rigour, or that quantitative methods such as social network analysis are myopic and dehumanising, need to be overcome for the benefit of organisation development. Beyond personal preferences for one or the other, today's cyberconnected world of work would be incomplete without both.

HUMANS FIRST

Today's technology will be outdated before the ink on this book is dry. Shifting technological boundaries are not just the amount of data available and the speed at which it can be processed, but also the ease with which these new capabilities and new ideas can be combined and recombined. Economic historians tell us that it took several decades for earlier breakthrough technologies, such as the steam engine or electricity, to reach the point of ubiquity and flexible application at which they fundamentally changed the way people lived and businesses operated.[4]

The big winners in this new era are the consumers who are able to buy a wider range of higher-quality goods and services at lower prices. The other winners are those who create and finance the new machines or figure out how best to use them to gain competitive advantage. Great wealth will be created in the process, provided that decision-makers understand and promote the human-centric approach, which in turn is to be mirrored in technology-induced products and services. Their development cycles are largely ICT-driven, and, typically 'from engineers by engineers for engineers'. To date, most conventional design methodologies consider the needs of humans as an input, but not as the purpose of the design and much less involve the people in the process. Their buy-in comes at a later stage in the development process; only seldom is it the root cause. The human-centric focus enables the inclusion of diverse interests, needs and expectations, typically for the benefit of profit maximisation.

THE DISTINCTIVENESS OF MY OFFERING

Technological developments have undoubtedly made the world of work more interconnected but less human. Pulling together seemingly opposing ideas focuses on the human perspective in today's cyberconnected world and allows approaches to become more human-centric again.

Part I of this book combines the disciplines, their offerings and solutions needed in response to the challenges people face when building and developing organisations building interconnectivity among social, technological and cultural boundaries.

---

4   Brynjolfsson, McAfee 2014:14.

THE BUILDING PROCESS

Part II of the book presents you with the strategic framework you need for building interconnectivity: The Three Lenses of Diversity, designed to organise thinking in the navigation of technological, cultural and social boundaries. The framework consists of:

- The Lens of Multiple Identity for the exploration of people's coexisting and overlapping identities;

- The Lens of Perception for the examination of potential stereotypes and their impact on the interaction;

- The Environmental Lens for the analysis of the geopolitical, cultural, financial and business environment.

This part of the book walks you step-by-step through the lenses:

The Lens of Multiple Identity introduces you to the details of people's identity maps, offering you the option for reflection and exploration of your personal identity map and those of others. This allows room for the changes in our identity maps which will come in the future as our identity elements shift in relative importance.

The Lens of Perception equips you with ways forward to break through possible preconceptions and stereotypes in order to create commonness, even on shifting and contradictory identity maps your business partner might bring.

The Environmental Lens offers you a human-centric, strategic analysis of the environment in which your business endeavours take place.

THE TRANSITION FROM ICT-DRIVEN DEVELOPMENT TO INCLUSION

Part III concentrates on the transition from conventional product and service design methodologies to grassroots design approaches. Whilst the former considers the needs of humans as an input, the grassroots design understands the needs of human as its purpose by means of co-creation and mobilisation.

Root-cause design and customisation in organisation development happen through collaborative formats such as co-creation, the mobilisation approach and engagement through gamification. Online communication and collaboration technology act as initiators or enablers for these development processes and as accompanying tools for the mobilisation or co-creation process. In innovative organisations, they have long been wedded.

In essence, you now have the tool to understand the coexisting and occasionally contradicting identity maps of your interaction partners. Once you understand the identity maps you can align your behaviour to build effective business relationships and help others build them, to contribute to organisation development.

Bibliography

Abbas, AJ. 2005. *Islamic Perspectives on Management and Organization*. New Horizons in Management Series. Cheltenham, UK, Northampton, MA, USA: Edward Elgar.

Abraham, P.E. 1999. Cross Cultural Training: LeviStrauss for Managers. Occasional Paper of Copenhagen Business School: Department of Intercultural Communication and Management. Frederiksberg.

Abraham, P.E. 2005. Hightech MigrantInnen in Oesterreich, in *Herausforderung MigrationBeitraege zur Aktions und Informationswoche der Universitaet Wien anlaesslich des 'UN International Migrant's Day'*, edited by S. Binder, G. Rasuly Paleczek, and M. SixHohenbalken, Vienna: in *Abhandlung zur Geographie und Regionalforschung*, edited by K. Husa, C. Vielhaber, H. Wohlschlaegl, Band 7, the Institut für Geographie und Regionalforschung der Universität Wien 132–144.

Abraham, P.E. 2010. Contributions from Diversity. Objectives and Realities in a Large International Project. Doctoral Thesis, University of Vienna.

Abraham, P., Cassels-Brown, E. 2007. Looking in a Distorted Mirror: Western Mis-perceptions of Eastern Managers. SIETAR EUROPA Congress, April.

Abrams, D., Vasiljevic, M. 2013. Future Identities: Changing Identities in the UK – the Next 10 Years. DR 11: What Happens to People's Identity When the Economy is Suffering or Flourishing? University of Kent.

Ackerman, C. 2008. *Chefen och medarbetaren. Tankar om personlig utveckling och samspel på arbetsplatsen*. Stockholm: Ekerlids Förlag.

Adler, N. 2002. *International Dimensions of Organizational Behavior*, 4th edition. Cincinnati, OH: South-Western College Publishing.

Aguilera, F. 1996. Is Anthropology Good for the Company? *American Anthropologist*, New Series, 98 (4), 735–742.

Amin, G. 2003. *Whatever Else Happened to the Egyptians?* Cairo: The American University in Cairo Press.

Appaduri, A. 1996. *Modernity at Large: Cultural Dimensions of Globalisation.* Minneapolis: Public Worlds, Volume 1. University of Minnesota Press.

Appaduri, A. (Ed.) 2001. *Globalisation.* Durham: Duke University Press.

Appaduri, A. 2006. *Fear of Small Numbers. An Essay on the Geography of Anger.* Durham and London: Duke University Press.

Appiah, K.A. 2005. *The Ethics of Identity.* Princeton, NJ: Princeton University Press.

April, K. Shockley, M. (Eds) 2007. *Diversity. New Realities in a Changing World.* Basingstoke and New York: Palgrave Macmillan.

Argyris, C. 1990. *Overcoming Organizational Defenses.* London: Prentice Hall.

Atwater, E. 1992. *I Hear You.* New York: Walker.

Baba, M.L. 2001. The Globally Distributed Team. Learning to Work in a New Way, for Corporations and Anthropologists Alike. *Practicing Anthropology,* 23 (4)./Fall 2001. 2–8. Society for Applied Anthropology.

Baba, M. 2006. Anthropology and Business in *Encyclopedia of Anthropology,* edited by H. James Birx. Thousand Oaks, CA: Sage Publications, 83–117.

Bate, P. 1994. *Strategies for Cultural Change.* Oxford: Butterworth Heinemann.

Bate, P. 1996. Towards a Strategic Framework for Changing Corporate Culture. *Strategic Change,* 5(1), 27–42.

Baumann, G., Gingrich, A. (Eds) 2004. *Grammars of Identity/Alterity. A Structural Approach.* New York, Oxford: Berghahn Books.

Bennet-Alexander, D. 2000. Ten Ways to Value Diversity in your Workplace and Avoid Potential Liability in the Process. *Employee Rights Quarterly,* 1 (2), 57–64.

Boyd, D., Crawford, K. 2011. Six Provocations for Big Data. A Decade in Internet Time: Symposium on the Dynamics of the Internet and Society, September 2011.

Briggs, P. 2013. Future Identities: Changing Identities in the UK – the Next 10 Years. DR 4: Will an Increasing Element of Our Identity be 'Devolved' to Machines? Northumbria University.

Brynjolfsson, E., McAfee, A. 2014. *The Second Machine Age: Work, Progress, and Prosperity in a Time of Brilliant Technologies.* New York: W.W. Norton & Company Inc.

Burnett, T., Kettleborough, S. 2007. New Frontiers for Diversity and Inclusion, in *Diversity. New Realities in a Changing World,* edited by K. April, M. Shockley. Basingstoke and New York: Palgrave Macmillan.

Capgemini Consulting. 2013. Digital Leadership. An interview with Erik Brynjolfsson and Andrew McAfee. MIT Center for Digital Business, http://capgemini-consulting.com (Accessed December 2013).

Celko, J. 1999. *Data and Databases: Concepts in Practice.* San Francisco, CA, USA, Morgan Kaufmann Publishers.

Cornelius, N. (Ed.) 2002. *Building Workplace Equality. Ethics, Diversity, and Inclusion.* London: Thomson.

Cushner, K., Brislin, R.W. 1996. *Intercultural Interactions: A Practical Guide.* Thousand Oaks, CA: Sage Publications, Inc.

Czarniawska, B. 2007. On Time, Space, and Action Nets, in *The Anthropology of Organisations,* edited by A.C. Jimenez. Aldershot: Ashgate, 525–545.

Dahlen, T. 1997. *Among the Interculturalists. An Emergent Profession and its Packaging of Knowledge.* Stockholm: Stockholm Studies in Social Anthropology, 38. Department of Social Anthropology, Stockholm University. Gotab.

Data Breach Investigation Report. 2014. Verizon. www.verizonenterprise.com (Accessed June 2014).

Dignan, A. 2011. *Game Frame. Using Games as a Strategy for Success.* New York: Free Press.

Droro, G.S., Meyer, J.W., Hwang, H. (Eds) 2007. *Globalization and Organization: World Society and Organizational Change.* Oxford: Oxford University Press.

Eichenberg, T., Abraham, P., Hayward, I. 2012. Unterstützung von Veränderungsprojekten durch Qualifizierung beteiligter Führungskräfte. Das International Leadership Program im IT-Bereich von E.ON, in *Leadership – Best Practices und Trends* (German Edition), edited by H. Bruch, Krummaker, S., Vogel, B. Wiesbaden: Springer Gabler.

Ellison, N. 2013. Future Identities: Changing Identities in the UK – the Next 10 Years. DR 3: Social Media and Identity? Michigan State University.

Foresight Future Identities. 2013. Final Project Report. London: The Government Office for Science.

Friedrich, R., LeMerle, M., Peterson, M., Koster, A. 2010. *The Rise of Generation C: Implications of the World of 2020*. Booz and Company (Accessed July 2013).

Fukukawa, K., Balmer, J.M.T., Gray, E.R. 2007. Mapping the Interface between Corporate Identity, Ethics, and Corporate Social Responsibility, *Journal of Business Ethics*, 76, 1–5.

Future State 2030: The Global Megatrends Shaping Governments. 2013. KPMG International, kpmg.com/government (Accessed March 2014).

Gagnon, S., Cornelius, N. 2002. From Equal Opportunities to Managing Diversity to Capabilities: A New Theory of Workplace Equality? in *Building Workplace Equality. Ethics, Diversity, and Inclusion*, edited by N. Cornelius, London: Thomson, 13–58.

Gardenswartz, L., Rowe, A. 2003. *Diverse Teams at work. Capitalizing on the Power of Diversity*. Alexandria, VA: Society for Human Resource Management.

Geertz, C. 1973. *The Interpretation of Culture*. New York: Basic Books.

Ghannam, F. 2006. Keeping Him Connected: Labor Migration and the Production of Locality in Cairo, Egypt, in *Cairo Cosmopolitan. Politics, Culture, and Urban Space in the New Globalized Middle East*, edited by D. Singerman, P. Amar, Cairo, New York: The American University in Cairo Press, 251–266.

Golbeck, J. 2013. *Analyzing the Social Web*. MA, USA, Morgan Kaufman.

Golia, M. 2004. *Cairo. City on Sand*. Cairo: The American University in Cairo Press.

Hampden-Turner, C., Trompenaars, F. 2000. *Building Cross-Cultural Competence. Building CrossCultural Competence: How to Create Wealth from Conflicting Values*. Oxford: Butterworth Heinemann.

Hampden-Turner, C., Trompenaars, F. 2002. *21 Leaders for the 21st Century. How Innovative Leaders Manage in The Digital Age*. New York: McGraw-Hill.

Hannerz, U. 1996. *Transnational Connections: Culture, People, Places*. London: Routledge.

Hannerz, U. 2003. Being There ... and There ... and, *Ethnography*, 4 (2), 201–216.

Harb, Z. 2011. Arab Revolutions and the Social Media Effect. *Journal of Media and Culture (M/C Journal)*, 14 (2), http://journal.media-culture.org.au/index.php/mcjournal/article/viewArticle/364 (Accessed November 2013).

Harvey, D. 1989. *The Condition of Postmodernity*. Oxford: Basil Blackwell.

Herstatt, C., Von Hippel, E. 1992. From Experience: Developing New Product Concepts Via the Lead User Method: A Case Study in a 'Low Tech' Field. *Journal of Product Innovation Management*, 1992(9), 213–221.

Hofstede, G. 1980. *Culture's Consequences: International Differences in Work-related Values*. Newbury Park, CA: Sage.

http://alltogethernow.org.au/news/campaigns/everydayracism/ Accessed March 2014).

http://blogs.hbr.org/2013/11/dont-rate-your-employees-on-a-curve/(Accessed November 2013).

http://www.computerhistory.org/timeline/?year=1964 (Accessed October 2013).

http://www.forbes.com/sites/gartnergroup/2013/01/21/the-gamification-of-business/(Accessed February 2014).

http://www.google.com/loon/ (Accessed December 2013).

http://research.gigaom.com/report/proximity-based-mobile-social-networking-outlook-and-analysis/?utm_source=tech&utm_medium=editorial&utm_campaign=auto3&utm_term=795661+when-it-comes-to-new-markets-one-size-does-not-fit-all&utm_content=gigaguest (Accessed February 2014).

http://reviews.mtbr.com/the-angry-singlespeeder-why-strava-sucks (Accessed February 2014).

http://smalldatagroup.com, December 11, 2013 (Accessed December 2013).

https://swisseducation.educa.ch/en/vocational-education-and-training-0 (Accessed January 2014).

http://www.teachthought.com/trends/flipped-classroom-trends/10-conditions-for-achieving-success-with-blended-learning/ (Accessed September 2014).

http://techcrunch.com/2014/01/23/facebook-losing-users-princeton-losing-credibility/ (Accessed January 2014).

http://www.theguardian.com/commentisfree/2013/nov/10/germany-third-gender-birth-certificate.

http://www.theguardian.com/technology/shortcuts/2014/feb/16/facebook-should-remove-all-gender-options (Accessed February 2014).

http://www.theguardian.com/world/2013/dec/23/stores-agree-end-gendered-toys-displays-campaign (Accessed January 2014).

ICSPA. International Cyber Security Protection Alliance 2013. Project 2020. Scenarios for the Future of Cybercrime – White Paper for Decision Makers. European Cybercrime Centre, EC3, Europol (Accessed March 2014).

International Survey on Aesthetic/Cosmetic Procedures Performed in 2011. International Society of Aesthetic Plastic Surgeons (ISAPS), www.isaps.org (Accessed April 2014).

Jack, R.E., Garrod, O.G.B., Yu, H., Caldara, R., Schyns, P.G. 2012. Facial Expressions of Emotion are Not Culturally Universal. *Proceedings of the National Academy of Sciences of the United States of America*, 109 (19), 7241–7244.

Jansen, B.J., Moore, K., Carman, S. 2013. Evaluating the performance of demographic targeting using gender in sponsored search. *Information Processing and Management*, 49 (1), 286–302.

Jimenez, A.C. (Ed.) 2007. *The Anthropology of Organisations*. Aldershot: Ashgate.

Jones, E.E. 1986. Interpreting Interpersonal Behaviour: The Effects of Expectancy. *Science* 234 (4772), 41–46.

Jordan, A.T. 2003. *Business Anthropology*. Long Grove, IL: Waveland.

Krawinkler, S. 2008. Teilnehmende Beobachtung als Tool in der Organisationsentwicklung. Universitaet Wien: Diplomarbeit.

Kriwet, K.K. 1997. Inter – an Intraorganizational Knowledge Transfer. Bamberg: Dissertation.

Lee, T.L., Fiske, S.T. 2008. Stereotyping, in *International Encyclopedia of the Social Sciences*, edited by W.A. Darity (2nd edition, Vol. 8). Detroit: Macmillan Reference USA, 136–139.

Lévi-Strauss, C. 1998. *Traurige Tropen*. Frankfurt am Main: Suhrkamp.

Lewis, R.D. 1996. *When Cultures Collide: Managing Successfully across Cultures*. London: Nicholas Brealey Publishing Limited.

Lindberg, K., Czarniawska, B. 2006. Knotting the Action Net, or Organizing between Organizations, *Scandinavian Journal of Management*, 22, 292–306.

Marcus, G. 1998. *Ethnography through Thick and Thin*. Oxford: Butterworth Heinemann.

Mayer-Schoenberger, V., Cukier, K. 2013. *Big Data: A Revolution That Will Transform How We Live, Work, and Think*. New York: Houghton Mifflin Harcourt Publishing Company.

Mayo, E. 1933. The Human Problems of an Industrial Civilization. New York: Macmillan Co.

Merton, R.K. 1948. The Self-Fulfilling Prophecy. *The Antioch Review*, 8 (2), 193–210.

Mintzberg, H., Waters, J. 1998. Of Strategies, Deliberate and Emergent, in *The Strategy Reader*, edited by S. SegalHorn, Milton Keynes: Blackwell Publishing.

Moon, H., Min Wotipka, C. 2007. The Worldwide Diffusion of of Business Education, 1881–1999: Historical Trajectory and Mechanisms of Expansion, in *Globalization and Organisation: World Society and Organisational Change*, edited by G.S. Drori, J.W. Meyer, H. Hwang (Eds). Oxford: Oxford University Press.

Muenz, R., Reiterer, A. 2009. *Overcrowded World? Global Population and International Migration*. London: Haus Publishing Ltd.

Mullins, L. 2002. *Management and Organisational Behaviour*. Harlow: Pearson Education Limited.

Nydell, M.K. 1996. *Understanding the Arabs. A Guide for Westerners*. Yarmouth, ME: Intercultural Press.

Pheysey, D.C. 2003. *Organisational Culture and Identity*. London: Sage Publications.

Polzer, J.T., Caruso, H.M. 2008. Identity Negotiation Processes Amidst Diversity, in *Diversity at Work*, edited by A.P. Brief, Cambridge, NY: Cambridge University Press, 89–126.

Polzer, J.T., Milton, L.P., Swann, W.B. Jr. 2002. Capitalizing on Diversity: Interpersonal Congruence in Small Work Groups. *Administrative Science Quarterly*, 47 (2), 296–324.

Powell, J.L., Steel, R. 2011. Revisiting Appadurai: Globalizing Scapes in a Global World – the Pervasiveness of Economic and Cultural Power. *International Journal of Innovative Interdisciplinary Research*, 2011 (1), 74–80.

Reicher, S., Hopkins, N. 2013. *How Will Issues of Power, Conflict, and Prejudice and Discrimination Impact upon Notions of Identity?* London: Government Office for Science. In: Future Identities.

Roth, G., Turrini, P. 1981. *Bruno Kreisky*. Berlin: Nicolaische Verlagsbuchhandlung.

Rothbart, M. 1978. From Individual to Group Impressions: Availability Heuristics in Stereotype Formation. *Journal of Experimental Social Psychology*, 14, 237–255.

Roethlisberger, F.J., William J., Dickson, W.J. 1939. *Management and the Worker*. Cambridge, MA: Harvard University Press (Oxford University Press). In 1941 *The Economic Journal* 51 (202/203) 306–308.

Sassen, S. 2001. Spatiality and Temporality of the Global, in *Globalisation*, edited by A. Appadurai, Durham: Duke University Press, 260–278.

Savir, U. 1999. *The Process. 1,100 Days That Changed the Middle East*. New York, Toronto: Vintage Books.

Schwartz, S.H. 2012. An Overview of the Schwartz Theory of Basic Values. *Online Readings in Psychology and Culture*, 2(1), http://dx.doi.org/10.9707/2307-0919.1116 (Accessed October 2013).

Schwartzman, H.B. 1993. *Ethnography in Organizations*. Newbury Park, CA: Sage Publications Inc.

Scollon, R., Wong Scollon, S. 1995. *Intercultural Communication. A Discourse Approach*, 2nd edition. Oxford: Blackwell Publishing.

Sen, A. 2006. *Identity and Violence: The Illusion of Destiny*. London: Norton.

Shore, C., Nugent, S. (Eds) 2002. *Elite Cultures. Anthropological Perspectives*. ASA Monographs 38. London, New York: Routledge.

Simmel, G. 1949. The Sociology of Sociability. *American Journal of Sociology*, 55(3), 254–261.

Smircich, L. 1983. Concepts of Culture and Organizational Analysis. *Administrative Science Quarterly*, 28 (3), 339–358.

Soderberg, M. 2003. *Merging at Cross-Borders: People, Cultures, and Politics*. Copenhagen: Business School Press.

Spencer, L.M., Spencer, S.M. 1993. *Competence at Work: Models for Superior Performance*. New York: John Wiley & Son, Inc.

Swiss Adult Education Survey (CH-EAS 2011) 2013. Continuing Education in Switzerland 2011. Federal Statistics Office, Neuchatel, Swiss Confederation. www.bfs.admin.ch (Accessed January 2014).

Tajfel, H. 1981. *Human Groups and Social Categories Studies in Social Psychology*. Cambridge: Cambridge University Press.

The Deloitte Millenial Survey. 2014. Big Demands and High Expectations. www.deloitte.com/MillenialSurvey (Accessed March 2014).

The Future of Work. Jobs and Skills in 2030. 2014. UKCES Evidence Report 84. February 2014. www.ukes.org.uk (Accessed April 2014).

The Rise of Generation C: Implications of the World of 2020. 2010. Booz and Company. booz.com.

Tomlinson, J. 1999. *Globalisation and Culture*. Oxford: Polity Press (Accessed July 2013).

Toossi, M. 2012. Labor Force Projections to 2020: A More Slowly Growing Workforce. Bureau of Labor Statistics, Monthly Labour Review, January 2012, www.bls.gov (Accessed March 2014).

Turner, J.C. 1985. Social categorization and the Self-concept: A Social Cognitive Theory of Group Behavior, in *Advances in Group Processes: Theory and Research*, edited by E.J. Lawler, Greenwich, CT: JAI Press, Vol. 2, 77–122.

Turner, J.C., Giles, H. (Eds) 1981. *Intergroup Behaviour*. Oxford: Blackwell.

Ward, N.G., Al Bayyari, Y. 2010. American and Arab Perceptions of an Arabic Turn-Taking Cue. *Journal of Cross-Cultural Psychology*, 41, 2, 270–275.

Weick, K.E. 1985. The Significance of Corporate Culture, in *Organizational Culture*, edited by P. Frost, L.F. Moore, M.R. Louis, C.C. Lundberg, J. Martin. Beverly Hills, CA: Sage, 381–390, 382; cited in Schneider S.C. and J.-L. Barsoux (2003), *Managing across Cultures*, 2nd edition. Harlow, UK: Pearson Education Ltd, 118.

Wharton, A.S. 2012. *The Sociology of Gender: An Introduction to Theory and Research*. Chichester. Wiley-Blackwell.

Wiener, N. 1950. *The Human Use of Human Beings: Cybernetics and Society*. Boston, MA: Da Capo Press.

Williams, J. 1998. *Don't They Know its Friday. Cross-Cultural Considerations for Business and Life in the Gulf*. London: Motivate Publishing.

Willis, J., Todorov, A. 2006. First Impressions. Making Up Your Mind after a 100-Ms Exposure to a Face. *Psychological Science*, 17 (7), 592–598.

Wright, S. 1994. Culture in Anthropology and Organizational Studies, in *Anthropology of Organizations*, edited by S. Wright, London and New York: Routledge, 1–34.

Zichermann, G., Cunningham, C. 2011. Gamification by Design: Implementing Game Mechanics in Web and Mobile Apps. Sebastopol, CA: O'Reilly Media.

Index

For Product Safety Concerns and Information please contact our EU
representative GPSR@taylorandfrancis.com Taylor & Francis Verlag GmbH,
Kaufingerstraße 24, 80331 München, Germany

Printed and bound by CPI Group (UK) Ltd, Croydon, CR0 4YY
01/05/2025
01858434-0004